Methodist Christology

From the Wesleys to the Twenty-First Century

Jason E. Vickers and
Jerome Van Kuiken
General Editors

Methodist Christology: From the Wesleys to the Twenty-First Century

The General Board of Higher Education and Ministry leads and serves The United Methodist Church in the recruitment, preparation, nurture, education, and support of Christian leaders—lay and clergy—for the work of making disciples of Jesus Christ for the transformation of the world. Its vision is that a new generation of Christian leaders will commit boldly to Jesus Christ and be characterized by intellectual excellence, moral integrity, spiritual courage, and holiness of heart and life. The General Board of Higher Education and Ministry of The United Methodist Church serves as an advocate for the intellectual life of the church. The Board's mission embodies the Wesleyan tradition of commitment to the education of laypersons and ordained persons by providing access to higher education for all persons.

Wesley's Foundery Books is named for the abandoned foundery that early followers of John Wesley transformed, which later became the cradle of London's Methodist movement.

Methodist Christology: From the Wesleys to the Twenty-First Century

HIGHER EDUCATION & MINISTRY
General Board of Higher Education and Ministry
THE UNITED METHODIST CHURCH

Contents

Preface v

1
Early Methodist Christology

Chapter 1. "Practical Christology" in John and Charles Wesley
Paul W. Chilcote 3

Chapter 2. Early Methodist Christology Beyond the Wesleys
Mark K. Olson 37

Chapter 3. Nineteenth-Century Methodist Dogmaticians
Thomas H. McCall 55

2
Methodist Christologies through the Twentieth Century

Chapter 4. Personalism in Methodist Christology
Reginald Broadnax 75

Chapter 5. Christology "Human End Foremost":
Albert Outler and John Deschner
Jerome Van Kuiken 91

Chapter 6. The Christology of John B. Cobb Jr.
Michael Lodahl 109

3
The Futures of Methodist Christology

Chapter 7. The Image of God Is a Black Woman:
Feminist and Womanist Christologies
Christina M. Smerick 129

Chapter 8. Jesús Was Born in Guatemala:
Toward a Latinx Wesleyan Christology
Edgardo Colón-Emeric 143

Chapter 9. Essential Kenosis Christology
Thomas Jay Oord 161

Chapter 10. Why Did God Become a Man of the Spirit?
Toward a Wesleyan Pentecostal Spirit-Christology
Chris E. W. Green 179

Chapter 11. Methodist Christology after Barth
John L. Drury 193

Chapter 12. Methodist Christology after Oden
Justus H. Hunter 219

Chapter 13. William Burt Pope and the Future of Wesleyan Theology:
The Work of Christ in Dogmatic Perspective
Jason E. Vickers 237

Contributors 253

Preface

The first sign of Christology was not a cross but a question mark. In the Synoptic tradition, Jesus of Nazareth asked his gathered disciples, "Who do you say that I am?" They replied, "You are the Christ" (Mark 8:29 and parallels). Only after this confession do his crucifixion and exaltation come into view (Mark 8:31–9:13 and parallels) to redefine the meaning of the term *Christ*. Its pre-Christian associations with God-anointed leadership and deliverance took on fresh significance in light of the early Christian conviction that Jesus had died a criminal's death not for his own sins but for others' and that God had raised him to life and to heaven's throne as divine Lord and Savior, from whence he was to return to judge the world. This became the confessional framework for mainstream Christology from the late ancient era to early modern times, when Methodism arose.

The history of Christology in the Methodist tradition—which, in our usage, includes the whole range of pan-Wesleyan bodies and movements—likewise starts with a question. The query comes not from Jesus but from Jaroslav Pelikan, the eminent church historian: What happened to Methodist Christology after Wesley?[1] This volume begins sketching an answer by taking soundings in the history and current expressions of Methodist/ Wesleyan Christology. Our purpose is to stimulate further research toward a full-bodied reply to Pelikan. We wish to learn from the past and explore the present in order to chart a future for Methodist Christology. In every generation, the question of Christ remains the most vital inquiry that his

---

1 Pelikan's inquiry caps off his commendatory blurb on the back cover of John Deschner, *Wesley's Christology: An Interpretation* (Dallas: Southern Methodist University Press, 1960, 1985): "Question: What has happened to all this Christological substance in the subsequent history of Methodist theology?"

followers can undertake, for the answer shapes (or ought to shape) their understanding of God, themselves, and God's intention for the world.

Pelikan's question relies on the fact that Wesley himself had a Christology that he bequeathed to Methodism. Accordingly, our first three chapters investigate early Methodist Christology. The rise of Wesley studies in the mid-twentieth century has brought with it a variety of interpretations of John Wesley's Christology, while more recently Charles Wesley's theological contributions have begun to receive serious attention. Senior Wesley scholar Paul W. Chilcote devotes his opening chapter to assessing and applying this harvest of studies on the Wesley brothers' views of Christ.

In chapter 2, Mark K. Olson examines the doctrine of Christ held by the Wesleys' contemporaries in early Methodist leadership, particularly John Fletcher, Joseph Benson, and Thomas Coke. Olson finds that, like the Wesleys, their lieutenants were generally committed to traditional orthodoxy and especially emphasized Christ's deity in the face of eighteenth-century threats to it. This conservation of classical orthodoxy reaches mature, systematic expression in the following century's works of dogmatics by Methodist theologians, as Thomas H. McCall documents in chapter 3.

The following trio of chapters signals a significant shift in Methodist theology from the late nineteenth century on.[2] No longer content to work within the paradigm of the past, the subjects of these chapters all sought to rethink the received doctrine of Christ in a fresh framework. For the Boston personalists of chapter 4 (by Reginald Broadnax) and the process theologian John Cobb in chapter 6 (by Michael Lodahl), that framework was a new philosophical metaphysic. For Albert Outler, the framework was modern historiography and psychology, while for John Deschner it was Barthian sensibilities, as described in chapter 5 (by Jerome Van Kuiken). The mostly unified Christology of early Methodism gave way to the Christological pluralism of the late nineteenth through twentieth centuries.

---

2 Cf. Thomas A. Langford, *Practical Divinity: Theology in the Wesleyan Tradition* (Nashville: Abingdon Press, 1983), 101, 110, 119–24, 127–29, 171–73, 193–96; Thomas H. McCall and Keith D. Stanglin, *After Arminius* (Oxford: Oxford University Press, forthcoming), chap. 4, §§ ii.a., iii.c, ix.

While historical studies make up the former half of this volume, the latter half pivots to proposals for the new millennium. So far, the pluralism that characterized the previous century of Methodist theology persists through the first quarter of the twenty-first century. We foresee, broadly speaking, two possible futures for Methodist Christology: one of increasing pluralism and fragmentation or another of increasing consensus and integration. Each of the following proposals makes a bid (consciously or not) toward one of these futures. We begin with contextual theologies representing viewpoints other than the false universal of European male perspective. In chapter 7, Christina M. Smerick presents the history and ongoing challenge of feminist and womanist theologies for Christology. In chapter 8, Edgardo Colón-Emeric does the same with Latino/-a/-x theology.

Constructive Christological proposals continue in the next two chapters. Each queries the nature and significance of the divine kenosis displayed in the Incarnation. In chapter 9, Thomas Jay Oord draws on process and open theism's resources for a model of an eternally noncoercive and reciprocal God-world relation. In chapter 10, on the other hand, Christopher E. W. Green harks back to the classical theistic tradition in order to furnish Charismatic Spirit-Christology with a noncompetitive account of God-world and intratrinitarian relations.

Yet another pair of chapters probes the potential for building on the legacies of two titans of twentieth-century theology. John L. Drury uses chapter 11 to explore the "impossible possibility" of doing Wesleyan theology under the tutelage of Karl Barth. By contrast with Barth's so-called neo-orthodoxy, Methodist scholar Thomas Oden pursued a project of "paleo-orthodoxy." Justus H. Hunter's chapter 12 asks how Oden's agenda of retrieving consensual Christian tradition may be advanced.

Both Barth and the Great Tradition offer doctrinal order and objectivity to Wesleyans weary of the subjective excesses of their own heritage. Yet that heritage is not without its own resources in these areas. Jason E. Vickers concludes this volume by holding up nineteenth-century Methodist dogmatician William Burt Pope as an example. Imitating his theological penchants for good order and humility, Vickers believes, should cure our besetting tendency toward "anxious narcissism."

Readers familiar with Methodist historical theology or the contributors to this volume may be struck by certain lacunae. Regarding historical theology, these chapters do not cover every variation on Methodist Christology; for instance, there is no coverage of Sri Lankan Methodist D. T. Niles's transposition of Christology into an East Asian idiom or American Methodist Schubert Ogden's Christological blend of process, Bultmannian, and liberationist elements.[3] Concerning the contributors, the preponderance of males of European descent raises the question of tokenism in relation to those who do not fit that mold. The editors' defense is twofold: First, this volume as originally planned had a greater diversity of subject matter and contributors. Alas, not all those who were to contribute did so! Second, as noted earlier, this volume's aim is not to exhaust its topic but to spark new research. As one example, the late nineteenth-century paradigm shift from classical dogmatics to philosophical metaphysics deserves further scrutiny. As another example, the affinity of process and liberation theologies to traditional Methodist theological interests begs for more exploration.

We conclude this preface by dedicating this book to the memory of Dr. John Deschner of Perkins School of Theology. His landmark monograph *Wesley's Christology: An Interpretation* blazed the trail for subsequent studies of the topic and, by implication, of Methodist Christology generally. The year 2020 marks the sixtieth anniversary of his monograph's original publication, the thirty-fifth anniversary of its reprinting, and the twentieth anniversary of its author's death. We are grateful for his life and legacy.

— **Jason E. Vickers**
and Jerome Van Kuiken, General Editors

---

3   For brief synopses, see Creighton Lacy, "The Legacy of D. T. Niles," *International Bulletin of Missionary Research* (October 1984): 174–78; Sam Hodges, "Theologian Ogden Pushed Himself and His Students," *UM News* (June 11, 2019), https://www.umnews.org/en/news/theologian-ogden -pushed-himself-and-his-students; Langford, *Practical Divinity*, 232–35 (Ogden), 248–50 (Niles).

Early
Methodist
Christology

"Practical Christology" in John and Charles Wesley

Paul W. Chilcote

n spring 1725, John Wesley, a student at Oxford at that time, contemplated taking Holy Orders. He wrote to his father about his plans, but his mother's reply contained a statement that most certainly set the trajectory of his theological vision for years to come:

> I approve the disposition of your mind. I think this season of Lent the most proper for your preparation for Orders, and I think the sooner you are a deacon the better, because it may be an inducement to greater application in the study of practical divinity, which of all other I humbly conceive is the best study for candidates for Orders. Mr. Wesley differs from me, and would engage you, I believe, in critical learning (though I'm not sure), which though of use accidentally and by way of concomitance, yet is in no wise preferable to the other. Therefore I earnestly pray God to avert that great evil from you, of engaging in trifling studies to the neglect of such as are absolutely necessary.[1]

Susanna's appeal fixed a distinction in John's mind, and certainly in Charles's mind as well, between practical and speculative divinity. The brothers took their mother's advice seriously and committed themselves to the pursuit of a form of theological inquiry that would make a difference in the lives of real people in real time. In his preface to his first volume of

---

1   John Wesley, *The Works of John Wesley*, vol. 25, *Letters I, 1721–1739*, ed. Frank Baker (Oxford: Clarendon Press, 1980), 160.

Sermons on Several Occasions, John revealed this approach in his typically terse style: "I design plain truth for plain people."[2]

It should be no surprise that neither John nor Charles devoted any energy to the production of treatises or poetic collections dedicated specifically to Christology—to an explication of the person and work of Jesus Christ. On the other hand, it would be a serious mistake to conclude that Christology does not pervade the corpus of both Anglican theologians. The sermons and treatises of John the preacher and the hymns of Charles the poet reflect their deep concern to understand who Jesus Christ was (is) and what he has done for the redemption of God's creation. Nothing, in fact, was more core to their theology. Any effort to categorize their Christological vision, therefore, requires a process of discernment, ferreting out their leading ideas from the extremely broad spectrum of material they produced. But this exercise, if it produced nothing but clear labels, would mitigate their own vision of the purpose of theology.

In my teaching of theology, I have often noticed the way the declarations of the Council of Constantinople (381) bring a sense of "closure" among my students with regard to the Christological debates of the early church. The first great ecumenical Council of Nicaea (325) essentially addressed the question of Jesus's divinity with a definitive statement about his being *homoousion* (of one substance) with the Father, over against movements (such as Arianism) that denied his divinity or overstressed his humanity. Later in the fourth century, Constantinople reasserted Jesus's full humanity over against those who overemphasize his divinity (primarily the Apollinarians, who drew a distinction between Jesus's humanity and our own). By the end of the fourth century, in other words, the church definitively answered the question, Who is Jesus Christ? "Jesus Christ," the Council declared, "is fully divine and fully human." The well-known formula, "Jesus is one person in two natures," later codified this conclusion.

I find that my students are happy with this resolution of the issue and

---

2   John Wesley, *The Works of John Wesley*, vol. 1, *Sermons I, 1–33*, ed. Albert C. Outler (Nashville: Abingdon Press, 1984), 104.

feel little need to go beyond this. But, having answered the primary question about Jesus, two subsequent councils (Ephesus, 431) and (Chalcedon, 451) address a secondary question: If Jesus Christ is fully divine and fully human, then how do these two natures in Christ relate to one another? Instinctively, I think, my students generally sense a leap from the practical to the speculative at this point and view the subsequent debates accordingly. As they have engaged the intricacies and nuances of Nestorianism (which emphasized the distinction between the two natures) and Monophysitism (which emphasized the unity of the person of Jesus, blurring the distinction between the natures), for example, I think they reflect something of the reticence of the Wesleys to plunge too deeply into these mysteries. Like the Wesleys, while affirming the later Chalcedonian formulas of *hypostatic union* and *communicatio idiomatum*, their preference is to reside at Constantinople rather than Ephesus or Chalcedon.

To state it rather bluntly, they can discern the practical "so what?" factor related to a disproportional emphasis on either Jesus's humanity or his divinity. But speculative attempts to explain the natures' interrelationship leave my students without clear practical guidance for their journey into the fullest possible love of God and neighbor. I sense a similar disposition of mind and heart in the Wesleys. Given this essay's leading position in this volume and in an effort to more fully understand the Wesley brothers' "practical Christology," I first offer a comprehensive examination of the literature related to the Wesleys' vision of Christ and the "Christological sources" in each brother's corpus.[3] Second, I address four key themes in their writings related to their vision of the person and work of Christ and identify the respective implications of their "practical Christology" as these relate to the quest for holiness of heart and life.

---

3   This task was undertaken with regard to John Wesley by Richard M. Riss in 2010. His annotated bibliographical essay remains the most thorough survey of the literature on this topic: "John Wesley's Christology in Recent Literature," *Wesleyan Theological Journal* 45, no. 1 (Spring 2010): 108–29. He examines the material in chronological order. Given this previous documentation, the scholarly review of John provided here follows but augments the analysis of Riss. Given that no such review has been provided previously for Charles Wesley in this regard, more space and greater detail are devoted to the study of his Christology.

Studies and Sources Related to the Wesleys' Christology

"A study of Wesley's Christology is faced by one great difficulty," A. Raymond George once claimed, "namely that Wesley was interested primarily, not in Christology, but in soteriology."[4] While referring to older brother John, this statement most certainly exemplifies the lyrical theology of Charles as well. Given this fact, it is somewhat surprising that the vast majority of studies in this arena revolve around the question of whether John Wesley, in particular, maintains an "orthodox" view of the person of Christ. They address a fairly direct question: Does Wesley demonstrate a tendency toward Monophysitism? Does a purported emphasis on the divinity of Jesus lead to a diminution of his humanity in Wesley's teaching? Is Jesus's humanity lost in the sea of his divinity? Scholars have focused their attention more on the person, in other words, than the work of Christ with regard to John's Christology.

As regards Charles Wesley, much less effort has been expended on his Christology, to say nothing of his theology in general. Only in recent years— with a growing literature that has elevated the importance of "lyrical theology"—have scholars turned their attention to Charles's theological vision. Some have raised questions, however, of whether hymnody even affords a proper platform for a "first order" theological topic such as Christology.[5] Despite the more speculative nature of some of these questions, the debates of twentieth-century scholars are of "use accidentally and by way of concomitance" (to borrow Susanna Wesley's phrase) in an effort to more fully appreciate the Wesleys' practical theological perspective.

A Review of Studies on John Wesley's Christology

The question of John's "functional" or "practical Monophysitism" can be traced back to *Wesley's Christology: An Interpretation*, the fruit of John Deschner's doctoral studies at Basel under the direction of the neo-orthodox

---

4 A. Raymond George, "Review of John Deschner, *Wesley's Christology*," *Journal of Theological Studies*, New Series 12, no. 2 (October 1961): 382.

5 See, for example, Thomas A. Langford, "Charles Wesley as Theologian," in *Charles Wesley: Poet and Theologian*, ed. S T Kimbrough Jr. (Nashville: Kingswood Books, 1992), 97–105.

theologian Karl Barth.[6] This study remains the most thorough, careful, and perceptive examination of this topic. A single sentence articulates his ultimate conclusion succinctly: "Wesley betrays a decided emphasis on the divine nature and a corresponding underemphasis on the human."[7] Despite Deschner's cogent arguments regarding Wesley's Monophysite tendency—following the viewpoints of David Lerch and Robin Scroggs before him[8]—Geoffrey Wainwright's critique merits serious consideration. Attending to both Wesley's context and his wider corpus, he simply viewed Wesley's position "as a healthily Alexandrian view of Christ's Person."[9] Regardless, ever since the publication of Deschner's study in 1960, a host of other scholars have echoed his concerns or have sought to support them.

Among those who affirm this purported tendency of Wesley to overemphasize Jesus's divinity, Albert Outler stands out as one of the most significant scholars.[10] While Randy Maddox echoes some of the same concerns, he does not embrace them fully.[11] More recently, Matthew Hambrick and Michael E. Lodahl, over against Maddox and because of his defense of Wesley's position, have pressed the claim of Wesley's aberrant Christological views even further.[12] In their efforts to confirm Deschner's earlier conclusion, all these scholars resorted primarily to Wesley's

---

6   John Deschner, *Wesley's Christology: An Interpretation* (Dallas: Southern Methodist University Press, 1960).

7   Deschner, *Wesley's Christology*, 6.

8   David Lerch, *Heil und Heiligung bei John Wesley, Dargestellt unter Besonderer Berücksichtigung Seiner Ammerkungen zum Neuen Testament* (Zürich: Christlichen Vereinsbuchhandlung, 1941); Robin Scroggs, "John Wesley as Biblical Scholar," *Journal of Bible and Religion* 28, no. 4 (October 1960): 415–22.

9   Geoffrey Wainwright, "Review of John Deschner, *Wesley's Christology*," *Perkins Journal* 39, no. 2 (April 1986): 55.

10   Outler advances his argument primarily in his editorial commentary on Wesley's sermons. In particular, see his introductory comments to "On Knowing Christ after the Flesh," one of the very few places in Wesley's corpus where he actually attacks a Christological heresy; *The Works of John Wesley*, vol. 4, *Sermons IV, 115–51* (Nashville: Abingdon Press, 1987), 97–106.

11   Randy L. Maddox, *Responsible Grace: John Wesley's Practical Theology* (Nashville: Kingswood Books, 1994), 94–118; esp. 114–18.

12   Matthew Hambrick and Michael E. Lodahl, "Responsible Grace in Christology?: John Wesley's Rendering of Jesus in the Epistle to the Hebrews," *Wesleyan Theological Journal* 43, no. 1 (Spring 2008): 86–103.

Notes on the New Testament and a number of his sermons: "The Lord Our Righteousness," "Sermon on the Mount I," "The End of Christ's Coming," "Spiritual Worship," and "On Knowing Christ after the Flesh," in particular.[13]

Interestingly, references to Wesley's redaction of the Thirty-Nine Articles of Religion, his *Notes on the New Testament,* and the sermon "Spiritual Worship" in particular, feature prominently as evidence on both sides of this debate. John R. Renshaw,[14] William R. Cannon,[15] Charles R. Wilson,[16] Kenneth J. Collins,[17] Thomas C. Oden,[18] Timothy L. Boyd,[19] John R. Tyson,[20] David A. Graham,[21] Rob DeGeorge,[22] and Edgardo Rosado[23] all used these sources to counter the Monophysite claim and to portray Wesley as an

---

13 Wesley's abridgment of the writings of Ignatius of Antioch in the *Christian Library* also figures in the argument.

14 John R. Renshaw, "The Atonement in the Theology of John and Charles Wesley" (Ph.D. thesis, Boston University, 1965).

15 William R. Cannon, *The Theology of John Wesley with Special Reference to the Doctrine of Justification* (Lanham, MD: University Press of America, 1984).

16 Charles R. Wilson, "Christology," in *A Contemporary Wesleyan Theology,* vol. 1, ed. Charles W. Carter (Grand Rapids: Francis Asbury Press, 1983), chap. 9.

17 Kenneth J. Collins, *A Faithful Witness: John Wesley's Homiletical Theology* (Wilmore, KY: Wesley Heritage Press, 1993) and *The Theology of John Wesley* (Nashville: Abingdon Press, 2007).

18 Thomas C. Oden, *John Wesley's Scriptural Christianity: A Plain Exposition of His Teaching on Christian Doctrine* (Grand Rapids: Zondervan, 1994), 177–90.

19 Timothy L. Boyd, *John Wesley's Christology: A Study in Its Practical Implications for Human Salvation, Transformation, and Its Influences for Preaching Christ* (Salem, OH: Allegheny, 2004).

20 John R. Tyson, ed., *Charles Wesley: A Reader* (New York: Oxford University Press, 1989). Tyson is one of the limited number of Wesley scholars who has sought to examine Wesleyan theology through the lens of both brothers. He depicts John Wesley's Christology as robust, orthodox, and Anglican; his discussion of Charles's lyrical Christology will be discussed later in the chapter.

21 David A. Graham, "The Chalcedonian Logic of John Wesley's Christology," *International Journal of Systematic Theology* 20, no. 1 (January 2018): 84–103. One of the most significant defenders of Wesley's orthodox perspective, Graham gives particular attention to the way his antagonism to the deistic cultural context shaped his theology.

22 Rob DeGeorge, "Rehabilitating John Wesley's Christology in the Book of Hebrews: A Response to Hambrick and Lodahl," *Wesleyan Theological Journal* 53, no. 2 (Fall 2018): 165–93.

23 Edgardo Rosado, *John Wesley's Christology: A Social Approach to the Presentation of the Gospel of Christ* (independently published, 2019). A very recent publication, this English translation of the original Spanish work explores the implications of Wesley's Christology for social witness and action in the face of injustice and deprivation.

orthodox Anglican theologian. Jerome Van Kuiken provides the most up-to-date distillation of all the evidence surrounding the Monophysite controversy and demonstrates, in my view, the myth of Monophysitism, Docetism, or Apollinarianism in Wesley.[24] At the time Deschner's claims first surfaced, A. Raymond George[25] and Geoffrey Wainwright,[26] among others, both challenged his conclusions in formal responses to his work. Wesley's *Letter to a Roman Catholic*—a document Randy Maddox has described as "Wesley's most compact summary of his Christological commitments"—provides some of the most compelling evidence supporting his Chalcedonian perspective.[27]

A Review of Studies on Charles Wesley's Christology

Very little discussion, to say nothing of debate, has arisen with reference to Charles Wesley's Christology because so few studies have focused on his theology or this particular aspect of it. In general, most scholars who have addressed this topic in any way have depicted him as classically Anglican, embracing the robust Chalcedonian view of Jesus Christ articulated in the Articles of Religion, and describe his view of Christ's redemptive work through the broadest possible lens of biblical imagery. No scholar has attended exclusively to the topic of Christology in Charles Wesley's theology. As was the case with regard to John, given Charles's cultural context and the teleological orientation of his theology, he tends to emphasize the divinity of Christ without compromising his humanity.

J. Ernest Rattenbury, the most distinguished of the early twentieth-century students of Charles Wesley, addressed primary Christological themes in two chapters of his monumental *Evangelical Doctrines of Charles Wesley's*

---

24   Jerome Van Kuiken, "Deschner's Wesley and the Monophysite Meme," *Wesleyan Theological Journal* 54, no. 2 (Fall 2019): 37–55.

25   George, "Review," 382–84.

26   Wainwright, "Review," 55–56.

27   Maddox, *Responsible Grace*, 303.

Hymns.[28] In a chapter titled "Our Lord Jesus Christ," he reflected particularly on Wesley's hymns related to the Lord's birth, resurrection and ascension, and the Trinity. He detected a strong Lutheran element in this constellation of lyrical material, emphasizing God's unique self-revelation in the person of Jesus Christ. "Jesus Christ was to him God manifest in the flesh, the second person of the Trinity, 'our God contracted to a span,' 'Jehovah crucified.' . . . Not only is God seen through Him, but He is God."[29] In Rattenbury's examination of the Christological imagery of these hymns, he devoted more energy to Charles's articulation of Jesus's humanity than any other issue because of the following explicit concern:

> The problem of Charles Wesley's view of the Person of Christ is what he meant by His humanity. What he meant by His Deity is made clear by hundreds of allusions and by innumerable implications in his verses, but the humanity is so differently conceived from that of the human portraits of Jesus which are painted by modern students that some of them might wonder whether Wesley had any true view of the humanity at all.[30]

He argued that "no one has realized the true humanity of Jesus more literally than Charles Wesley."[31]

The hermeneutical key that unlocks these mysteries for Rattenbury was Charles's "kenotist" view of Jesus and his identification with "suffering humanity." He illustrates this theme with a hymn text drawn from the 1749 collection of *Hymns and Sacred Poems* titled "Desiring to Love":

> Quite from the manger to the cross
> Thy life one scene of sufferings was,
>   And all sustain'd for me:

---

28 J. Ernest Rattenbury, *The Evangelical Doctrines of Charles Wesley's Hymns* (London: Epworth Press, 1941), 152–72. In the absence of any review of the literature relating to this issue in Charles Wesley's theology, a fuller exploration of the primary sources that include a discussion of this topic is included herein.

29 Rattenbury, *Evangelical Doctrines*, 153–54.

30 Rattenbury, 156.

31 Rattenbury, 158.

> O strange excess of love divine!
> Jesus, was ever love like thine!
> Answer me from that tree![32]

He noted the way all aspects of Wesley's Christology ultimately revolve around the central conception of love divine—a love that will go to such great lengths to redeem and restore. "Thus we learn how from the manger to the cross," Rattenbury concluded, "Charles Wesley saw in Christ God manifest in the flesh and realized never more than at the manger that the flesh with which God clad Himself was very human."[33]

Rattenbury also devoted an entire chapter in this work to "The Atonement."[34] He examined both the "finished" and the "unfinished" work with illustrations drawn primarily from what he describes as Wesley's three theological hymn-books: *Hymns on God's Everlasting Love* (1741, 1742), *Hymns on the Lord's Supper* (1745), and *Hymns on the Trinity* (1767). "In the hymns on God's Everlasting Love the doctrine of the Atonement is relatively incidental," he wrote. "The scope and extent of the Atonement are emphasized rather than its content. In the eucharistic hymns, the Lord's Supper is incidental to the Atonement—an instrument for remembering and applying it."[35] After examining the various Christological images Wesley employed in these hymns—all of which reflect the full range of atonement theories—he concluded, "The fact to be most noted is that all these allusions to satisfaction, substitution, penal suffering, and the like are dominated by the central truth of God's love in the Cross; they are regarded as expressions of that love, and of the manner in which it acted. Love, however it is

---

32 Charles Wesley, *Hymns and Sacred Poems*, 2 vols. (Bristol, UK: Farley, 1749), 1:61. All hymn texts throughout this essay are cited from the website of the Center for Studies in the Wesleyan Tradition, Duke Divinity School: http://divinity.duke.edu/initiatives-centers/cswt/wesley-texts, with thanks to Randy and Aileen Maddox.

33 Rattenbury, *Evangelical Doctrines*, 172.

34 Rattenbury, 188–203. Rattenbury also provides an analysis of "the Wesleys' doctrine of the atonement and the modern mind" in a subsequent chapter of that title (pp. 204–14), which carries the discussion beyond the scope of this present exploration.

35 Rattenbury, 189.

explained, is the central doctrine of the Cross."[36] All the various images of atonement coalesce in the stellar hymn "All Ye That Pass By," a hymn that actually displaced "O for a Thousand Tongues to Sing" as the opening selection in the 1785 Methodist pocket hymnbook.[37] It fully explicates Wesley's view of Christ's "finished work," demonstrated by a selection of lines:

> Your ransom and peace, / Your surety he is . . .
> For what you have done / His blood must atone . . .
> He dies to atone / For sins not his own . . .
> Your debt he hath paid, / and your work he hath done.

> Ye all may receive
> The peace he did leave,
>   Who made intercession, "My Father forgive!"

Charles's hymn "Arise, My Soul, Arise" perfectly illustrates the importance of the "unfinished work of Christ" in his Christology.

> Arise, my soul, arise,
>   Shake off thy guilty fears,
> The bleeding sacrifice
>   In my behalf appears;
>   Before the throne my surety stands;
>   My name is written on his hands.

> He ever lives above
>   For me to intercede,
> His all-redeeming love,
>   His precious blood to plead;
> His blood atoned for all our race,
> And sprinkles now the throne of grace.[38]

---

36 Rattenbury, *Evangelical Doctrines*, 192.

37 First published in Charles Wesley, *Hymns on the Great Festivals* (London: for M. Cooper, 1746), 8–10, from which the selections that follow are drawn.

38 John and Charles Wesley, *Hymns and Sacred Poems* (Bristol, UK: Farley, 1742), 264–65. Quoting

"The 'unfinished' work of Christ's priestly intercession," wrote Franz Hildebrand and Oliver Beckerlegge, "the blood of sprinkling, the joint witness of Spirit and blood, the name written on his hands are central themes for Wesley."[39] In Rattenbury's estimation:

> The two hymns, "Arise, my soul, arise" and "All ye that pass by," taken together, condense in a few verses the substance of Wesley's teaching about the Atonement, about the finished and the unfinished work of Christ. In the latter the Atonement, once for all made for the human race, is the basis of the appeal to sinful men to come to Christ; in the former the work is conceived as unfinished, as being carried on in Heaven by Christ, so that individuals may receive the benefits for which He died.[40]

For Charles, Jesus's eternal intercession must also be considered a crucial aspect of his atoning work.

In his *Wesley Hymns as a Guide to Scriptural Teaching*, John Lawson provides limited commentary on the divine Son, the Incarnation, the two natures of Christ, the cross, Christ as victor and sacrifice vis-à-vis atonement, and Christ as high priest.[41] Wesley's hymn "We Know, by Faith," Lawson claimed, demonstrates Charles's view that in Jesus "God came not only to reveal something, but supremely to do something, to perform an historic divine saving act within our world, as a member of the human race, and on behalf of our race. By consequence our Lord is to be confessed as the eternal divine Son."[42] He argued that in Wesley's poetry the profound truth of the divine-human Person—the mystery of the Incarnation—is "set forth in

---

here the first two stanzas of the hymn, see also Rattenbury's full explication of all five verses in *Evangelical Doctrines*, 198–200.

39 John Wesley, *The Works of John Wesley*, vol. 7, *A Collection of Hymns for the Use of the People Called Methodists*, ed. Franz Hildebrand and Oliver A. Beckerlegge (Oxford: Clarendon Press, 1983), 324.

40 Rattenbury, *Evangelical Doctrines*, 198–99.

41 John Lawson, *The Wesley Hymns as a Guide to Scriptural Teaching* (Grand Rapids: Francis Asbury Press, 1987).

42 Lawson, *Wesley Hymns*, 46.

the language of daring paradox, to be interpreted symbolically."[43] Lawson, like Rattenbury, illustrated Wesley's robust conception of atonement with Charles's two hymns, "Arise, My Soul, Arise" and "All Ye That Pass By." He identified more than a hundred scriptural allusions in these hymns, ranging from Leviticus to Revelation, all of which demonstrate Wesley's emphasis on the symbiosis of sacrifice and victory in the cross.[44] According to Lawson, Charles's hymn "Entered the Holy Place Above" demonstrates that "there is eternally within the nature of the God of glory One who knows what it is to be frail and tempted, and of whose sympathy we may be sure."[45]

John R. Tyson's several explorations of Christological themes in Charles Wesley's hymns, sermons, journals, and letters demonstrate his focus on the work of Christ within the larger matrix of soteriology. His two-volume doctoral dissertation, "Charles Wesley's Theology of the Cross," actually argues that Wesley's entire theological project revolves around the "atonement-redemption nexus."[46] He concluded that, while Wesley contributes nothing new to the standard theological content of the doctrine, he presented his conception of redemption in fresh and daring lyrical forms that are simultaneously biblical and balanced. He based this conclusion largely, though not exclusively, on an examination of Wesley's use of individual words. Tyson only alluded to Christology in his *Charles Wesley: A Reader*.[47] He described Wesley's view as "robust," employing the traditional devices for describing the person and work of Christ. But the fifty different Christological titles Tyson identified in Charles's hymn corpus also demonstrate his lyrical creativity and versatility in explicating the doctrine.[48] He

---

43 Lawson, *Wesley Hymns*, 53.

44 Lawson, 62–63.

45 Lawson, 71.

46 John R. Tyson, "Charles Wesley's Theology of the Cross: An Examination of the Theology and Method of Charles Wesley as Seen in His Doctrine of the Atonement" (PhD diss., Drew University, 1983). His research supersedes the earlier work of Renshaw, "The Atonement," primarily in terms of its scope and breadth. For a redacted form of this research, see John R. Tyson, *Charles Wesley on Sanctification: A Biographical and Theological Study* (Salem, OH: Schmul, 1992).

47 Tyson, *Charles Wesley: A Reader*, 40–43.

48 Tyson, 491.

identified the patristic conception of "recapitulation" (particularly as developed in Irenaeus) as a key that unlocks the mystery of Jesus's person and work in Wesley's Christological vision, the restoration of the image of Christ in the believer being "the one thing needful."

In a reflection on Wesley's *Hymns for our Lord's Resurrection*, Tyson returned to these themes, describing Charles's robust Christology and his doctrine of atonement/redemption as two of three persistent theological constants in this collection.[49] He explored all these themes further in *The Way of the Wesleys*, in which he devoted two chapters to Christological concerns, "Risen with Healing in His Wings: Jesus Christ" and "An Interest in My Savior's Blood: The Atonement."[50] He argued cogently that Wesleyan Christology can only be understood properly within the larger context of soteriology, that in the context of English Deism an emphasis on the divinity of Christ was to be expected of anyone claiming to be a "Bible Christian," and that Charles's vision of the restoration of humanity to health and freedom followed a Christological pattern reminiscent of the ancient Eastern Church Fathers.[51]

No person has contributed more to an appreciation for and understanding of Charles Wesley's lyrical theology in the past quarter century than S T Kimbrough Jr. In recent years he has devoted much energy to a

---

49 John R. Tyson, "The Lord of Life is Risen: Theological Reflections on *Hymns for our Lord's Resurrection* (1746)," *Proceedings of The Charles Wesley Society* 7 (2001): 81–99.

50 John R. Tyson, *The Way of the Wesleys: A Short Introduction* (Grand Rapids: Eerdmans, 2014), 80–90, 105–17.

51 Charles Yrigoyen Jr. was commissioned to prepare a popular volume on Charles Wesley's theology for the use of the church on the occasion of the tercentenary of his birth: *Praising the God of Grace: The Theology of Charles Wesley's Hymns* (Nashville: Abingdon Press, 2005). His chapter on "Jesus, God Incarnate" includes a discussion of classical Christological themes drawn from the Christmas hymn "Hark! The Herald Angels Sing": Jesus as prophet, priest, and king; the concept of "veiled in flesh;" and the imagery of Christ as "Prince of Peace" (pp. 25–33).

collaborative study of the ways Charles opened a window to the East.[52] His own contributions to these ongoing discussions reflect his keen concern for particular Christological themes in Wesley's corpus, particularly the issues of *kenosis* and *theosis*. In an exploration of the nativity hymns vis-à-vis Charles Wesley and Ephrem the Syrian, he argued that "both view God's self-emptying, self-limitation, and self-effacement in the Incarnation of Jesus Christ as the foundational foci for Christian spirituality."[53] The critical Christological themes emerging from this research—those elements that shaped Wesley's thought and expression—include the centrality of mystery (the unfathomable), paradox (the irreconcilable), and participation (the teleological).

In an article exploring the theme of *theosis*, primarily in Wesley's *Hymns for the Nativity of Our Lord*—hereinafter *Nativity Hymns*—and *Hymns on the Lord's Supper,* Kimbrough demonstrated an interrelatedness of the Incarnation and the Eucharist in Wesley's Christology.[54] "One may approach 'being made divine' only in the context of the ultimate Mystery," he averred, "which cannot be fully comprehended. How one is transformed into the divine nature remains a mystery for Wesley."[55] While he does not offer commentary in his *Lyrical Theology of Charles Wesley* on Christological questions

---

52 See S T Kimbrough Jr., "Charles Wesley and a Window to the East," in *Charles Wesley: Life, Literature and Legacy,* ed. Kenneth G. C. Newport and Ted A. Campbell (Peterborough, UK: Epworth Press, 2007), 165–83. Kimbrough edited three significant volumes devoted to this quest, *Orthodox and Wesleyan Spirituality* (Crestwood, NY: St. Vladimir's Seminary Press, 2002), *Orthodox and Wesleyan Scriptural Understanding and Practice* (Crestwood, NY: St. Vladimir's Seminary Press, 2005), and *Orthodox and Wesleyan Ecclesiology* (Crestwood, NY: St. Vladimir's Seminary Press, 2007), which consist of presentations from four consultations on "Orthodox and Wesleyan Spirituality" convened at St. Vladimir's Orthodox Theological Seminary and sponsored jointly by the seminary and the United Methodist General Board of Global Ministries under Kimbrough's leadership.

53 S T Kimbrough Jr., *"Kenosis in the Nativity Hymns of Ephrem the Syrian and Charles Wesley,"* in Kimbrough, *Orthodox and Wesleyan Spirituality,* 265.

54 S T Kimbrough Jr., *"Theosis in the Writings of Charles Wesley,"* *St. Vladimir's Theological Seminary Quarterly* 52, no. 2 (2008): 199–212.

55 Kimbrough, "Wesley and the East," 166. In this article Kimbrough provided an "Annotated Bibliography" (165–71) which, while not directly related to Christology, sheds light on important ancillary research. Of particular significance in this regard is the work of A. M. Allchin, Michael Christensen, Geoffrey Wainwright, and Kenneth Carveley on the doctrines of deification, Trinity, and Incarnation.

per se, his careful selection of hymn texts on "The Grace of Jesus Christ" reflect these same concerns and even identify *kenosis* as a central theme.[56] *Partakers of the Life Divine* represents his most comprehensive treatment of the Incarnation and *theosis*.[57] In this work he demonstrates the inseparable connection between the person and work of Christ in Wesley's Christology—how the incarnation of God in the person of Jesus Christ enables salvation and how redemption culminates in a mystical participation in God.[58] Following the lead of Gordon Wakefield, Kimbrough finds the fullest expression of this interrelation in Charles's hymn on the Incarnation, "Let earth and heaven combine."

> He deigns in flesh t' appear,
> Widest extremes to join,
> To bring our vileness near,
> And make us all divine;
> And we the life of God shall know,
> For God is manifest below.[59]

Incarnation conceived as *kenosis* and participation conceived as *theosis* constitute the primary elements of Wesley's Christology.[60]

Several other studies that include some discussion of Charles's Christology,

---

56 S T Kimbrough Jr., *The Lyrical Theology of Charles Wesley* (Eugene, OR: Cascade Books, 2011), 130–37.

57 S T Kimbrough Jr., *Partakers of the Life Divine: Participation in the Divine Nature in the Writings of Charles Wesley* (Eugene, OR: Cascade Books, 2016).

58 See Kimbrough, *Partakers of the Life Divine*, 37–44 in particular.

59 [Charles Wesley], *Hymns for the Nativity of Our Lord* (London: [Strahan], 1745), 8.

60 Paul Chilcote pursued this same line of argument in two chapters of *A Faith That Sings: Biblical Themes in the Lyrical Theology of Charles Wesley* (Eugene, OR: Cascade Books, 2016), in particular, chapter 1, "Incarnation: The Word Became Flesh," and chapter 2, "Redemption: The Lamb That Was Slain." He touched indirectly on Christological issues, particularly *kenosis* and *theosis*, in several articles: "'Claim Me for Thy Service': Charles Wesley's Vision of Servant Vocation," *Proceedings of The Charles Wesley Society* 11 (2006–2007): 69–85; "John and Charles Wesley on 'God in Christ Reconciling,'" *Methodist History* 47, no. 3 (April 2009): 132–45; "Charles Wesley's Lyrical Credo," *Proceedings of The Charles Wesley Society* 15 (2011): 41–67, and "'All the Image of Thy Love': Charles Wesley's Vision of the One Thing Needful," *Proceedings of The Charles Wesley Society* 18 (2014): 21–40.

either directly or tangentially, deserve at least brief mention here. Wesley's *Hymns on the Trinity* (1767) figure prominently, of course, in terms of his view of the person of Christ. He drew inspiration for these hymns from a prose work of William Jones, titled *The Catholic Doctrine of the Trinity*.[61] This collection represents a lyrical exposition of Jones's work—following the structure and content rather compulsively—the purpose of which was to combat the neo-Arian tendencies of Deism, which overemphasized Jesus's humanity. The collection includes an opening section of fifty-seven hymns (one-third of the volume) on "the divinity of Christ." In 1989 Wilma J. Quantrille provided a detailed analysis of this collection in which Christological concerns naturally emerged.[62] She concluded that, while Wesley sought to affirm orthodox teaching with regard to Christ throughout the collection, his primary concern was doxological and not theological; he was more interested in words sung *to* God in praise than words *about* God in the hymns. The hymns reflect a portrait of Christ as the One who embraces fallen humanity with divine love, effects the work of salvation, restores the believer to the original image of God, and indwells the faithful, bringing the joys and blessings of divine love to each through the body of Christ, the church.

Charles Wesley not only produced hymns; he preached. Kenneth G. C. Newport's definitive edition of his sermons, therefore, provides an important corpus of material frequently neglected in the articulation of Wesley's theology.[63] Having said this, however, it must be acknowledged that Newport's intention was not to provide theological analysis of these prose texts; rather, he purposed to provide definitive texts. Regardless, his limited theological reflection on these sermons can be summarized in a terse statement about the collection as a whole. "With all these texts," he observed,

---

61 For a more thorough examination of Wesley's dependence on Jones, see Randy Maddox's introduction in *"Trinity Hymns* (1767)," accessed May 21, 2020, https://divinity.duke.edu/sites /divinity.duke.edu/files/documents/cswt/67_Trinity_Hymns_%281767%29.pdf.

62 Wilma J. Quantrille, "The Triune God in the Hymns of Charles Wesley" (PhD diss., Drew University, 1989).

63 Kenneth G. C. Newport, *The Sermons of Charles Wesley: A Critical Edition with Introduction and Notes* (Oxford: Oxford University Press, 2001).

"the one overriding concern is salvation and how it is achieved, and the one consistent answer given is that it is by faith in Christ, who has paid the price of human sin."[64]

While the tercentenary volume that Newport coedited with Ted Campbell provides several points of entry with regard to theological discourse, attention to Christological concerns remains indirect. S T Kimbrough's essay, "Charles Wesley and a Window to the East" (165–83) has already been discussed. Likewise, John Tyson's discussion of Charles Wesley and redemption (204–228) rehearses his well-worn themes. Ted Campbell's portrait of "Charles Wesley, *Theologos*" (264–77) infers throughout that he used precise language of historic Christian teaching with regard to his own doctrinal formulations. In his reflections on Charles's doctrine of the Trinity (278–98), Jason Vickers concludes that Wesley's view of the person of Christ can be understood as an aspect of economic trinitarian thinking, that in his hymns Charles captured the mystery and ineffability appropriate to divine transcendence, and that he "summons his readers to praise, adoration, thanksgiving and love for God."[65]

In his review of Deschner's study of John Wesley's Christology, Geoffrey Wainwright hinted at an arena begging for further exploration. "By deliberately limiting himself to the Standard Sermons, the Notes on the New Testament, and the Articles," he opined, "Deschner effectively minimized the attention given to an important dimension in Wesley, namely the sacramental."[66] Francis Frost advanced this agenda in two articles published in the *Proceedings of The Charles Wesley Society*.[67] Two of his insights related to the Wesleys' eucharistic theology confirm earlier Christological perceptions. First, while confessional statements were critical for the Wesleys, the

---

64 Newport, *Sermons of Charles Wesley*, 62.

65 Jason E. Vickers, "Charles Wesley and the Revival of the Doctrine of the Trinity: A Methodist Contribution to Modern Theology," in Newport and Campbell, eds., *Charles Wesley*, 292.

66 Wainwright, "Review," 56.

67 Francis Frost, "The Veiled Unveiling of the Glory of God in the Eucharistic Hymns of Charles Wesley: The Self-Emptying Glory of God," *Proceedings of The Charles Wesley Society* 2 (1995): 87–99; and "The Christ-Mysticism of Charles Wesley: The Eucharist and the Heavenly Jerusalem," *Proceedings of The Charles Wesley Society* 9 (2003–2004): 11–26.

brothers were perennially reaching beyond them to the heart of scripture, the gospel, and the community of living faith centered in Christ and the Eucharist. Second, Charles, in particular, showed that "intimate union with Jesus, in communion at the sacramental memorial of his Supper, is the deepest experience of our earth-bound existence and, as such, is not only the surest guarantee of the fullness to come, but also the most efficacious means of growing towards it." Frost described this as Wesley's "Christ-Mysticism." The sacrament, in other words, focuses the attention of the faithful on the supreme importance of the Incarnation—the "alpha event" related to Christ's being—and the "omega event"—the culmination of the process of participatory redemption in the restoration of Christlike love through union with Christ.

Christological Principles in the Wesleys' "Practical Theology"

Three principles related to the Wesleys' engagement with specifically Christological concerns or questions shaped their practical understanding of the person and work of Christ.

1) The Wesleys employed a *"distinct, but not separate" principle* in two critical areas. First, in explicating the person of Christ, they viewed the divine and the human natures as distinct, but not separate. Second, they retained a dynamic understanding of the interrelationship of Christ's person and work as distinct, but inseparable as well. Who Jesus is affected their understanding of what he does; Jesus's purpose and mission lived out in history shaped their vision of who he is.

2) Given the soteriological focus of Wesleyan theology, in general, both brothers viewed Christology through the lens of redemption and thereby tended to place greater *emphasis on the redemptive work of Christ.* In this arena of Christological discourse—as opposed to that concerned more with the person of Christ—the existential "so what?" factor becomes all the more apparent. Despite the inseparability of the person and work of Christ, the brothers' theology revolves around God's ultimate mission of redemption and how Jesus Christ fits into the larger salvific mission of the triune God.

3) Both John and Charles Wesley went to great lengths to exhibit the

full range of biblical imagery related to the person and work of Christ, with only limited explication of these themes or discussion of nuances that would divert their attention from the primary themes of redemption. They employed the language, analogies, and iconography of scripture to proclaim a more richly textured and robust view of Christ's redemptive work. They devoted less energy to the task of elucidating the more elusive aspects of Christ's person. A concern for transformation, rather than information, drove their theological vision and program.

The Wesleys on the Person of Christ

Four primary themes characterize the "practical Christology" of John and Charles Wesley. The first two reflect concerns related to the person of Christ; the third and fourth relate to their vision of Christ's redemptive work.[68]

John and Charles Wesley embraced a robust understanding of the person of Christ as articulated in the historic creeds of the church and affirmed in their Anglican tradition. Both brothers exhibited a keen interest in *kenosis* as a means of explicating the mystery of the Incarnation.

Christology Within The Bounds Of Nicene Orthodoxy

"God in the Person of his Son"[69]
"See in that Infant's face / The depths of Deity"[70]

John and Charles Wesley explicitly affirmed a traditional Chalcedonian understanding of Jesus Christ. Thomas Oden, in *John Wesley's Scriptural Christianity*, declares that "Wesley effortlessly employed the language of Chalcedon in phrases such as 'Real God, as real man,' 'perfect, as God and as man.'"[71] In his sermon "Scriptural Worship," John ascribed to Jesus "all

---

68 In these summative statements I make no effort to survey or discuss the breadth of the Wesleys' discussion of these themes; rather, my intention is to illustrate conclusions drawn from their primary Christological sources and to illustrate these with clear statements from their works.

69 [Charles Wesley], *Hymns on the Trinity* (Bristol, UK: Pine, 1767), 5.

70 Wesley, *Nativity Hymns*, 7.

71 Oden, *John Wesley's Scriptural Christianity*, 177.

the attributes and all the works of God. So that we need not scruple to pronounce him God of God, Light of Light, very God of very God, in glory equal with the Father, in majesty coeternal."[72] John defended the humanity of Jesus, as well, particularly in his *Notes on the New Testament*, describing him as "real man, like other men," whose human existence culminates in death and burial.[73] In his redaction of Article 2 of the Articles of Religion—the primary standard of doctrine and practice that shaped his life and ministry as well as his theology—he declared that "two whole and perfect natures, that is to say, the Godhead and Manhood, were joined together in one Person, never to be divided, whereof is one Christ, very God, and very man."[74]

Charles Wesley composed literally hundreds of hymns on the Incarnation. In these lyrical articulations of his Christology, he described Jesus Christ, the second person of the Trinity, as the friend of humanity. In Jesus Christ, God enters human history, comes close, lives with us, and offers friendship through a human person to every person. Many of Charles's nativity hymns, as in the case of the following example, underscore this understanding of the person of Christ:

Glory be to God on high,
    And peace on earth descend;
God comes down and bows the sky,
    And shows himself our friend!
God the invisible *appears*,
    God the blest, the great I AM
Sojourns in this vale of tears,
    And Jesus is his name.[75]

---

72 John Wesley, *The Works of John Wesley*, vol. 3, *Sermons III, 71–114*, ed. Albert C. Outler (Nashville: Abingdon Press, 1986), 91.

73 See John Wesley, *Explanatory Notes upon the New Testament* (Salem, OH: Schmul, 1975), Mark 6:6; Luke 2:40, 43, 52; John 4:6; Phil 2:7–8; and Heb 2:17 in particular.

74 John Wesley, *The Sunday Service of the Methodists in North America*, ed. James F. White (Nashville: The United Methodist Publishing House, 1984), 306.

75 Wesley, *Nativity Hymns*, 5–6.

He affirms Jesus as true God and true human, a commitment illustrated, as well, in a hymn on "The presence of the Lord," based on Matthew 1:23:

> God is in our flesh revealed,
>> Earth and heaven in Jesus join,
> Mortal with Immortal filled,
>> And human with Divine.
>
> Fulness of the Deity
>> In Jesus's body dwells.[76]

The Wesleys were familiar with all the Christological debates in early church history. They adhere firmly to the orthodox view of the person of Christ defined at the Council of Nicaea (325), later refined in the Nicene Creed, and reiterated in the theology and doxology of their Anglican tradition. They carefully avoided all forms of Arianism that view Jesus as anything less than fully divine. Likewise, they avoided a gnostic or docetic understanding that denies Christ's full humanity. The practical implications are clear. If Jesus is not fully divine, then he simply provides guidance to those seeking recovery and restoration by means of his example. If Jesus is not fully human, then God does not truly enter into the realities of human life with redemptive power. On the other hand, in "Jesus our Savior" we encounter the true God—love incarnate. And in "Jesus our brother" we discover our true selves—agents of love in God's world.

Paradox, Mystery And *Kenosis*

> Being's source *begins to be*, / And God himself is
>> BORN![77]
>> "He emptied himself of all but love" [78]

---

76   Charles Wesley, MS Matthew, 4 (see n. 34).

77   Wesley, *Nativity Hymns*, 6.

78   Wesley, MS Hymns Old Testament, 29 (see n. 34).

John and Charles Wesley both framed their understanding of who Jesus is in terms of paradox and mystery. Rather than attempting to explain the Incarnation in philosophical terms as if to master the inexplicable, they simply described the lengths to which God's love will go to reach people wherever they are. In his sermon "God's Love to Fallen Man" John proclaimed:

> "Beloved, what manner of love is this," wherewith God has loved us! So as to give God's only Son! In glory equal with the Father; in majesty co-eternal! What manner of love is this wherewith the only-begotten Son of God has loved us! So as to "empty himself," as far as possible, of his eternal Godhead! As to divest himself of that glory which he had with the Father before the world began! As to "take upon him the form of a servant, being found in fashion as a man!" And then to humble himself still farther, "being obedient unto death, yea, the death of the cross!"[79]

Charles also used the concept of *kenosis* (self-emptying) as a metaphor to more fully understand the nature of God's mysterious act of Incarnation.[80] A lyrical medium, perhaps, provides a more appropriate form of discourse in which to express this great mystery, and Charles Wesley possessed unique gifts in this arena. He viewed God's self-emptying, self-limitation, and self-effacement in the incarnation of Jesus Christ—described in the hymn embedded in Philippians 2:5–11—as the primary building blocks of Christian theology and spirituality. His most profound exposition of the kenotic theme comes in a hymn exploring the titles of Christ:

> Equal with God, most high,
> He laid his glory by:
> He, th' eternal God was born,
>   Man with men he deign'd t' appear,
> Object of his creature's scorn,
>   Pleas'd a servant's form to wear.

---

79 John Wesley, *The Works of John Wesley*, vol. 2, *Sermons II, 34–70*, ed. Albert C. Outler (Nashville: Abingdon Press, 1985), 428.

80 See Kimbrough, *"Kenosis."*

> He left his throne above
> Emptied of all, but love:
> Whom the heav'ns cannot contain
>   God vouchsaf'd a worm t' appear,
> [81]Lord of glory, *Son of man*,
>   Poor, and vile, and abject here.[82]

Two practical implications emerge from this kenotic paradigm related to humility and self-sacrifice in the Christian journey of discipleship. Both these practices figure prominently in the brothers' appeal to all followers of Jesus to "imitate Christ." The paragraph quoted above from John's sermon based on Romans 5:15 concludes with the following admonition: "If God so loved us, how ought we to love one another!"[83] The qualities of humility (obedience) and self-emptying love (service) shaped Wesley's portrait of Christ. Throughout Christian history, devout followers of Jesus have prayed intentionally and cooperated with God's grace in a quest to realize these lofty virtues in their lives. To imitate Christ—to have the same mind in you that was in Christ (Phil. 2:5 NRSV), to grow to the measure of the full stature of Jesus (Eph. 4:13 NRSV), to be a letter of Jesus written on the tablet of the human heart (2 Cor. 3:3 NRSV)—meant to become like Jesus in his humility and self-sacrificial service.

The Work of Christ

John and Charles Wesley display the full range of biblical imagery with regard to the work of Christ. Charles's hymn "Desiring to Love," published jointly by the brothers in their 1742 collection *Hymns and Sacred Poems* (hereinafter *HSP*), demonstrates the breadth of their vision:

---

81 See a helpful discussion of this conception of Christian discipleship in Paul W. Chilcote's annotations to Thomas à Kempis, *The Imitation of Christ: Selections Annotated & Explained* (Woodstock, VT: SkyLight Paths Publishing, 2012).

82 John and Charles Wesley, *Hymns and Sacred Poems* (London: Strahan, 1739), 165, 167.

83 Wesley, *Works*, 2:428.

What shall I do my God to love,
    My Saviour, and the world's to praise?
Whose bowels of compassion move
    To me, and all the fallen race;
Whose mercy is divinely free
For all the fallen race, and me.

I long to know, and to make known
    The heights and depths of love divine,
The kindness thou to me hast shewn,
    Whose every sin was counted thine:
My God for me resign'd his breath,
He died, to save my soul from death.

All souls are thine: and thou for all
    The ransom of thy life hast given,
To raise the sinner from his fall,
    And bring him back to God and heaven,
Thou all the world hast died to save,
And all may thy salvation have.

How shall I thank thee for the grace,
    On me, and all mankind bestow'd!
O that my every breath were praise,
    O that my heart were fill'd with God!
My heart would then with love o'erflow,
And all my life thy glory shew.[84]

In this hymn, the Wesleys directly tie the Incarnation to its primary purpose—the atonement of all and reconciliation with God. Their doctrine of the redemptive work of Christ is richly textured, reflecting all the classical theories of atonement drawn from various strands of the bib-

---

84 Wesley, *HSP* (1742), 24–25.

lical witness. The reference to Christ taking the sin of humanity upon himself resonates with a *substitutionary or satisfaction theory*. Their conception of Christ's victory over death reflects a more ancient *Christus victor theme*, as does Charles's reference to the metaphor of ransom and release. They alluded to the *moral influence theory* of atonement in their explication of "love divine" and its implied power to transform. Given the full breadth of the biblical imagery they used, "one is tempted to describe this," avers Randy Maddox, "as a Penalty Satisfaction *explanation* of the Atonement which has a Moral Influence *purpose*, and a Ransom *effect*."[85]

While all these themes pervade their sermons and hymns, the Wesleys explicated the work of Christ primarily through reference to the threefold office of Christ as prophet, priest, and king. Both brothers exhibited a keen interest in *theosis* as a means of explicating redemption as the restoration of the image of God and the role of Eucharist in this process.

The Threefold Office of Christ

"Jesus to you his fulness brings / Pardon, and
holiness, and heaven"[86]

"Make, O make my heart thy seat / Christ, be
Lord, be King to me!"[87]

The breadth of their soteriological concerns "led the brothers to emphasize relating to Christ 'in all his offices,'" claims Maddox, "not just as the priest who atones for guilt, but also as the prophet who teaches the ways in which we are to live, and as the king who oversees the restoration of wholeness in our lives."[88] Likewise, Oden described John's focus on the

---

85 Maddox, *Responsible Grace*, 109.

86 [Charles Wesley], *Hymns for Those That Seek and Those That Have Redemption in the Blood of Jesus Christ* (London: Strahan, 1747), 63.

87 Wesley, *HSP* (1739), 174.

88 Randy L. Maddox, "Theology of John and Charles Wesley," in *T&T Clark Companion to Methodism*, ed. Charles Yrigoyen (New York: T&T Clark International, 2010), 29.

offices of Christ as the crux of his Christology.[89] In John's *Letter to a Roman Catholic*, he summarized his teaching in this regard:

> I believe that Jesus of Nazareth was the Saviour of the world, the Messiah so long foretold; that, being anointed with the Holy Ghost, he was a *prophet*, revealing to us the whole will of God; that he was a *priest*, who gave himself a sacrifice for sin, and still makes intercession for transgressors; that he is a *king*, who has all power in heaven and in earth; and will reign till he has subdued all things to himself.[90]

This Christological formula figures prominently in his sermon "The Law Established by Faith, II," as well, with a fuller explication of the meaning of each office:

> We must . . . proclaim Christ in all his offices. To preach Christ as a workman that needs not to be ashamed is to preach him, not only as our great *High Priest*, "taken from among men, and ordained for men, in things pertaining to God," as such, "reconciling us to God by his blood" and "ever living to make intercession for us."—but likewise as the *Prophet of the Lord*, "who of God is made unto us wisdom," who, by his word and his Spirit, is with us always, "guiding us into all truth;"—yea, and as remaining a *King* forever, as giving laws to all whom he has bought with his blood, as restoring those to the image of God whom he had first re-instated in his favor, as reigning in all believing hearts until he has "subdued all things to himself,"—until he hath utterly cast out all sin and brought in everlasting righteousness.[91]

John drew here upon a long-standing tradition in Western theology (owing much to John Calvin) that conceived Jesus's work through the lens of these particular roles.[92] While Wesley was concerned about how to

---

89 See Oden, *John Wesley's Scriptural Christianity*, 187–90.

90 Albert C. Outler, ed., *John Wesley* (New York: Oxford University Press, 1964), 404.

91 Wesley, *Works*, 2:37–38.

92 See my discussion of these concepts in *John and Charles Wesley: Selections from Their Writings and Hymns* (Woodstock, VT: SkyLight Paths Publishing, 2011), 90–91; cf. Maddox, *Responsible Grace*, 109–14.

properly interpret the "past" or "finished" work of Christ—his redemptive work that made atonement possible—he emphasized with equal or even greater vigor the "present" work of Christ. Despite the foundational nature of "Christ dying for us," he was equally concerned about "Christ reigning in us." In other words, he did not view Christ's atoning death as the totality of his redemptive work; rather, he viewed the cross as the foundation of God's present and transforming work through Christ in the life of the believer. Following the order of the offices that Wesley seems to have preferred, Christ's role as priest—through which God mediates the experience of pardon—precedes his culminating work of restoration. As prophet, Christ reveals the moral image of God and initiates the renewal of Christlike character. The present work of Christ comes to fruition through the office of Christ as king (or physician).[93] Christ as Lord rules in all believing hearts and enables full conformity to his own image as the believer grows into the fullest possible love of God and neighbor. Christ as priest forgives (pardon); Christ as prophet guides (holiness); Christ as king restores (heaven).

Charles Wesley replicated this Christological paradigm in the concluding stanzas of a "Hymn to the Son":

> Prophet, to me reveal
> Thy Father's perfect will.
> Never mortal spake like thee,
>   Human prophet like divine;
> Loud and strong their voices be,
>   Small and still and inward thine!

> On thee my priest I call,
> Thy blood aton'd for all.
> Still the Lamb as slain appears,
>   Still thou stand'st before the throne,
> Ever off'ring up my pray'rs,
>   These presenting with thy own.

---

93 See Maddox, *Responsible Grace*, 112–13.

> Jesu! Thou art my King,
> From thee my strength I bring!
> Shadow'd by thy mighty hand,
> > Saviour, who shall pluck me thence?
> Faith supports, by faith I stand
> > Strong as thy omnipotence.[94]

In other hymns Charles demonstrates his full alignment with his brother's understanding of the kingly role of Christ in terms of restoration—the recovery of God's image in the believer and the reign of love in all believing hearts. The suppliant cries:

> I pant to feel thy sway
> And only thee t' obey.
> Thee my spirit gasps to meet,
> > This my one, my ceaseless pray'r,
> Make, O make my heart thy seat,
> > O set up thy kingdom there![95]

One might easily expect three primary implications from this exposition of the offices of Christ. First, the priestly role of Christ reveals that God graciously forgives and reconciles those who have no claim to pardon. Our trust in the fact that God has already accepted us and loves us defines living faith. Christ came to demonstrate this amazing love to us. Second, salvation means more than forgiveness of sin. Christ as prophet reveals that the purpose of a life reclaimed by faith is the recovery of God's image. Faith is the means to love's end. In other words, the Christian life moves toward the goal of holiness of heart and life and ever greater conformity to the image of Christ. Third, the kingly rule of Christ reveals salvation as *therapeia*—divine therapy that heals the child of God. The goal of the way or process of salvation is the fullest possible restoration to health in those who put

---

94 Wesley, *HSP* (1739), 110.

95 Wesley, 174.

their trust in Christ. The Wesleys' concept of ultimate spiritual health is *theosis*—the fullest possible participation of the believer in God. The goal of the redemptive work of Christ is the fullest possible love of God and others.

Partaking of the Life Divine in the Eucharist

"To rise restor'd, and throughly pure, / In all the image of thy love"[96]
"That I thy nature might partake"[97]

Everything in John and Charles Wesley's concept of redemption aligns toward the goal of fully restored love. While affirming the forensic or juridical aspects of the work of Christ, they also understood the human need for divine *therapeia*; freedom from slavery to sin provides a foundation for the restoration of the living presence of God in the believer. For the Wesleys, the work of Christ culminates in the fullest possible recovery of the *imago Dei*. Whether influenced directly or indirectly by patristic sources, *theosis*—God became like us so that we might become like God—defines the primary purpose or *telos* of Christ's work.[98]

"Ye know that the great end of religion," John would repeat on a number of occasions, "is to renew our hearts in the image of God, to repair that total loss of righteousness and true holiness which we sustained by the sin of our first parents."[99] He defined this theotic goal as "Christian perfection."[100] In "The Scripture Way of Salvation," he provided one of his most succinct definitions of this vision: "The word [i.e., "perfection"] has various senses: here it means perfect love. It is love excluding sin; love filling

---

96 Wesley, *HSP* (1749), 2:187.

97 John and Charles Wesley, *Hymns on the Lord's Supper* (Bristol, UK: Farley, 1745), 39.

98 In the foreword to his 1985 reprint edition of his original *Wesley's Christology*, John Deschner acknowledged that it was important to take the Eastern theme of *theosis* more seriously in order to understand Wesley (ix).

99 Wesley, *Works*, 2:185.

100 For a full discussion of this Wesleyan concept, see the introduction to Wesley's Christian perfection corpus in *The Works of John Wesley*, vol. 13, *Doctrinal and Controversial Treatises, II*, ed. Paul Wesley Chilcote and Kenneth J. Collins (Nashville: Abingdon Press, 2013), 3–25.

the heart, taking up the whole capacity of the soul. It is love 'rejoicing ever-more, praying without ceasing, in everything giving thanks.'"[101] "This great gift of God, the salvation of our souls," he averred in his *Plain Account of Christian Perfection*, "is no other than the image of God fresh stamped on our hearts. *It is a renewal of believers in the spirit of our minds, after the likeness of him that created them.*"[102] John articulated his vision of *theosis*—participation in the divine nature—in his translation of a Gerhardt hymn in which the singer pleads for love to fill one's whole being:

> O grant that nothing in my soul
>> May dwell, but thy pure love alone!
> O may thy love possess me whole,
>> My joy, my treasure, and my crown;
> Strange flames far from my heart remove—
> My every act, word, thought, be love.[103]

This concept of *theosis* also shaped Wesley's understanding of Eucharist, a connection exploited more fully by his younger brother.

The concluding stanza of Charles Wesley's famous redemption hymn "Love Divine, All Loves Excelling," celebrates redemption's lofty goal:

> Finish then thy new creation,
>> Pure and sinless let us be,
> Let us see thy great salvation,
>> Perfectly restor'd in thee;
> Chang'd from glory into glory,
>> Till in heaven we take our place,
> Till we cast our crowns before thee,
>> Lost in wonder, love, and praise![104]

---

101 Wesley, *Works*, 2:160; emphasis original.

102 Wesley, *Works*, 13:150.

103 Wesley, *HSP* (1739), 156.

104 Wesley, *Hymns for Those That Seek and Those That Have Redemption in the Blood of Jesus Christ*, 12.

Kimbrough noted how the concern of *theosis* "surfaces time and again in Charles Wesley's poetry in concert with many of the Early Fathers of the Church."[105] Wesley encapsulated this vision in a simple couplet from his hymn on Philippians 2:5: "I shall fully be restored / To the image of my Lord."[106] The twin themes of incarnation and restoration find profound expression in one of his nativity hymns:

> Made flesh for our sake,
> That we might partake
> The nature divine,
> > And again in his image, his holiness shine;
>
> And while we are here,
> Our King shall appear,
> His Spirit impart,
> > And form his full image of love in our heart.[107]

In his lyrical corpus, three corollaries of *theosis* receive repeated attention: the claim that the Spirit restores the image of Christ in the believer, that transformed disciples of Jesus will be like him, and that this kind of transformation enables them to radiate the glory of God.[108]

"The eucharistic hymns especially exhibit a *participatory* understanding of our relation to Christ," observes Geoffrey Wainwright. "Charles Wesley's Easter hymn expresses it exactly: 'Made like Him, like Him we rise! Ours the cross, the grave, the skies!'"[109] For Charles the sacrament of Holy Communion functions as a focal point for "the one thing needful," namely, the restoration of the divine image in the believer. The Lord's Supper both presents a vision of holiness and, perhaps even more important, offers

---

105 Kimbrough, *Lyrical Theology*, 89; cf. Kimbrough's most fully developed examination of this theme, *Partakers of the Life Divine*.

106 Wesley, *HSP* (1742), 223.

107 Wesley, *Nativity Hymns*, 12.

108 See the discussion of these themes in Chilcote, "'All the Image of Thy Love,'" 21–40.

109 Wainwright, "Review," 56.

sanctifying grace to the faithful on their journey toward holiness of heart and life. In his incisive study of Wesley's *Hymns on the Lord's Supper* (hereinafter *HLS*), Daniel Stevick examines the conjunction of forgiveness and holiness in this collection and affords this summative comment:

> In describing Wesley's understanding of redemption, it should be remarked that for him, salvation and holiness of life—justification and sanctification—are inseparable. If the sacrament conveys the very reality of Christ's atonement, it brings forgiveness of sins; but forgiveness necessarily inaugurates a new creation. If a life of holiness does not follow from faith, it is as though Christ had died in vain.[110]

The concept of "partaking in the life divine" comes into clear focus in these hymns.

Three particular insights related to this divine partaking surface in Charles's hymns. First, he simply affirmed that participation in the Eucharist shapes the fullest possible love in the disciple of Jesus.

> O what a soul-transporting feast
> Doth this communion yield!
> Remembering here thy Passion past
> We with thy love are fill'd.[111]

Second, the fullest possible infilling of love ultimately means conformity to the cross. The "suffering servants" of God are called to take up their crosses daily in multifarious acts of self-sacrificial love. Wesley repeatedly described the full extent of solidarity with the crucified Lord:

> His servants shall be
> With Him on the tree,
> Where Jesus was slain
> His crucified servants shall always remain.[112]

---

110 Daniel B. Stevick, *The Altar's Fire: Charles Wesley's Hymns on the Lord's Supper, 1745 Introduction and Exposition* (Peterborough, UK: Epworth Press, 2004), 36.

111 Wesley, *HLS*, 82.

112 Wesley, 120.

To possess the mind of Christ, to be fully restored in love, means to be shaped in the form of the cross.

Thirdly, he also communicates a profound, corporate dimension with regard to his vision of conformity to the divine. The Eucharist shapes the followers of Jesus into a community that suffers with others for the sake of love. The Eucharist "forms the Savior in the soul," to use Charles's own phrase; that formation takes place not only in the individual heart of the believer, but in the heart of the church. Holy Communion enables the believer to realize participation in the divine:

> Saviour, thou didst the mystery give
>> That I thy nature might partake,
> Thou bidst me outward signs receive,
>> One with thyself my soul to make,
> My body, soul and spirit to join
> Inseparably one with thine.[113]

The singular, practical implication of John and Charles Wesley's vision of Christ's redemptive life and work in which God invites us to partake of the divine nature could not be any clearer. Christ is the true light of the world whose radiance transcends all darkness, and when it floods the soul, all manner of darkness vanishes. Living into this light and this love is the chief end of life. So, Charles prayed for the in-breaking of the glorious light of the One "whose glory fills the skies":

> Visit then this soul of mine,
>> Pierce the gloom of sin, and grief,
> Fill me, radiancy divine,
>> Scatter all my unbelief,
> More and more thyself display
> Shining to the perfect day.[114]

---

113 Wesley, *HLS*, 39.

114 Wesley and Wesley, *Hymns and Sacred Poems* (London: Strahan, 1740), 25.

2

Early Methodist Christology Beyond the Wesleys

Mark K. Olson

Early Methodists were in love with Jesus. Their devotion to Christ was celebrated in sermons, tracts, letters, diaries and journals, and especially in their hymns. In the following stanzas Sarah Jones (d. 1794) expressed what many Methodists felt toward their Savior:

> O Christ, the God of love
> Teach me the holy art,
> In love to rise, and walk above,
> And give thee all my heart!
>
> Thus all that's good agree
> In Christ, as all in all
> For time, and to eternity
> Adore him, O my soul![1]

On a popular level early Methodists did not champion any new teachings about Jesus.[2] Firmly committed to trinitarian Christology, they understood Christ to be the eternal Son of God, who became incarnate as a human being to purchase our salvation through his death and resurrection.

---

1 Lester Ruth, ed., *Early Methodist Life and Spirituality: A Reader* (Nashville: Kingswood Books, 2005), 40–41.

2 See Ruth, 31–66; Paul Wesley Chilcote, *Early Methodist Spirituality: Selected Women's Writings* (Nashville: Kingswood Books, 2007).

Jesus Christ was a divine Savior who came to earth to "save his people from their sins" (Matt. 1:21 NRSV). Methodist Christology was therefore largely shaped by its soteriology. As Lester Ruth observed, Methodists were "obsessed with salvation." It was the "one concern around which all other convictions orbited."[3] John Wesley taught his followers they had "nothing to do but to save souls."[4] Thus, Methodists proclaimed a Savior who died for every person and stressed the personal dimension of salvation—Jesus had died for *me*. Faith in Jesus was more than a creed; it was a life-changing encounter with the crucified and risen Lord, bringing assurance of salvation in this present life.

Rise of Heterodox Christologies

Soteriology was not the only source for early Methodist statements on Christology. In the seventeenth and eighteenth centuries, heterodox views on the Trinity arose in England that challenged traditional teachings on Christ's person and work.[5] There were three that most concerned early Methodists: Deism, Arianism, and Unitarianism, also known as Socinianism. Deism was a popular movement among intellectual classes that promoted a rationalistic faith grounded on Enlightenment principles. Rejecting divine revelation, Deism affirmed a supreme being but considered Christianity a corruption of an original, pure, natural religion. One of the most influential deistic works was Matthew Tindal's *Christianity as Old as the Creation*, published in 1730. Arianism was a fourth-century heresy that taught that Christ was the first created being, second in rank to the Father, but inferior by nature. Prominent supporters of Arianism in the early modern period were the poet John Milton (d. 1674), mathematician and historian William Whiston (d. 1752) and scholar Samuel Clarke (d. 1729).[6] But in the latter half

---

3   Ruth, *Early Methodist Life and Spirituality*, 31.

4   Thomas Jackson, *The Works of John Wesley*, 14 vols. (London: Wesleyan Conference, 1872), 8:310.

5   Philip Dixon, *Nice and Hot Disputes: The Doctrine of the Trinity in the Seventeenth Century* (New York: T&T Clark, 2003).

6   Dixon, *Nice and Hot Disputes*, 101, 181–83.

of the eighteenth century, Unitarianism was considered the most danger-ous by Methodists. The father of English Unitarianism was John Biddle (d. 1662), who was influenced by the teachings of Faustus Socinus (d. 1604).[7] Socinianism was an anti-trinitarian movement that spread from Italy to Po-land in the sixteenth century and then to England by the 1640s. It stressed God's singularity and denied Christ's deity and incarnation. In contrast to Arianism, Socinianism viewed Christ as only a human being. Like Deism, it rejected the doctrines of original sin and Christ's death as an atonement for sin. Early Methodists used the terms *Socinian* and *Unitarian* interchangeably.

Whereas the appeal of Deism and Arianism was mostly to individu-als, Unitarianism was a different matter. The first English Unitarian chapel opened in April 1774, and over the next several decades the movement gained strength in England and America, leading to the birth of a Meth-odist Unitarian Movement in the nineteenth century.[8] In the 1770s a new preacher of Unitarian doctrine rose to prominence in England. Joseph Priest-ley (d. 1804) was famous as a scientist, philosopher, and scholar. His pub-lished works numbered around 150, and his achievements included the discovery of oxygen and other gases. He moved in high circles and wrote on philosophical, political, and theological issues of the day. Raised in En-glish dissent, Priestley converted to Arianism before settling as a Unitarian. He represented a new kind of Unitarian, one who appealed to historical scholarship to make his case. According to Priestley, the Christian faith was at first Jewish and Unitarian, and belief in Christ's preexistence was intro-duced by Christian apologists in the second century who relied on Greek philosophy to guide their theology. Drawing on Peter's statement in Acts 2:22—Christ was a "man approved by God" (WEB)—Priestley famously as-serted that Jesus was a "mere man." In late 1782 Priestley published his broadside against trinitarian Christology and other perceived corruptions of the faith in a massive two-volume work, *An History of the Corruptions*

---

7   Socinus was the Latin form of his last name. The Italian spelling was Sozzini.

8   Robert E. Schofield, *The Enlightened Joseph Priestley: A Study of His Life and Work from 1773 to 1804* (University Park: The Pennsylvania State University, 2004), 26, 267; H. McLachlan, *The Methodist Unitarian Movement* (London: Manchester University Press, 1919).

of Christianity.[9] In this tome Priestley presented all the standard Unitarian doctrines under the guise of historical scholarship. Four years later he followed this up with a more massive, four-volume work, *An History of Early Opinions concerning* Jesus *Christ . . . Proving That the Christian Church Was at First Unitarian.*[10]

Given Priestley's reputation, many Christians felt that a response was necessary. By the summer of 1783, critical reviews from Anglican leaders appeared in the press. A heated debate ensued between Priestley and Anglican bishop Samuel Horsley (d. 1806) that lasted for several years. Even at their deaths twenty years later, their families and supporters argued over which side had won the debate. It was not only Anglican leaders who felt compelled to respond. John Fletcher, vicar of Madeley, was a leading early Methodist scholar. His *Checks to Antinomianism* and other writings were seminal in early Methodist theology. By March 1784 Fletcher had written several letters to Priestley defending Christ's divinity, but later decided that a more thorough response was required. John Wesley told Fletcher that Priestley was "one of the most dangerous enemies of Christianity" and encouraged Fletcher to write a full refutation of the Unitarian's teachings.[11]

To answer Priestley's two main assertions—the doctrine of the Trinity is irrational, and the biblical authors teach only a human messiah—Fletcher planned a two-part response. Over the next several months, he wrote the introduction, an expostulatory letter, and the first four chapters of the first part, *A Rational Vindication of the Catholic Faith*, before unexpectedly passing away in August 1785. With Wesley's recommendation, Mrs. Fletcher gave the manuscript to Joseph Benson to prepare for publication. Benson (d. 1821), who had been a close colleague of Fletcher for

---

9   Joseph Priestley, *An History of the Corruptions of Christianity, in Two Volumes* (Birmingham, UK: Piercy and Jones, for J. Johnson, 1782).

10   Joseph Priestley, *An History of Early Opinions concerning* Jesus *Christ, Compiled from Original Writers, Proving That the Christian Church Was at First Unitarian* (Birmingham, UK: Pearson and Rollason, for the author), 1786.

11   W. Reginald Ward and Richard P. Heitzenrater, eds., *The Works of John Wesley: Journal and Diaries* (Nashville: Abingdon Press, 1995), 6:299; John Telford, ed., *The Letters of John Wesley, A.M.*, 8 vols. (London: Epworth Press, 1931), 7:265.

many years, added ten chapters to Fletcher's four to complete the argument against Priestley's Unitarian Christology.

Some comment on the development of Benson's Christology is relevant at this point. In the 1770s he embraced the idea of the preexistence of Christ's human soul, which he derived from Isaac Watts's book *The Glory of Christ as God-Man*.[12] The purpose of Watts's work was to counter Socinian views by showing that the theophanies in the Old Testament were Christophanies. Yet, Watts went so far as to claim that the angel of the Lord was Christ's preexistent human soul. When Benson was assigned the task of preparing *A Rational Vindication* for publication, Wesley cautioned him against including speculative theories. He mentioned Watts's views and how it led him to adopt Arian beliefs. Wesley counseled Benson to stay close to scripture and to not try to solve all the difficulties related to the subject.[13] From Benson's memoirs we learn that Wesley's counsel was persuasive, for he reexamined the subject while preparing the manuscript and concluded there was no scriptural support for the preexistence of Christ's human soul.[14]

A Rational Vindication was published in 1788 and again in 1790.[15] The next year Benson published Fletcher's eight letters addressed to Priestley, along with eleven of his own. Titled *Socinianism Unscriptural*, it was the second part of Fletcher's planned response to Priestley.[16] The aim of this work was to show that the biblical authors taught a divine messiah by providing a running commentary on each book of the Bible. However, nothing new

---

12 Isaac Watts, *The Glory of Christ as God-Man Display'd, in 3 Discourses. With an Appendix* (London: for J. Oswald at the Rose and Crown, 1746).

13 Telford, *Letters of John Wesley*, 8:89.

14 Richard Treffry, *Memoirs of the Rev. Joseph Benson* (New York: Lane and Sandford, 1842), 78.

15 John Fletcher and Joseph Bentley, *A Rational Vindication of the Catholick Faith Being the First Part of a Vindication of Christ's Divinity; Inscribed to the Reverend Dr. Priestley* (London: Hull, 1788; New-Chapel, City-Road, 1790). To locate *Rational Vindication*, see John Fletcher, *The Works of the Reverend John Fletcher*, 4 vols. (New York: Waugh and Mason, 1844), 3:377–497 (hereafter *Works*).

16 John Fletcher, *Socinianism Unscriptural* (Birmingham, UK: E. Jones, in Bull Street, 1791). To locate *Socinianism Unscriptural*, see Fletcher, *Works*, 3:499–619.

regarding their Christology was offered in the second work. Therefore, in this study we will focus on *A Rational Vindication* to expound their Christology and reference the second work when needed. The importance of these two works was that they represented the first full exposition of Methodist Christology according to scripture, tradition, reason, and experience.

A Rational Vindication of the Catholic Faith

The primary concern of Fletcher and Benson was that Priestley's low Christology undermined the gospel. By robbing Christ of his divinity, Priestley had shredded the gospel of its saving power, for a "mere man" could never atone for human sin nor be the source of eternal life to fallen humanity. Since Priestley did not deny Christ's humanity, their rebuttal centered on a rational explanation of his deity. In this sense, the authors' approach was like the apostle Paul's; the apostle showed less interest in the details of Christ's human life and focused on Jesus as a divine Savior who assumed human nature to save us from sin and death. Nevertheless, as we will see, Fletcher and Benson did affirm Christ's full humanity, including a rational soul and physical body. Also, by titling the work a defense of the "Catholic Faith" the authors intended their readers to understand their firm adherence to the ancient ecumenical councils at Nicaea (CE 325) and Chalcedon (CE 451), which were embodied in the Anglican Articles of Religion. Therefore, their use of the word "Catholic" signified the historic faith of the universal church reaching back to the apostles.

Fletcher opened with a general explanation of the Catholic faith regarding the nature of God. There is one "Supreme Being," one "infinite and eternal Mind," "One Creator over numberless creatures," and one "boundless" and "living God." In this sense, Fletcher acknowledged, "true Christians are all Unitarians."[17] He then added with carefully chosen words, this "one eternal and perfect essence subsists, without division or separation, under three adorable distinctions, which are called sometimes the Father,

---

17 Fletcher, *Works*, 3:398.

the Son, and the Holy Ghost; and sometimes the Father, the Word, and the Spirit."[18] Moreover, Fletcher explained that trinitarians do not confound the persons or the divine essence by claiming the "three persons are one person, or three gods are one God." Instead, quoting 1 John 5:7 Fletcher explained, "These three Divine subsistences are one substance. These three Divine persons are one Jehovah."[19]

By clarifying the doctrine of the Trinity, Fletcher could define the nature of Christ's divine sonship. Central to his argument was to demonstrate that Jesus was a "proper Son" of the Father. In the Bible, wrote Fletcher, the term "son" is used in several senses. First, there are "created sons," like the angels and Adam. Second are listed "reputed sons," which refers to everyone who has a "filial reverence" of God. Third are "titular sons," who by their office exercise authority given them by God. This includes human leaders and judges (Psalm 82). Unitarians, like Priestley, defined Christ's sonship in this sense. Fourthly, there are sons by adoption, which includes believers in Jesus and those who participate in the future resurrection.[20] By contrast, Jesus was unique as a "proper Son of God."[21] He was the "only begotten Son," who as the *Logos* (Word) was "in the beginning with God," and "was God" (John 1:1, 2 KJV).[22] He was a "Son by nature," not by creation or adoption, and in passages such as John 17:5, Jesus spoke of God the Father as "his proper and natural Father."[23] His generation was eternal since "all of the Son's Deity came from his Divine Father" and there was a "real communication of divinity" from the Father to the Son.[24] Furthermore, Jesus

---

18 Fletcher, *Works*, 3:398–99.

19 Fletcher, 3:399–400. Fletcher quotes from 1 John 5:7, "For there are three that bear record in heaven, the Father, the Word, and the Holy Ghost: and these three are one" (KJV). This portion is now recognized as an interpolation and not original.

20 Fletcher, 3:409.

21 Fletcher, 3:408.

22 Fletcher, 3:407. Since early Methodists used the King James Version of the Bible, this is the version used in this chapter.

23 Fletcher, 3:408.

24 Fletcher, 3:411, 537, 545, 550.

possessed the "incommunicable attributes of the Supreme Being" and thus was "perfectly equal to the Father."[25] Existing in the "most perfect unity with his Father who precedes him," as the apostle John wrote, the Son does the "very works of his Father jointly with him" and executes judgment on behalf of the Father, so that all may "honour him as they honour the Father."[26]

Besides defining Christ's eternal sonship, Fletcher recognized that Jesus was a "created Son of God, as well as Adam, with respect to his humanity."[27] He was "miraculously and supernaturally formed from the substance of his virgin mother" so that he was a "real man."[28] This theme was developed further in *Socinianism Unscriptural*. As the Son of Man, Fletcher held that Christ fulfilled the offices of prophet, priest, and king.[29] He mediated between God and sinful humanity by laying down his "human life" in his sufferings and death.[30] Regarding his human character, Jesus was a "man approved of God" and in "his form of a servant, a loving, humble man."[31] Though Fletcher did not go into detail about the Incarnation or the particulars of Christ's human life, his writings demonstrate belief in the doctrine of the hypostatic union of the two natures in the one person, Jesus Christ.[32] In his introductory letter he drew on an argument first used by Saint Augustine that the hypostatic union can be rationally understood by the "immortal soul and the mortal body" that form "one man."[33]

With Christ's divine and human sonship defined, Benson provided a series of rational arguments based on scripture and scholarship to support

---

25   Fletcher, *Works*, 3:410–11.

26   Fletcher, 3:412.

27   Fletcher, 3:409.

28   Fletcher, 3:409, 545.

29   Fletcher, 3:517–18, 533, 539.

30   Fletcher, 3:550, 553.

31   Fletcher, 3:550, 553.

32   Fletcher, 3:408–9, 545–46.

33   Fletcher, 3:391. Boniface Ramsay, ed., *The Works of Saint Augustine: Letters 100–155* (Hyde Park, NY: New City Press, 2003), 218–19 (Letter 137). For a sermon outline that summarizes Fletcher's Christology, see *Works*, 4:207.

that definition. A wide range of authorities were included. Most quoted were Anglican scholars George Bull (d. 1710), Gilbert Burnet (d. 1715), and John Pearson (d. 1686); yet he also appealed to Nonconformist commentator Philip Doddridge (d. 1751) and French Protestant minister Jakob Abbadie (d. 1727). Several church fathers were quoted, like Athenagoras (d. 190), Irenaeus (d. 202), Origen (d. 254), and the *Epistle to Diognetus* (c. 200), which Benson incorrectly attributed to Justin Martyr. Finally, Benson included several Jewish sources: the philosopher Philo of Alexandria (d. 50), the Jewish Targums, and the *Book of Wisdom* (also known as the *Wisdom of Solomon*). The wide range of sources, both contemporary and ancient, reveals the level of scholarship that Benson included in his section of *A Rational Vindication*.

Benson began his argument with a series of observations about Christ as the *Logos* of God in John 1:1–14 (ch. 5). Benson noted that the *Logos* was a person, eternally distinct from the Father, "not a titular god, or a god by office" as the Unitarians claimed, but "God by nature, partaking of a real and proper Deity, in unison with the Father, whose Word he was."[34] The *Logos* was therefore the Creator of all things, the source of life and spiritual illumination.[35] He was the one who appeared in the theophanies of the Old Testament. Since the Father in his "Divine essence" cannot be seen, it was the role of the only begotten Son to reveal God to humans (John 1:18).[36] Thus, contrary to the Arian position, the Son was by nature superior to the angelic realm and the proper heir of God's kingdom.[37] Christ, as a proper Son, was shown to be Jehovah, the God of the Old Testament, in the next three chapters. Benson argued that Old Testament passages that refer to Jehovah (ch. 6), divine titles and incommunicable attributes that pertain to Jehovah (ch. 7), and the divine works of creation and providence

---

34 Fletcher, *Works*, 3:416–71.

35 Fletcher, 3:417.

36 Fletcher, 3:418, 428–30. In *Socinianism Unscriptural* Fletcher made the same argument about the Father's unseen essence and the Son's role as revealer (Fletcher, *Works*, 3:508).

37 Fletcher, 3:420–22.

are all applied to Christ in the New Testament (ch. 8). Benson wrapped up his argument for Christ's divinity by showing that the Son will execute final judgment (ch. 10) and received divine worship while on earth and after the resurrection (ch. 11).

Though the central aim of *A Rational Vindication* was to establish Christ's divinity, in chapter twelve Benson addressed the Incarnation, "The true catholic Church has allowed, and believed, in all ages; that he who is God is also *man*."[38] Jesus was fully human, "subsisting" of a "reasonable soul, and human flesh."[39] He experienced the normal stages of development, from conception to adulthood, and was subject to all natural human weaknesses and affections, such as hunger, thirst, weariness, joy, and sorrow.[40] As a human being, he physically died, rose from the dead, and ascended to heaven.[41] In keeping with the Chalcedonian Definition, Benson maintained that the two natures were "preserved distinct" and not mixed or changed to form one nature, as Eutyches taught.[42] Nor did the two natures suggest there were two persons—one divine and one human—as Nestorius taught.[43] Regarding the hypostatic union, Benson affirmed the communication of properties, which he defined as when "one nature speaks things, or has things spoken of it, which are only proper to the other nature."[44] He then quoted Burnet's *Exposition of the Thirty-Nine Articles* to assert that the union of both natures could be understood by the analogy of the soul-body union, which came from Saint Augustine.[45] Finally, when answering Unitarian objections in chapter 13, Benson affirmed the eternal generation of the Son by stating that "as the branch

---

38 Fletcher, *Works*, 3:475, emphasis his.

39 Fletcher, 3:475, 477, 481.

40 Fletcher, 3:475.

41 Fletcher, 3:483.

42 Fletcher, 3:477–78.

43 Fletcher, 3:483.

44 Fletcher, 3:482.

45 Fletcher, 3:482.

is from the root, and river from the fountain, so the Son is from the Father."[46] And, "the Father, therefore, is the fountain of Deity . . . the source and principle, both of the Word and Spirit."[47] Therefore, within the Trinity it is the Father who is the head and source of deity for the Son and Holy Spirit.

What we see in *A Rational Vindication* is a Methodist Christology in full harmony with the universal faith expressed at Nicaea and Chalcedon and articulated in the Anglican standards. However, subtle shifts in Methodist Christology would begin in the 1780s that would open the door for divergent Christologies to emerge in the nineteenth century.

Thomas Coke and Methodist Christology

At the same time Fletcher was preparing to write *A Rational Vindication*, across the Atlantic another Methodist leader preached a powerful sermon on Christ's deity at the first General Conference of the Methodist Episcopal Church, on December 26, 1784. Thomas Coke (d. 1817) was a committed Deist as an undergraduate at Oxford until he was convinced of the trustworthiness of the Bible and Christian doctrine through his reading of Thomas Sherlock's *Trial of the Witnesses of* Jesus.[48] From there he went on to earn a doctorate and was ordained a priest in the Church of England. Coke was introduced to the Methodists through Fletcher's writings and met John Wesley in August 1776. He joined the Methodists and soon rose in the ranks to become one of the first general superintendents of the Methodist Episcopal Church in America. Coke served as Wesley's assistant and is considered today the father of Methodist missions.

Probably in reaction to his prior life as a Deist, Coke was a zealous proponent of Christ's deity as full equality with the Father. This led him in 1779 to accuse several Methodist ministers of Arian sentiments, notably Joseph Benson. We saw earlier that Benson had embraced Watts's views on the

---

46 Fletcher, *Works*, 3:486.

47 Fletcher, 3:487.

48 John Vickers, *Thomas Coke: Apostle of Methodism* (Nashville: Abingdon Press, 1969), 14–15.

preexistence of Christ's human soul and had freely shared these ideas with others. Coke accused Benson of subordinationism and of not believing that Jesus Christ was the "One, Supreme, eternal, independent, Self-existent God" and in the "most extensive and unlimited sense of the Word *Eternal* with the Father."[49] In response, Benson accused Coke of Sabellianism by questioning whether he denied the Father of "any proper Godhead" and meant to "confound the Persons of the Father and the Son."[50] At the heart of this exchange were differences of opinion over the immanent Trinity and the doctrine of the Son's eternal generation from the Father. The matter came before the 1780 conference, with Benson cleared of any charge of advocating Arianism. Coke apologized and the two men were reconciled. This ended the heresy-hunting phase of Coke's ministry, but not his zeal to defend Christ's supreme Godhead.

The sermon delivered at the General Conference in 1784 was titled "On the Godhead of Christ" and was published the next year at the request of the Conference.[51] The text was taken from the third line in John 1:1 ("the Word was God") and encapsulated Coke's high Christology at the time. Alarmed at the rising popularity of Arianism and Socinianism (Unitarianism) in America as well as in England, Coke sought to "prove that the Lord Jesus" was "God in the fullest and highest sense."[52] He agreed with Fletcher and Benson that Christ was "God by nature and not only by office" and applied the same arguments to establish Christ's deity according to scripture.[53] The Incarnation was assumed throughout the sermon with

---

49 John A. Vickers, *The Letters of Dr. Thomas Coke* (Nashville: Kingswood Books, 2013), 14, 19, emphasis his. It is notable that Samuel Bradburn used the exact same language in a letter to Coke defending his belief in Christ's divinity (J. A. Vickers, 18).

50 J. A. Vickers, 19. Sabellianism, or modalism, was an ancient heresy that denied the Father, Son, and Holy Spirit are three eternal persons in the one Godhead.

51 Thomas Coke, *The Substance of a Sermon on the Godhead of Christ* (London: J. Paramore, 1785). An 1810 edition titled it *A Sermon on the Supreme Godhead of Christ* (J. A. Vickers, *Thomas Coke*, 377).

52 Coke, *Godhead of Christ*, 8. Coke likened the rise of Arian and Socinian views to a plague (p. 6).

53 Coke, 19–20. Coke made similar arguments based on divine titles, attributes, and works of creation, preservation, and redemption (pp. 11–12, 14–15).

numerous references to Christ's human life and ministry.[54] But whereas Coke's sermon contained similar arguments and content as found in *A Rational Vindication*, it differed in tone and emphasis. The Son's equality with the Father was magnified to the point that his divinity was no longer "derived" from the Father, but both "co-eternally" existed in glory and worked equally in the regeneration and salvation of believers.[55] To argue otherwise was to support a "subtle" form of Arianism.[56] As the "Most High God," the creator and sustainer of all things, Christ was independent, self-sufficient, and hence not subordinate to anyone.[57] Even during his earthly ministry, Jesus was not dependent on anyone, for "all his miracles were wrought in his own name, or by his own immediate power."[58] Coke further minimized the Spirit's role in Christ's ministry by reminding his audience that he was called the "Spirit of Christ."[59] Allowing for limitations of a single homily to express one's full Christology and that Coke was refuting heterodox Christologies that demeaned Christ's deity, the sermon magnified the Godhead of the Son at the expense of the other two members of the Trinity. It therefore lacked the balance established in the early ecumenical creeds and found in the Anglican Articles of Religion.

For the newly formed Methodist Episcopal Church in America, John Wesley produced an abridgment of the Anglican Book of Common Prayer and the Thirty-Nine Articles of Religion. *The Sunday Service of the Methodists in North America* (1784) was presented to the same General Conference at which Coke preached his famous sermon on the Godhead of Christ. Except for two minor changes,[60] the article on Christology in

---

54 Coke, *Godhead of Christ*, 8–10, 22.

55 Coke, 16, 19.

56 Coke, 19.

57 Coke, 10, 14–15.

58 Coke, 15.

59 Coke, 16.

60 In Article II the word *which* was altered to *who* and the line "of her substance" was struck out following the words "Virgin Mary." The first change added clarity and the second removed unnecessary verbiage.

The Sunday Service followed the Anglican article word for word, preserving the balance between the Son's derived essence and inseparable union with the Father—"begotten from eternity of the Father . . . of one substance with the Father."[61] Jason Vickers discovered that the clause concerning the Son's eternal generation was removed in succeeding editions beginning in 1786.[62] Henry Wheeler noted that the clause was also removed from *A Sunday Service* for the English Wesleyans.[63] The circumstances surrounding its removal remain a mystery. Scholars have suggested Wesley's editing or a printer's error, but Vickers noted these remain unconvincing since Wesley taught the doctrine of eternal generation and it was highly unlikely that a typological error would not have been corrected.[64] Both Vickers and James White explained that Coke served an editorial role in the original and succeeding editions of *The Sunday Service.*[65] Wesley later stated that Coke made "two or three little alterations" in the first edition without his knowledge, but said nothing about the removal of the eternal generation clause.[66] Vickers proposed that while the evidence pointing to Coke was not conclusive, it was plausible.[67] Given that Coke championed Christ's divinity as underived equality with the Father, that he served as editor of *The Sunday Service*, and that the other options appear untenable, the argument makes sense. Even though the circumstances surrounding the clause's removal remain uncertain and Coke's role inconclusive, the change in the article did portend

---

61   James F. White, ed., *John Wesley's Prayer Book: The Sunday Service of the Methodists in North America* (Akron, OH: OSL Publications, 1991), 306.

62   Jason E. Vickers, "'Begotten from Everlasting of the Father': Inadvertent Omission or Sabellian Trajectory in Early Methodism?", *Methodist History* 44, no. 4 (2006): 251–61.

63   Henry Wheeler, *History and Exposition of the Twenty-Five Articles of Religion of the Methodist Episcopal Church* (New York: Eaton & Mains, 1908), 68 n. 1.

64   Jason E. Vickers, "Begotten from Everlasting," 253–55.

65   Vickers, 255; White, *John Wesley's Prayer Book*, 3–4. Also, editions in the 1790s included commentary by Coke and Francis Asbury. Given that Coke published more material than Asbury, it is safe to assume he was largely responsible for the commentary (e.g., Thomas Coke and Francis Asbury, *The Doctrines and Discipline of the Methodist Episcopal Church, in America: With Explanatory Notes*, 10th ed.) (Philadelphia: Henry Tuckniss, 1798).

66   Telford, *Letters of John Wesley*, 8:144–45.

67   Vickers, 257.

developments in the nineteenth century, as some leading Methodist scholars openly rejected the doctrine of the Son's eternal generation.[68]

Coke's sermon and possible involvement in the clause's removal, however, were not his last word on the subject. In 1803 he released his two-volume *Commentary on the New Testament*.[69] Throughout the two volumes, and here in Coke's comments on John 1:1–3, Coke emphasized the Son's equality with the Father: "It is observable, that St. John's discourse here rises by degrees: he tells us, first that the Word in the beginning of the world existed; thus asserting his eternity: next, that he existed *with God*, thus asserting his co-eternity: and then, that he *was God*, and made all things: thus asserting his co-equality."[70]

Quoting Augustine on John 10:30 ("I and the Father are one"), Coke pointed out the errors of both Arianism and Sabellianism: "'One' delivers you from Arius, who denies the eternal divinity of Christ: 'Are' delivers you from Sabellius, who denies a distinction of persons in the godhead." Though none of his remarks on the Gospels on Jesus as the "only begotten" mentioned his eternal generation,[71] Coke's later comment on the Son as "the brightness of his glory" (Heb. 1:3 KJV) clearly affirmed the doctrine:

> But to raise their thoughts of the matter, the apostle sets forth this *Light*, by which he describes the Father, under the title of *Glory*; the design of which is, to express the purity, perfection, and lustre of all his attributes. Suitably to this account of God the Father, he represents the Son, as a splendor or ray eternally and essentially derived or proceeding from the Father: and as the beams or rays cannot be separated from the sun, that great fund of light, so neither can the nature and the glory of the divine

---

68 Notably, Adam Clarke and Bishop David Wasgatt Clark (J. E. Vickers, "Begotten from Everlasting," 257–58).

69 Thomas Coke, *A Commentary on the New Testament*, 2 vols. (London: For the author, 1803). John Vickers stated that the published date was marked 1803 but the commentary was not completed until 1807 (*Thomas Coke*, 376).

70 Coke, *A Commentary on the New Testament*, 1:699, italics his.

71 For example, on John 1:14 Coke referred "only begotten" to the incarnation, when the "Word was made flesh." On this point, see J. E. Vickers, "Begotten from Everlasting," 256.

Son be separated from that of the Father: he is "Light of Light, very God of very God."

In contrast to his sermon twenty years earlier, Coke now stated the Son does derive his divine essence from the Father and quoted the Nicene Creed for support. In opposition to Arian and Socinian opinions, Coke argued in the general preface for the Son's eternal generation by appealing to Psalm 2:7 ("Thou art my son; this day have I begotten thee," KJV) and Proverbs 8:24 ("When there were no depths, I was brought forth," KJV).[72] He also referenced the doctrine in his "Reflections" on Colossians 2.[73] Assuming Coke wrote his commentary by following the general order of the New Testament (Gospels and Acts; Pauline Epistles; General Epistles; Revelation), the fact that his statements on the Son's eternal generation do not appear until the later books suggests that his Christology possibly continued to mature as he studied and wrote the commentary.

Besides expressing his settled views on Christ's deity, the *Commentary* allowed Coke to articulate his mature position on the Incarnation. Sounding almost Apollinarian, Coke wrote that the *Logos* had his divine nature, the shekinah glory, dwell, or "tabernacle," in a "human body" (see John 1:14). Yet, in keeping with trinitarian Christology, Coke expressed his firm belief in the hypostatic union and the communication of properties between the two natures. He spoke of the "adorable mystery of the union of the divine and human natures, in the person of the glorious Emmanuel" (see Col. 2:9), and defined the communication of properties as "what is proper to the divine nature is spoken concerning the human, and what is proper to the human, is spoken of the divine" (see John 3:13).[74] Coke explained that in the Incarnation Christ did not "empty himself" of his divine nature, "but of the glories and majesties belonging to him" (Phil. 2:8). Taking the "form of a servant," Jesus was a "complete and perfect man . . . having the same

---

72 Coke, *A Commentary on the New Testament*, 1:xxiii.

73 Coke, *Commentary*, 2:502. Coke ends each chapter with "Inferences" and then "Reflections."

74 On hypostatic union, see Coke, 1:xxvi, John 1:17, Phil. 2:7–8, and Col. 2:19, and Col. 2 Inferences. On communication of properties, Coke also listed Acts 20:28 and 1 Cor. 2:8.

common nature, distinguished by the same specific differences, but united to his own eternally divine nature" (see Phil. 2:7). As a human being, Christ was inferior to the angels (see Heb. 2:9) and united himself to "our inferior miserable nature, with all its innocent infirmities" (see John 1:14). He "underwent all kinds of trials, sufferings, and temptations," without "falling away from the truth, or doing anything amiss" (see Heb. 4:15).

In the end, Coke professed Jesus Christ to be Son of God and Son of Man, both divine and human—the "God-man."[75] Though his earlier sermon *On the Godhead of Christ* suggested otherwise, by the time he wrote his *Commentary on the New Testament* Coke had fully embraced Nicene and Chalcedonian Christology, including the doctrines of the Son's eternal generation, the hypostatic union, and the communication of properties.

Closing Thoughts

In an age that valued natural reason as a primary criterion for truth, the doctrine of Christ's deity came under scrutiny from several quarters. Deists, Arians, and Unitarians attacked the doctrine as illogical and offered alternative Christologies that early Methodists felt undermined the evangelical message of salvation in Christ. Most concerning to Methodists in the last quarter of the eighteenth century was the sudden rise of a Unitarian gospel that proclaimed a human Jesus as the true faith of the apostles. In response, Methodists carved out Christologies that aimed at defending on rational and scriptural grounds the doctrine of the eternal Son of God who became incarnate in the man Jesus for our salvation from sin and death. In keeping with the ancient ecumenical creeds, early Methodists taught the Son's deity as equal in nature to the Father and the hypostatic union of the two natures in the one person Jesus Christ.

Even with this common ground there remained important differences in their Christologies. John Fletcher carefully preserved the delicate balance between the Son's derived essence and his shared equality with the

---

75 Coke, *Commentary*, 1:xxvii.

Father, while affirming the created essence of Jesus's humanity as the Son of Man. In this way he articulated a trinitarian Christology that was faithful to the Anglican Articles of Religion and to the ancient ecumenical creeds. At first, Joseph Benson adopted the novel idea of the preexistence of Christ's human soul before becoming convinced of its error according to the scriptures and Christian tradition. He then espoused the same view as Fletcher in their two-volume response to the Unitarian Joseph Priestley.

Thomas Coke, on the other hand, was a zealous advocate for Christ's divinity as full equality with the Father. In contrast to Fletcher and Benson, Coke rejected the notion of the Son's derived essence from the Father. As editor of *The Sunday Service* and one of the two general superintendents of the Methodist Episcopal Church, Coke was possibly involved in the removal of the eternal generation clause in the Articles of Religion. Although he later moderated his views by embracing the Son's eternal generation, it can be argued that his sermon on Christ's supreme Godhead and possible involvement in the removal of the eternal generation clause had a more lasting influence on Methodist Christology.

3

Nineteenth-Century Methodist Dogmaticians

Thomas H. McCall

Throughout the growth of Methodism and the corresponding develop-ment of Wesleyan doctrine, the proclamation of Jesus Christ was cen-tral. Jesus Christ, the Son of God incarnate, lived and died—and rose to life again—for the salvation of wretched sinners. The person of Christ is absolutely central to the gospel message proclaimed by Methodist preach-ers. But just who is Jesus Christ? At one level, the answer seemed very straightforward and the answers rather predictable (from the perspective of traditional Christian orthodoxy). But as the massive intellectual shifts of modernity rose and crested in the nineteenth century, the question be-came more challenging and the answers grew more complicated.

The Challenging Nineteenth Century

The theologians of Methodism were proclaiming and confessing the gos-pel of Jesus Christ, and, in many cases, they were doing so to unlettered and "plain" people. They were also, however, doing so in contexts of rad-ical intellectual and social upheaval. They were formulating Christian doc-trine while faced with a set of powerful challenges to received doctrine.

Background: Two Centuries of Controversies

Among the many currents of rapid intellectual change, several elements stand out as particularly important with respect to the background of Wesleyan Christological thought. The first of these is the residual impact of Socinianism and Unitarianism upon received Christian doctrine. During the "long seventeenth century," the rise and spread of Socinianism exerted great pressure on the theology of the creedal tradition. As the century progressed, the arguments in favor of Socinianism became increasingly sophisticated and influential. These movements called for widespread reformation of Christian doctrine. In particular, they were decidedly and energetically non-trinitarian and even anti-trinitarian in theology proper as well as anti-creedal in Christology. Arguments against the traditional doctrines were drawn from biblical exegesis as well as renewed interest in historical theology and philosophy. The Socinians argued from the Bible by contending that the creedal and confessional formulations far outstripped any purported biblical support; even when interpreted most generously, there simply are no biblical passages that bring us anywhere close to the formulations of the Niceno-Constantinopolitan Creed and the Chalcedonian formula. More importantly—and more aggressively—the Socinians also argued that the confessional statements go directly *against* biblical teaching: not only do we lack good biblical warrant to believe in the divinity of the Son, we also have explicit testimony to the subordination and weakness of the Son. As we move later into the seventeenth century, however, the Socinians and their Unitarian allies also made arguments from patristic theology. They argued that the witness of major ante-Nicene theologians not only fails to support the conclusions of the ecumenical creeds but also, in many cases at least, goes directly against such conclusions. Similarly, they argued with the use of philosophical tools (including resources drawn from innovations in modern philosophy) to the conclusion that the traditional doctrines are, quite literally, nonsensical and thus necessarily false.

The responses of theologians in the broadly "Remonstrant" and Anglo-Arminian traditions to such challenges were varied. Some Remonstrant theologians showed considerable sympathy to the Socinians. It is not always completely clear just how we should interpret such sympathy; in some cases it looks simply as though the Remonstrants were arguing that the Socinians should not be persecuted, in other cases it seems plain that they were insisting that while the Socinians are wrong, their errors were not nearly so consequential as the Reformed took them to be, while in other cases it is not hard to discern notable shifts in Remonstrant theology in the direction of Socinianism. In other cases, however, Arminian theologians mounted very strong counterattacks against Socinian arguments. And when they did so, they sometimes took very different approaches.

Consider, by way of example, the controversies at the turn of the seventeenth and eighteenth centuries. In direct response to Socinian attacks on traditional doctrine, William Sherlock (dean of St. Paul's) mounted a forceful and extended defense of the classical formulations.[1] He defended the traditional doctrine, but he did so in a novel way: he employed a distinctly Cartesian metaphysics of personhood and identity. For his efforts, he was rewarded with very sharp criticisms and charges of heresy as Robert South and other Reformed theologians argued that his defense of traditional doctrine actually devolves into rank tritheism. The debate raged throughout the last decade of the seventeenth century: Sherlock charged South with modalism, South alleged that Sherlock taught tritheism, and Stephen Nye and the other Unitarians exulted over the controversy. The debate was officially halted by a formal decree, but shortly thereafter Samuel Clarke revived controversy by defending what can only be understood as a subordinationist account that closely resembles mid-fourth-century proposals often called "Semi-Arian." Perhaps predictably, the responses to Clarke were both varied and passionate. Among the Anglo-Arminians,

---

1 A brief overview of Sherlock's career and involvement in various controversies can be found in Sydney Lee, *Dictionary of National Biography,* vol. 52 (London: Smith, Elder, & Co., 1897), 95–97. Sherlock's theology and the debates occasioned by it are discussed in R. S. Franks, *The Doctrine of the Trinity* (London: Duckworth, 1953), 149–51; Edmund J. Fortman, *The Triune God: A Historical Study of the Doctrine of the Trinity* (Philadelphia: Westminster Press, 1972), 245; Jason E. Vickers, *Invocation and Assent: The Making and Remaking of Trinitarian Theology* (Grand Rapids: Eerdmans, 2008), 85–118; Udo Thiel, *The Early Modern Subject: Self-Consciousness and Personal Identity from Descartes to Hume* (Oxford: Oxford University Press, 2011), 54–59; William C. Placher, *The Domestication of Transcendence: How Modern Thinking about God Went Wrong* (Louisville: Westminster John Knox Press, 1996), 175–76; Paul C. H. Lim, *Mystery Unveiled: The Crisis of the Trinity in Early Modern England* (Oxford: Oxford University Press, 2012), 203–15; Philip Dixon, *Nice and Hot Disputes: The Doctrine of the Trinity in the Seventeenth Century* (London: T&T Clark, 2003), 109–37; Stephen Hampton, *Anti-Arminians: The Anglican Reformed Tradition from Charles II to George I* (Oxford: Oxford University Press, 2008), 129–91; Jan Rohls, "Subjekt, Trinität und Persönlichkeit Gottes: Von der Reformation zur Weimar Klassik," *Neue Zeitschrift für Systematiche Theologie und Religionsphilosophie* (1988), 48–56.

Daniel Whitby rose to the defense of Clarke's account. At the same time, however, Daniel Waterland emerged as the champion of the traditionally orthodox account as he sharply and ably criticized Clarke's proposal.

Even from this brief rehearsal, we can see at least three different sorts of responses: the Anglo-Arminians who defended revisionist accounts (e.g., Whitby), those who defended traditional doctrine but who sought to do so with recourse to the newer philosophies (e.g., Sherlock), and those who mounted vigorous and decidedly traditional defenses of traditional doctrine (e.g., Waterland). These debates at Oxford were the immediate inheritance of the brothers Wesley as they studied there. Although the focused attention of John and Charles was not on the formal debates as such, it is not hard to discern where their sympathies and commitments lay. Despite some continuing (and unfortunate) controversy over the Christology of John Wesley, it is clear that both John and Charles were deeply committed to the classical accounts as encapsulated in the creeds.[2] It is also, of course, well known that they celebrated orthodox doctrines of the Trinity and Christology in their hymns and prayers; theirs is a rigorously doxological theology. Such theological commitments, and the debates that helped shape them, were then carried into the Wesleyan revivals throughout the eighteenth century and further into the early nineteenth century.

Criticism, Rationalism, and Idealism in the Nineteenth Century

The nineteenth century brought its own set of intellectual challenges to received doctrine. Again at the risk of oversimplification, we can identify the

---

2 On the continuing controversies with respect to the interpretation of John Wesley's Christology, some historians charge Wesley with commitment to various heresies (the usual culprits are docetism, Apollinarianism, monophysitism, and Nestorianism). See especially John Deschner, *Wesley's Christology: An Interpretation* (Dallas: Southern Methodist University Press, 1960); Randy L. Maddox, *Responsible Grace: John Wesley's Practical Theology* (Nashville: Kingswood Books, 1994), 117; Edward T. Oakes, *Infinity Dwindled to Infancy: A Catholic and Evangelical Christology* (Grand Rapids: Eerdmans, 2011), 285 n. 26, 288. For more sympathetic interpretations of Wesley, see especially Jason E. Vickers, "Christology," in William J. Abraham and James E. Kirby, eds., *The Oxford Handbook of Methodist Studies* (Oxford: Oxford University Press, 2009), 555–58; David A. Graham, "The Chalcedonian Logic of John Wesley's Christology," *International Journal of Systematic Theology* 20, no. 1 (2018): 84–103; Jerome Van Kuiken, "Deschner's Wesley and the Monophysite Meme," *Wesleyan Theological Journal* 54, no. 2 (2019): 37–55.

following streams as particularly important for subsequent theological and Christological development. At one level, the Methodist theologians were keenly aware of the ongoing challenges of Unitarianism and, more broadly, Deism. Accompanying these movements was a wave of critical studies of the Bible, and these threatened to undermine Christian confidence in what can be known about Jesus Christ. At the same time, the lingering impact of Remonstrant subordinationism is obvious. Beyond this, as the influence of Immanuel Kant became more pronounced, the Wesleyans felt compelled to address what they saw as a kind of moralism that was a beguiling substitute for the gospel. Kant offered ample discussion of the "Son of God"— but only as an ideal. He is famous for his statement that "the doctrine of the Trinity, taken literally, has no practical significance at all . . . The same holds true of the doctrine that one person of the Godhead became human."[3] Indeed, Kant argued vigorously that while the ideal or archetype of moral perfection is necessary, the actual instantiation of this in a distinct historical person is not and cannot be. Moreover, divinity would actually disqualify a potential savior from fittingness for a redemptive career.[4] Kant's thought triggered forceful (and largely negative) reactions from the Methodist theologians as they became aware of it. They also engaged with the reception of F. D. E. Schleiermacher. Schleiermacher placed heavy emphasis on human experience of the divine, and he employed the feeling or sense of absolute dependence as the central dogmatic criterion for theology. Accordingly, he subjected received Christological doctrine to scrutiny in this light. He wanted a truly Christian theology that is authentically modern to be "ever more completely purged of scholasticism."[5] He insisted that the received "ecclesiastical formulae concerning the Person of Christ need to be

---

3 Immanuel Kant, "The Conflict of the Faculties," in *Religion and Rational Theology,* trans. and ed. Allen W. Wood and George di Giovanni (Cambridge: Cambridge University Press, 1996), 264.

4 See the discussion in Thomas H. McCall, "Christology . . . within the Limits of Reason Alone?: Kant on Fittingness for Atonement," in Chris L. Firestone, Nathan A. Jacobs, and James H. Joiner, eds., *Kant and the Question of Theology* (Cambridge: Cambridge University Press, 2017), 213–27.

5 F. D. E. Schleiermacher, *The Christian Faith,* trans. H. R. Mackintosh and J. S. Stewart (Edinburgh: T&T Clark, 1989), 396.

subjected to continual criticism."[6] What do we find when we do such criticism? We find that the overall aim of the major creedal and confessional statements is laudable and well-intentioned, for indeed it is true that there God can be said to exist in Christ and thereby to mediate salvation. So, the "aim" is appropriate. But we also find that "there is almost nothing in the execution of this aim against which protest must not be raised, whether we regard the scientific character of the expression or its suitability for ecclesiastical usage."[7] In place of the traditional creedal formulae, Schleiermacher posited that "the Redeemer, then, is like all men in virtue of the identity of human nature, but distinguished from them all by the constant potency of his God-consciousness, which was a veritable existence of God in him."[8] Schleiermacher's revisions to traditional doctrine were attractive to Wesleyan theologians in some ways; after all, they shared together an emphasis on the importance of authentic religious experience. But his critical and revisionist account was also viewed with suspicion and even hostility. And the major Methodist theologians were very aware of—and concerned about the potential impact of—the rise of philosophical idealism more broadly. Within this variegated intellectual context, we see several engagements and developments that are particularly important.

The Curious Case of Adam Clarke: Clarke's Christology

Adam Clarke was a prominent biblical commentator whose work exerted significant influence within Methodist circles. He took and defended a rather novel view of the personal identity of the Son: he held that the second person of the Trinity, while eternally existent and eternally personal within the triune life, was not eternally or necessarily the Son but only became the Son at his incarnation.[9]

---

6 Schleiermacher, *The Christian Faith*, 389.

7 Schleiermacher, 391.

8 Schleiermacher, 385.

9 E.g., Adam Clarke, *Love of God to a Lost World, Demonstrated by the Incarnation and Death of Christ: A Discourse* (New York: Nathan Bangs and J. Emory, 1826).

His view is easily misunderstood. It was not a denial of the eternality or necessity of the Trinity. To the contrary, Clarke affirmed that God is tri-une; he held that there are three divine persons within the Godhead. So, he did not reject the eternal distinction of the personal identities. Nor did he reject the traditional affirmation that there is one divine substance. To the contrary, he believed that the three eternal divine persons are *ho-moousios.* Clearly, his view was not a version of Arianism, Socinianism, or Unitarianism. Nor is it to be confused with the theology of Samuel Clarke. Neither can it be considered a version of Sabellianism. On his proposal, the second person of the Trinity is eternally distinct and, of course, fully divine; this second person is the eternal Logos. In the Incarnation, the Logos be-came what he was not before: the Logos became *the Son.* For in becom-ing human the Logos-to-be-Son came to have a filial relationship with the first person of the Trinity, *the Father.* Sonship is thus a category of the di-vine economy. It is neither eternal nor ontological; instead it is to be un-derstood as a function of the economy of salvation that is related to the human nature of Christ.

A charitable reading of Clarke might see his position as not only non-Arian but indeed as radically *anti-Arian.* If one understands generation to equal or entail inferiority, then the theologian who wishes to resist any conclu-sions of ontological superiority and subordination will be resistant to any account of generation that is both eternal and ontological. If one takes the traditional doctrine of eternal generation to entail that the Father has an essential divine attribute (i.e., aseity) that the Son lacks, then one will be worried about the implications. In particular, one will be concerned that an affirmation of the eternal generation of the Son *qua divinity* will entail the denial of the venerable *homoousios.*

The Curious Case of Adam Clarke: Mainstream Methodist Responses

Clarke was an important figure within early Methodism, and the reach of his influence was broad. Despite his influence, however, his views on Christology and the doctrine of the Trinity did not gain a significant following.[10] Indeed, the fact that his Christological proposals and arguments were held at arm's length testifies to the strength and depth of the ingression of orthodox commitments within Methodism more broadly. His proposal was met with sharp responses, some of which were indirect while others were more direct and pointed in criticism. As an example of the former, observe the clear articulation and response from Samuel Wakefield. Without attaching a name to it, he clearly pinpointed Clarke's view when he said, "It is granted that some divines, truly decided on the question of our Lord's divinity, have rejected the Divine Sonship."[11] His verdict is also clear: in taking this position such divines "have gone contrary to the judgment of the Church of Christ of all ages, and would certainly have been ranked among heretics in her earliest and purest times."[12] Other theologians—including major figures such as Richard Watson—were much more direct and polemical in their rejection of Clarke's innovations. Watson chastised him in his textbook of doctrine, and he even devoted an entire treatise to the refutation of Clarke's position.[13] Throughout Watson insisted that the doctrine of eternal generation is both true and salutary. He directly followed Waterland in seeing the title "Son of God" as more than a reference to the Son's humanity and in seeing eternal generation as pertaining to both nature and will.[14] Indeed, he saw the doctrine of eternal generation and sonship as vital to the Christian faith, for it "contains a revelation of the Divinity of our Lord, as a person of the same *nature* and *essence* with the Father."[15]

---

10 This is not to say that his position was completely isolated. Jason E. Vickers has observed that Thomas Coke "affirmed Christ's eternality" but hesitated "over the term *sonship* or any other term that made Christ appear subordinate to the Father and therefore presumably less than fully divine." "Christology," 558.

11 Samuel Wakefield, *A Complete System of Christian Theology* (New York: Carlton & Porter, 1862; repr. Salem, OH: Schmul, 1985), 219.

12 Wakefield, *A Complete System of Christian Theology*, 219.

13 Richard Watson, "Remarks on the Eternal Sonship of Christ," in vol. 7 of *The Works of the Rev. Richard Watson,* 13 vols. (London: John Mason, 1847).

14 Richard Watson, *Theological Institutes* (New York: Phillips & Hunt, 1823, 1850), 1:561–62.

15 Watson, *Theological Institutes*, 562; cf. John Miley, *Systematic Theology* (New York: Hunt & Eaton, 1893; repr., Peabody, MA: Hendrickson, 1989), 1:235–39.

In retrospect, the depth and intensity of the Methodist rejection of Clarke's innovative proposal bears strong witness to the general Wesleyan commitment to traditional orthodoxy. Clarke was a powerful figure who commanded great respect, and the Wesleyans resisted his moves *in spite of* their profound respect for his abilities and their deep appreciation of his contributions. And we should not underestimate the strength of their negative response to his Christological proposal. As Wakefield wrote, "denial of the Divine Sonship destroys all *relation* among the persons of the Godhead."[16] He expressly followed deeply traditional teaching that the only relations between the three divine persons are those of paternity, filiation, and procession, and he argued that without these ontological relations the affirmation of three divine persons would certainly entail the existence of three autonomous and independent deities. So "Son" is not a merely honorific title; it is not merely referring to the virgin birth or humanity of Jesus. Instead, Wakefield concluded, "Son" is a "personal" (rather than merely "official") designation.[17]

Subordinationism And Kenoticism
In Methodist Theology

Methodist theology in the nineteenth century was impacted by two important currents: one is the partial continuation of a trend carried over from earlier Remonstrant teaching; the other is the result of engagement with important developments in continental Protestant theology. The first concerns the submission or subordination of the Son to the Father, while the second concerns the "emptying" of the Son in the Incarnation.

Subordinationism

The biblical witness to the submission or subordination of the incarnate Son is a perennial area of controversy in Christology. On one hand, Christians who assent to creedal orthodoxy embrace the venerable affirmation

---

16 Wakefield, *A Complete System of Christian Theology*, 220.

17 Wakefield, 211.

of *homoousios*—the Son is of the same essence or substance (or simply "being") as the Father (and the Holy Spirit). On the other hand, Christians also see ample biblical witness to the supremacy of the Father over the Son and the submission of the Son to the Father. Just what are we to make of this? Are we to follow the main lines of the tradition and hold that any subordination is to be understand as properly predicated of the Son *as incarnate*, of the Son *qua human nature*? In other words, is the subordination merely economic or functional? Or are we to follow the legacy of the various forms of "Arianism" in maintaining that the subordination is ontological—thus allowing the biblical witness to the Son's submission and the Father's supreme authority to pull us away from affirmations of *homoousios*? Or do we look for a third option, perhaps trying to carve out conceptual space for an account of something like "eternal functional subordination?"[18] The legacy of Remonstrant and Arminian theologies is rather mixed on this issue.

Some Remonstrant and Anglo-Arminian theologians indeed do show sympathies to Socinianism.[19] But many other Remonstrant and Anglo-Arminian theologians do not take this route. Many do, however, opt for a rather pronounced version of subordinationism. It is not to be confused with Socinianism or Arianism, but neither is it to be taken as an outright affirmation of classical orthodoxy. For instance, the trinitarian theology of the Remonstrant theologians Simon Episcopius and Philipp van Limborch was neither Arian or Socinian but clearly promoted a pronounced subordinationism. Thus Episcopius taught that there is subordination that includes order (*Ordine*), dignity (*Dignitate*), and authority (*Potestate, Dominio*).[20] Similarly, Limborch said that there is some sort of subordination between the divine persons that is not merely "economic" but indeed based on order within the Trinity.[21] Within Anglo-Arminian circles, Whitby made extensive

---

18 On this issue in recent theology, see Thomas H. McCall and Keith E. Yandell, "On Trinitarian Subordinationism," *Philosophia Christi 11* (2009), 339–58.

19 See the discussion in Thomas H. McCall and Keith D. Stanglin, *After Arminius* (Oxford: Oxford University Press, forthcoming).

20 Simon Episcopius, *Opera Theologica* (Amsterdam: 1650), 333–34.

21 Philipp van Limborch, *Theologia Christiana* (Amsterdam: 1686), 107.

arguments from the biblical witness to the obedience and subordination of the incarnate Son. This means that the Son's sovereignty and dominion is a "derived dominion," for the Father is the absolute and supreme God.[22] He concluded that "the Superiority of the Father to the Son, and the Subordination of the Son to the Father, are extremely evident."[23] But other theologians in the broadly "Arminian" tradition strongly resisted such subordinationism. William Sherlock deployed the newer Cartesian metaphysics while Daniel Waterland resisted such innovations, but neither embraced subordinationism. For all their differences, their intentions were clear and clearly the same: to defend the traditional orthodoxy as it is expressed in the creedal formulations.

The nineteenth-century Methodist theologians reflected this range of positions and arguments. Olin A. Curtis is representative of those theologians who tended toward a fairly strong account of subordination. He insisted that a proper understanding of Christ's subordination is what removes every hint of Sabellianism and thus saves the doctrine of the Trinity from heresy. As he resisted strictly idealist understandings of preexistence, so he also held that the subordination or submission of the Son to the Father is not merely according to Christ's human nature. It is not limited to the economy of salvation; to the contrary, it is eternally and necessarily true of the eternal and immanent Trinity.[24] But other important theologians—from the beginning of the century until the end—rejected such tendencies. Thus Watson, early in the century, set an important trend by insisting on the complete equality of the Son with the Father. He made plain that any commitment to orthodoxy includes (or at least entails) affirmation of the aseity of the Son. Against much of the received tradition, he denied that the Father or Spirit could have been incarnate; indeed, he went so far as to call such a view

---

22 Daniel Whitby, *The Last Thoughts of Dr. Whitby, Containing His Correction of Several Passages in His Commentary on the New Testament, To Which Are Added, Five Discourses*, 2nd ed. (London: 1728), 107.

23 Whitby, *Last Thoughts*, 109.

24 Olin Alfred Curtis, *The Christian Faith* (New York: The Methodist Book Concern, 1905), 488.

"violent and repulsive" to theology.[25] Nonetheless, his view was opposed to subordinationism. And much later in the century, John Miley maintained that the subordination of the Son pertains only to the "divine economies," and he insisted that the notion of subordination is exhausted "in the work of redemption."[26] Similarly, William Burt Pope followed the development of Christology from patristic and medieval formulations through the major Protestant (Lutheran and Reformed) confessions, and he criticized the Remonstrant theologians for their accounts of Christ's subordination.[27]

Kenoticism

The Methodist theologians of the nineteenth century were not immune to the challenges coming from the continent. Thus D. W. Clark observed in the middle of the century that various challenges from "modes of thought" that were "derived from a certain school in Germany" had "been gradually working their way into our metaphysical and speculative philosophy" and from there down into the "domain of theology."[28] Clark is representative of theologians who are both reluctant to reject traditional orthodoxy but who are also keenly aware of the pressing challenges of the age. Thus he rejected the proposals of Channing and Bushnell outright, but he also showed considerable sympathy for Schleiermacher's criticisms of the traditional creedal formulae as inadequate.[29] By the end of the century, Henry C. Sheldon noted that, in response to the challenges to the older doctrinal formulae and in increasing recognition of the limitations of the man Jesus Christ, "a few have resorted to a radical doctrine of kenosis, the theory of a

---

25 Watson, *Theological Institutes*, 1:556–67, 587. My claim that he went against much theology in the Latin theological tradition is supported by the argument of Richard Cross that, for all major medieval theologians, any of the divine persons could have become incarnate. See Cross, *The Metaphysics of the Incarnation: Thomas Aquinas to Duns Scotus* (Oxford: Oxford University Press, 2002), 179.

26 Miley, *Systematic Theology*, 1:239.

27 William Burt Pope, *A Compendium of Theology* (London: Wesleyan-Methodist Book-Room, 1880), 1:284; 2:105, 115, 154–55, 187–88.

28 D. W. Clark, "The Incarnation," *Methodist Quarterly Review* (1851): 114–15.

29 Clark, "The Incarnation," 123–26.

veritable depotentiation of the divine Logos in the incarnation."[30] Sheldon also observed that the radical view of kenosis is seen as much too radical by some, and he speculated that "the enormous metaphysical difficulties which pertain to the radical doctrine of kenosis, and the scanty exegetical support which it can claim, will restrict its progress among Methodist scholars."[31]

Sheldon referred to "radical" theories of kenosis. This calls for some clarification. There are more and less radical accounts on offer at the time. To summarize, all kenotic accounts hold that the Son, who was personally preexistent and wholly divine, gave up or surrendered or "emptied" himself of *something* in the process of being incarnate. The relatively less radical accounts suggest that what the Son gave up were any divine attributes that would have been inconsistent with his also being fully and completely human (or that would have interfered with his ability to fulfill his mission in the economy of salvation). The typical candidates for divestment, on these views, are the "omni-" attributes: omnipotence, omniscience, omnipresence, and so on. Sometimes it is said that the Son emptied himself of everything except the "moral attributes" (love, holiness, etc.). In other words, these might opt for a literal reading of the striking line from Charles Wesley's famous hymn "And Can It Be?": "emptied himself of all but love." The more radical theories (of which the theory of Gess is perhaps the boldest and thus understandably the most famous) hold that what the Son divested himself of in the Incarnation was nothing less than divinity itself.[32]

Curtis is a theologian who illustrated a willingness to rethink Christology in a modern key, and more specifically as someone who took a decidedly kenotic line to do so. He was keenly sensitive to those who, he said, had "honestly made up their minds, under the pressure of the new demands of science,

---

30 Henry C. Sheldon, "Changes in Theology among American Methodists," *The American Journal of Theology* 10 (1906): 40–41.

31 Sheldon, "Changes in Theology," 41.

32 See further Thomas R. Thompson, "Nineteenth-Century Kenotic Christology: The Waxing, Waning, and Weighing of a Quest for a Coherent Orthodoxy," in C. Stephen Evans, ed., *Exploring Kenotic Christology: The Self-Emptying of God* (Oxford: Oxford University Press, 2006), 74–111.

that the old Christianity is now untenable."[33] Curtis was unwilling to reject all the tenets of the older orthodoxy, and indeed he defended it against the criticisms of modern thought (perhaps most notably, Albrecht Ritschl, and behind Ritschl, Kant). But he did so with an openness to modern developments in both exegesis and metaphysics. More specifically, he directly followed J. B. Lightfoot's exegesis and the metaphysics of the noted Boston personalist Borden Parker Bowne. With these resources, Curtis rejected the most extreme (and specifically Gessian) accounts of kenosis but insisted nonetheless that Christian theology should be committed to a Christology "from above" that includes preexistence and the full divinity of Christ as well as a strong account of kenosis. What emerges is certainly not a repristination or defense of older orthodoxy, but neither is it a complete capitulation to the pressures of modern thought. Instead, it is a modified account of kenosis, one according to which the Son is personally and really preexistent as divine and yet who emptied himself of his self-consciousness of the possession of divine attributes. Therefore, while Christ is fully divine as well as fully human, as incarnate "the self-consciousness of the Son of God is now in total eclipse."[34] Curtis concluded that the Son "emptied himself of no divine thing save the personal experience of God"—and the Son did so for the salvation of sinners.[35]

The Steady Persistence of Chalcedonian Christology

Despite such longstanding attraction to subordinationism and occasional dalliances with kenotic theories, much mainstream Methodist theology exhibits a steady and loyal adherence to creedal orthodoxy. In the late eighteenth century, Richard Allen insisted that the triune God is "perfectly one and perfectly three, one essence and three persons."[36] As Sheldon looked

---

33 Curtis, *The Christian Faith*, 229.

34 Curtis, 244–47.

35 Curtis, 245.

36 Richard Allen, *The Life, Experience, and Gospel Labors of the Rt. Rev. Richard Allen, to Which Is Annexed The Rise and Progress of the African Methodist Episcopal Church in the United States of America, Containing a Narrative of the Yellow Fever in the Year of Our Lord 1793, with an Address to the People of Color in the United States* (Philadelphia: F. Ford and M. A. Riply, 1880), 29.

back over the nineteenth century from the beginning of the twentieth, he observed that "up until the seventh or eighth decade of the nineteenth century there was no considerable, if any, divergence from Richard Watson's quiet affirmation of the general terms of the Chalcedonian Creed."[37]

Sheldon was surely right, but it is also important not to overstate the changes that were taking place even as we approach the end of the century. As prominent and important examples, consider the proposals of Miley and Pope.

Miley saw the Christological issues as extremely important; the Christological question is not one "of mere speculative interest, but one that vitally concerns the central realities of Christianity itself."[38] He made careful and extended arguments for the full divinity and equality of Christ from exegesis of important New Testament passages. He insisted that there is only one incarnate person, and further that this person is the preexistent Son who took upon himself the fullness of human nature in becoming incarnate. For Miley, it was clear that there is no *tertium quid*, no hybrid entity that is somehow partly divine and partly human but not quite one with either God or humanity. He took a firm stand on the controverted issues related to the *communicatio idiomatum*: the attributes of the humanity are rightly attributed to and predicated of the person, and the attributes of the divine nature are rightly attributed to and predicated of the person of the Son. But the properties of the divinity are not to be predicated of the humanity, and the properties of the humanity are not to be predicated of the divinity.[39] He explicitly rejected not only Ebionism, Gnosticism, all versions of Arianism, Apollinarianism, Socinianism, Nestorianism, and Eutychianism but also criticized Lutheranism's account of the *communicatio* for coming too close to monophysitism.[40] Moreover, he unambiguously rejected the kenotic theories of Thomasius, Ebrard, Martenson, and Gess, and he was

---

37 Sheldon, "Changes in Theology," 40.

38 Miley, *Systematic Theology,* II:4.

39 Miley, 21–34.

40 Miley, 2:62.

forceful in his criticisms of such innovations. For to accept such kenotic theories would be to surrender the doctrine of divine immutability and enable the "subversion of the divine Trinity." Accordingly, these kenotic theories are "contrary to the deepest truths of Christianity."[41]

Miley did, however, evince a willingness to take leave of some elements of ecumenical Christological teaching on what he took to be more minor points—at least when those points are not supported by scriptural teaching and are judged actually to entail problematic conclusions. Thus he would not affirm the rejection of Monotheletism found in the Sixth Ecumenical Council, for the conclusion reached there was "really Nestorian, though not intended" as such.[42] He did, however, resolutely affirm Chalcedon (as well, of course, as the Christology of the Methodist Articles of Religion).[43]

Pope was even more scrupulously traditional. He adhered very closely to the formal affirmations of the orthodox tradition. Predictably, he argued from SCRIPTURE for the creedal conclusions. He drew together the main lines of the traditional—and truly *Methodist*—doctrine by saying that Christ is "anciently summed up as follows: Christ is truly God, perfectly Man, unconfusedly in two Natures, indivisibly in one Person."[44] He countered Clarke's proposal by insisting that the Sonship of Christ is both eternal and necessary. Throughout, he was overtly committed to the standards of creedal orthodoxy; he did not waver at all. He accepted and defended the Niceno-Constantinopolitan and Chalcedonian statements, but he did not hesitate in going further. In marked distinction from Miley, he tracked with the Sixth Ecumenical Council's rejection of Monotheletism.[45] The doctrine of the Incarnation is the "supreme fact in human history," and he was convinced that Chalcedonian Christology captures the key insights well.[46]

---

41 Miley, *Systematic Theology*, 2:62.

42 Miley, 2:9.

43 Miley, 2:7.

44 Pope, *Compendium of Theology,* 2:107.

45 Pope, 2:135–38.

46 Pope, 2:145.

Conclusion

The Methodist theologians of the nineteenth century were committed to a Christian vision of reality that was centered on the person and work of Jesus Christ as the sole and all-sufficient hope for sinful, helpless humans. They articulated this vision with confidence and clarity. They did so in a context that was marked by social upheaval and intellectual challenges.

With some notable exceptions, the Methodist theologians were generally committed to the Christological vision summarized in the great ecumenical creeds. Indeed, they often cited these creeds as authoritative.[47] As Miner Raymond said, these creeds "resulted not from an attempt to improve upon, much less add to, the teachings of the Scriptures; but from an effort so to state the Bible doctrine as to defend the Church against the incoming heresies."[48] They forcefully rejected the heretical alternatives to classical orthodoxy and also offered correction to those Wesleyans who strayed from the established paths of orthodoxy. Notably, they rejected not only Arian and other subordinationist views but also the "modern pantheism" of G. W. F. Hegel and other idealists as well as the "Sabellianised Pantheism" of Schleiermacher.[49] Jesus Christ is fully human and fully divine in the unity of his person. This is both true and salutary.

---

47   E.g., Miley, *Systematic Theology,* 1:227–29; Pope, *Compendium of Theology,* 1:275–78.

48   Miner Raymond, *Systematic Theology* (Cincinnati: Cranston & Stowe, 1877), 1:381.

49   E.g., Pope, *Compendium of Theology,* 1:280, 282.

Methodist Christologies through the Twentieth Century

4

Personalism in Methodist Christology

Reginald Broadnax

What is personalism? "Personalism is a philosophical perspective for which the person is the ontological ultimate and for which personality is the fundamental explanatory principle."[1] Personalism is the key to all philosophical problems, both about value, epistemology, and metaphysics. "To be is to be a person or self, or some act or experience of a person or self."[2] Theologian Albert C. Knudson wrote, "It is in personality that individuality finds its only adequate realization. It is personality alone that has the characteristics necessary to a basal unity. It is in personal agency that we have the source of the idea of causality and its only self-consistent embodiment. It is the reality of personality that constitutes the foil to the phenomenality of matter, space, and time and renders it intelligible."[3] It is in being a self (person) that all experience is interpreted, and it is within the experience of being a self that all problems of philosophy find resolution.

Knudson referred to personalism as a new name for an old philosophical way of thinking. The word was first used by the Germans. Schleiermacher used it in his *Discourses* in 1799; but it was also used by Goethe, who spoke of F. H. Jacobi as a "personalist."[4] However, the stream that is

---

1 Paul Deats and Carol Robb, eds., *The Boston Personalist Tradition in Philosophy, Social Ethics, and Theology* (Macon, GA: Mercer University Press, 1986), 2.

2 Edgar S. Brightman, "Personalism," in Vergilius Ferm, ed., *A History of Philosophical Systems* (New York: The Philosophical Library, 1950), 340.

3 Albert C. Knudson, *The Philosophy of Personalism* (Boston: Boston University Press, 1949), 237–38.

4 Knudson, *Philosophy of Personalism*, 17.

personalism has many tributaries. Knudson, in the final section of his book, outlined the different lines of thought that prepared the way for modern personalism: from Plato and Aristotle, through Augustine and Aquinas, to Descartes and Berkeley, Kant and Hegel, Lotze and then to Bowne. In speaking of these persons, Knudson acknowledged that there are many others who could have been listed in what he called a "personalistic Hall of Fame."[5] Edgar Sheffield Brightman identified Gottfried Wihelm Leibniz as the founder of modern personalism. Leibniz's "monadology represented the universe as consisting of simple psychic monads,[6] ranging from the most dimly conscious types to the sublime and consciousness of God. Every monad is active ('to be is to act') and all activity is conation of striving."[7] Monads are individual conscious experiences. Leibniz held that there is "one monad that is known to us with immediate certainty, namely, our own personal conscious being."[8]

It was American philosopher and clergyman Borden Parker Bowne who was the first to use the term *personalist* in English. Speaking of his own philosophy, Bowne wrote, "I largely agree with Lotze, but I transcend him. I hold half of Kant's system, but sharply dissent from the rest. There is a strong smack of Berkeley's philosophy, with a complete rejection of his theory of knowledge. I am a Personalist, the first of the clan in any thoroughgoing sense."[9] Bowne began as a critic of Herbert Spencer, who was a proponent of *un*critical Evolutionism (always with a capital *E*).[10] Particularly for our

---

5   Knudson, *Philosophy of Personalism*, 428–34.

6   A monad is a simple substance, by which is meant that it is without parts. All other things are composites, which are made up of monads. Because they are without parts, there can be neither extension nor divisibility. Monads are created (here meaning, part of the divine creation), and their end can only come by annihilation. Alfred N. Whitehead would later take Leibniz's understanding of monads and redefine them as *actual occasions*. For monads, see Gottfried Wilhelm Leibniz, *Discourse on Metaphysics and the Monadology*, trans. George R. Montgomery (Buffalo: Prometheus Books, 1992), 67.

7   Brightman, "Personalism," 342.

8   Edgar Sheffield Brightman, *An Introduction to Philosophy*, rev. ed. (London: Sir Isaac Pitman & Sons, 1951), 116.

9   Brightman, *Introduction to Philosophy*, 16, 18.

10   See Deats and Robb, *Boston Personalist Tradition*, 5.

purposes, Bowne was critical of Spencer's epistemology (which is materialistic) and his agnosticism. Materialism held that matter is the cause of every mental state and mental activity, and experience is not a basis for mental life. Spencer held that organisms produce thought (apart from experience) and are capable of correcting thought by natural selection. When an organism's thought came into conflict with its environment, it would not survive. However, those organisms that produced correct thought would survive to pass on those thoughts.[11] Spencer's epistemic materialism led to his agnosticism. Spencer believed that there were limits to knowledge and that because of those limits, one could not know about the Reality called God.[12]

Epistemology

For Bowne, the self in knowing and experiencing is always pointing to something outside of itself. The experience of knowing is to know other and beyond the self. This outward pointing is not just present in the finite mind itself, but in the content of its own thinking. "At the instant when the self seems to be most self-controlled in thinking, at that instant the content of its thought seems most truly given from outside."[13] Because the content of thinking and experience is given from outside the individual self, the basis for mental life is experience and not matter, as the materialists have said; but a key distinction must be made here. Knowledge is the relationship between thought and thing, the thing being objective and outside of the self. This relationship between thought and thing is known as *epistemic dualism*, that is, the relationship between the experienced object and the knower. What makes this relationship dualistic is not their union (between thought and thing), as monists believe, but rather their mutual otherness. As Bowne insisted, the dualism of thought and thing is ineradicable.[14]

---

11 Knudson, *Philosophy of Personalism*, 352–53.

12 Francis John McConnell, *Borden Parker Bowne: His Life and His Philosophy* (New York: Abingdon Press, 1929), 66.

13 McConnell, *Borden Parker Bowne*, 123.

14 See Knudson, 100–102.

It's upon this basis that all knowledge exists. "Without a duality of thought and object, knowledge could not be."[15] However, this duality of thought and object/thing is not a recognition of knowledge but rather an examination of knowledge. This examination is facilitated by the analytic-synoptic method. The analytic side of this method is a complete examination or analysis of perceived objects (things) and their constituent parts.[16] Synopsis means "the viewing of any object or complex of objects as a whole."[17] Each relevant part of an object must be analyzed to determine what is contributed to the whole and what is unique to the whole. "The analytic-synoptic method requires that we know the individual parts, their relations to each other, and their relations to the whole."[18] Thus, analysis and synopsis must be used together. "Synopsis without prior analysis is superficial and inarticulate; analysis without synopsis is the dissection of a corpse; synopsis and analysis combined yield the richest and completest knowledge of which the human mind is capable."[19] Notice that what is achieved is the "completest knowledge of which the human mind is capable." Personalism does not assert that there is certainty of either knowledge or truth. It instead asserts that the analytic-synoptic method yields the richest and completest knowledge of which the human mind is capable.

The reason that personalism does not make an assertion of the certainty of either knowledge or truth is because the knowledge of the knower and the direct object does not come without interpretation. It is by interpretation of that which we have in our conscious experience that we gain knowledge. Yet with interpretation is the possibility of error. "What is known must be open to reasonable interpretation. Indeed, since error cannot occur in what is known, error means that the mind in knowing is no passive

---

15 Brightman, *Introduction to Philosophy*, 86.

16 Brightman, 33.

17 Brightman, 39.

18 Rufus Burrow Jr., *Personalism: A Critical Introduction* (St. Louis: Chalice Press, 1999), 118.

19 Brightman, 40.

recipient."[20] If the mind is not passive, then it must be an active recipient, which means that experience is a basis for mental life (against materialistic epistemology); but it also means that there are limits to knowledge, even in experience. "Dualism gives a clear and adequate account of the fact of error. Our ideas refer to objects, but they often fail to reach the truth about them because they are based on insufficient observation, incoherent thinking, or distorted data arising from defects of our sense organs."[21] While dualism gives a clear and adequate accounting for error, error in no way invalidates the method. When error is encountered, one need only revise his or her thought concerning the immediate experience and move toward a clearer or even richer synopsis.

Personalism and Methodism

This epistemology is the foundation of what became known as Boston personalism; but it became known as Boston personalism by happenstance. Bowne came to Boston University as professor of philosophy in 1876 and became dean of the graduate school in 1888.[22] Bowne first identified himself (and his philosophy) as personalist in 1908. Knudson said that Bowne's 1908 publication was the first in English to use the name *Personalism*, but the book was a fresh restatement "of the philosophic system which for thirty years past he had expounded in various books and journals and in his classroom lectures in Boston University."[23] Social reformer Francis John McConnell came to Boston University in 1894. He was a student of Bowne and completed his PhD in 1897. McConnell wrote Bowne's biography in 1929. Albert. C. Knudson was a student of Bowne's and received his PhD in 1900. After teaching at several institutions, he returned to Boston University in 1906 as professor of Hebrew and Old Testament; and upon

---

20 See Deats and Robb, *Boston Personalist Tradition*, 58–59.

21 Brightman, *Introduction to Philosophy*, 93.

22 Knudson notes that Bowne came to Boston University in spite of attractive offers from other universities. Presumably, some other school could have been known for personalism. See Knudson, *Philosophy of Personalism*, 19n.

23 Knudson, 19n.

Bowne's death in 1910, Knudson succeeded him as professor of philosophy. Edgar Sheffield Brightman was a student of Bowne's before Bowne's death and completed his PhD in 1912. He joined the faculty of Boston University in 1919 as the Borden Parker Bowne Professor of Philosophy. From these four men, a series of students came to Boston to study personalism: Walter G. Muelder; Georgia Harkness; Peter A. Bertocci; S. Paul Schilling; John H. Lavely; L. Harold DeWolf, and Paul Deats.[24] Important for our study is that *all of these individuals were Methodists*. Thus, this school of thought became known as Boston personalism because Borden Parker Bowne first developed this philosophy while being the professor of philosophy at Boston University. From Bowne, Knudson and Brightman further developed the philosophy, and a series of students came to study under them. These students were predominantly Methodists.[25] However, these students did not go on to establish centers of personalist thought at other universities. In fact, the majority of these students returned to Boston to teach. Therefore, Boston University, being a Methodist-sponsored institution, played a significant role in the development of Methodist doctrine and theology in the twentieth century.

Thomas A. Langford referred to personalism as a change in direction in the Methodist movement at the beginning of the twentieth century away from the nineteenth century's doctrinal emphasis, particularly the doctrines of sanctification, holiness, and Christian perfection. Personalism was a turn toward Protestant liberalism, which became an emphasis of Methodist theology.[26] One such emphasis is that of social ethics. Multidisciplinary scholar Thomas Jay Oord refers to this as "personal morality and

---

24   There are bibliographies of these individuals in Deats and Robb's book.

25   One very important person was not a Methodist. A young Baptist student originally from Atlanta came to Boston to study personalism under Brightman in 1951. His name was Martin Luther King Jr. From his time at Boston, King was a thoroughgoing personalist, and it was at Boston that he developed his social ethic. Because of this, personalism played a significant role in the transformation not just of the United States, but of human rights around the world.

26   Thomas A. Langford, *Practical Divinity*, vol. 2, *Readings in Wesleyan Theology* (Nashville: Abingdon Press, 1999).

social responsibility."[27] Brightman, after encouragement from Muelder,[28] worked out a complete social ethic within his metaphysics, and Francis J. McConnell was instrumental in developing the *Social Creed* of 1908 and 1912. This emphasis on social ethics arises out of personalism's central focus on the centrality of the person. Personalism "stands alone in stressing the primacy and worth of the person and the need for all ethical principles to be conditioned by the highest conceivable estimate of the value of persons as such."[29] Thus, "the person is the ontological ultimate and . . . personality is the fundamental explanatory principle."

The Meaning of Person

We began with Knudson's understanding of personality: "It is in personality that individuality finds its only adequate realization. It is personality alone that has the characteristics necessary to a basal unity." The early personalists often used the words *person* and *personality* interchangeably, giving the impression that the two essentially are the same. However, with the advancement of psychology, we currently understand that person and personality are distinct and inherently different; therefore, we need to clarify these terms. Person is who someone is; personality is what is developed. Peter A. Bertocci recognized the distinction between the two and was explicit about their differences: "A personality is learned as a person interacts with other persons. More exactly, a person's personality is his more or less systematic mode of response to himself, to others, and to his total environment in the light of what he believes them to be, and what they actually are."[30] Because of this distinction between person and personality, it becomes necessary to clarify and define the meaning of *person*.

In his effort to do so, Brightman said, "A person, then, is a complex unity

---

27 Thomas Jay Oord, "Wesleyan Theology, Boston Personalism, and Process Thought," in Bryan P. Stone and Thomas Jay Oord, eds., *Thy Nature & Thy Name Is Love: Wesleyan and Process Theologies in Dialogue* (Nashville: Kingswood Books, 2001), 383.

28 See Deats and Robb, *Boston Personalist Tradition*, 110.

29 Burrow, *Personalism*, 188.

30 Burrow, 91.

of consciousness, which identifies itself with its past self in memory, determines itself by its freedom, is purposive and value-seeking, private yet communicating, and potentially rational."[31] A complex unity of consciousness is the monad discussed earlier. Individual monads form a complex unity. This complex unity is conscious and has experiences, is capable of memory and self-determination, and is purposive, value-seeking, private, and potentially rational. Brightman further clarified the meaning of *person* by saying, "A distinction is often made between self and person. A self is any complex unity of consciousness; a person is a self able to develop rationality and ideal values."[32] Brightman made this clarification of a self to distinguish between humans and other, nonhuman sentient beings. Other sentient beings are complex unities and have consciousness; but only a person is capable of developing rationality and ideal values.

This clarification of the distinction between person and personality gets us closer to what a definition of *person* should be today; but one important thing must be noted concerning this definition. Brightman said that a person is capable of memory, or in this sense, remembering. Memory or the ability to remember, allows us to locate one experience with another, whether that previous experience happened a moment ago, yesterday, or even last year. Being able to locate one experience with another is an important function within human experience. Bertocci noted this: "We must not miss the significance of remembering, for it points to an inexpressibly important fact. Without remembering, the unity of experience would be impossible as we 'flit' from moment to moment; without it no man can maintain his self-identity as he grows from infancy onward."[33] The unity of experience is both a connection and a collection of experiences; thus, memory is a reference point. It allows us to connect one experience with another. The ability to connect one experience with another is the predicate to the analytic-synoptic method. Without the ability to remember, to

31 Brightman, "Personalism," 341.

32 Brightman, 341.

33 Burrow, *Personalism*, 92.

connect experiences, one is unable to engage analysis because the analysis is not based on a single experience but on the set of experiences of the person. This is also true of the synopsis because the comprehensive view sought is predicated upon prior experiences and synopses. Therefore, without the ability of memory, a personalistic epistemology cannot go forward.

Returning to the definition of a person, Burrow posits, "A person is a self that is not only conscious, but is at least potentially self-conscious, rational, self-directed, and capable of establishing and striving toward the achievement of ideal value."[34] Burrow stated that one need not exhibit these characteristics in every waking moment, but that one need be capable of exhibiting these characteristics. However, even with this revision, the definition was problematic. Burrow recognized the dehumanization inherent in his definition. He identified these characteristics as being fundamentally basic human characteristics, but he also questioned whether these characteristics can be applied to the severely mentally challenged. If a severely mentally challenged individual is not fully capable of exhibiting these characteristics, then by definition we must question his or her personhood. On the other hand, how can we possibly question the personhood of a human being, no matter his or her mental capabilities? Knudson made this mistake in defining a person. He wrote, "But, strictly, 'person' is a narrower term. It applies only to selves that have attained a certain degree of intellectual and moral development; a slave is not a person, nor is a child."[35] Given human history, particularly in reference to the treatment of native/indigenous peoples by colonizing countries, the trans-Atlantic slave trade and the continued oppression of former slaves, and the general treatment of anyone deemed to be "other," this is a dangerous definition of a person. Burrow recognized this and stated that because God is Creator, God's intention for human beings is that they be "normal" human beings, whether they actualize that or not.

---

34 Burrow, *Personalism*, 97.

35 Knudson, *Philosophy of Personalism*, 83.

This raises the question, What is "normal"? Burrow acknowledged the problem of definition by saying, "Indeed, part of the way personalism characterizes what it means to be a person has left it open to the criticism that we can be selective about who is a person and who is not."[36] While Burrow recognized both the problem of the definition and the damage it can cause, he didn't provide a corrective. What he left us with is this: "For our purpose suffice it to say that it is God's intention that those given birth by human beings be persons in the fullest sense."[37] This, too, is problematic; however, it is beyond the scope of this essay to give a full correction to the problem of definition. While I acknowledge the problems and danger of personalism's definition of a person and the quandary it poses for the remainder of this essay, it remains the task of a future interpreter to posit a more adequate personalist definition of a person.

God as Person

Given personalism's definition of a person (and the complications we previously discussed), personalism asserts that God is both personal—in that one is capable of having a personal relationship with God—and that God is the epitome of what it is to be a person. God in God's essential nature is a personal being; a being with whom one could have fellowship and a personal relationship.[38] God was personal before God was regarded as absolute or given any other attribute.

God is a person, a unity of consciousness, self-conscious, rational, self-directed, and capable of having personal relationships with other beings. God's consciousness is God's active participation in and God's experience of creation. God experiences creation in the purest and most complete way, needing no analysis because God's synopsis needs no interpretation. God is the only person who can experience the whole of creation in its fullest manifestation. God's experience of creation also means that God

---

36 Burrow, *Personalism*, 97.

37 Burrow, 97.

38 Knudson, *Philosophy of Personalism*, 79.

is rational, but also that God has memory; however, this is an inadequate term to describe the concept. Memory, here in reference to God, means that each experience of the creation is held as a complete synopsis within the divine mind. It is to this extent that one can say that God is omniscient. God's omniscience is an expression of God's complete and full knowledge of the experiences of the creation, and each experience is held in the divine mind. What omniscience cannot mean is that God would have prior (fore) knowledge of the free, self-directed actions of creatures. There is, therefore, a limit to knowledge, and that limit is to the extent that other selves have the freedom of their own self-direction.[39]

To be self-directed means to be free in one's choices and decisions. To have such freedom means that one's actions are not determined by some being outside of the self. To be a person is to be free in one's decisions and actions. This freedom is metaphysical; it is a quality of all persons. Personalism holds that "to be is to act." "The fundamental nature of being is to act. To be is to act, or to be acted upon."[40] For God to be a person, God must be capable of being acted upon. "Personality is also social. It implies reciprocal intercourse with other persons. A completely isolated person would not be a person in the full sense of the term."[41] For this reason, the God of traditional theism must be rejected.[42] There is no reciprocal relationship between God and creation, no intimacy by which God can enter into personal relationships. True personhood means social ability: the ability to enter into social, personal relationships. It is by this that we say that God is *personal*. God is a person, a unity of consciousness, self-conscious, rational, self-directed, and capable of having personal relationships with other beings.

---

39 For a full expression of omniscience and freedom, see Knudson, *The Doctrine of God* (New York: Abingdon-Cokesbury Press, 1930), 317–19.

40 Burrow, *Personalism*, 93.

41 Knudson, *The Doctrine of God*, 297–98.

42 Traditional theism is predicated upon the Aristotelian *Unmoved Mover*. This deity, overly transcendent and without interaction with creation (immutable) is the basis of traditional theism; or, what Charles Hartshorne calls Classical Theism.

Personalist Christology

Personalist Christology follows from its theology. Because God in God's essential nature is both a person and personal, Jesus, the Christ, who is both fully divine and fully human, must be the perfect manifestation of both divine and human personhood. In Jesus, who is the Christ, we must see the full personhood of divinity, as well as the full personhood of humanity. Both essential qualities and characteristics are fulfilled in the unique person that is Jesus, the Christ.

In reference to Christology, Randy Maddox wrote that for Wesley, his focus was never on the question of the "Jesus of history." Wesley was suspicious of anyone who would posit Jesus as a "mere man." Neither was Wesley interested in the issues of the Incarnation. He believed that the debate over Christ's nature was "simply unwarranted imposition of philosophical conceptions on the simply-expressed teachings of Scripture and the earliest Church."[43] Wesley was only concerned with "Jesus as the Christ, the Saviour of the world. Put in technical terms, his focal Christological concern was with the *work* of Christ."[44] This Wesleyan concern is also a personalistic concern (attributive to the espousers of personalism also being Methodists).

Knudson believed that the best New Testament summary of Christology is in 2 Corinthians 5:19, "God was in Christ, reconciling the world unto himself" (KJV). The first part of the statement applies directly to the person of Christ, as relating to the doctrine of Incarnation; the other relating to the work of Christ, underlying the basic truth of the doctrine of atonement.[45] Knudson began a Christology with the two-natures doctrine as formulated at Chalcedon. He stated that belief in the divinity of Christ—the person of Christ—was due to the unique impression that Jesus made upon his disciples: there was something about his personality "which at times awakened

---

43   Randy L. Maddox, *Responsible Grace: John Wesley's Practical Theology* (Nashville: Kingswood Books, 1994), 94–95.

44   Maddox, *Responsible Grace*, 95 (italics original).

45   Albert C. Knudson, *Basic Issues in Christian Thought* (New York: Abingdon-Cokesbury, 1950), 127.

in others a sense of the 'numinous' or the divine."[46] However, more significant than Jesus's personality was his messianic consciousness, "or his unique filial relation to God."[47] When Peter proclaimed that Jesus was the Christ, the Son of the living God, Jesus ratified this in the strongest terms by saying that he would build his church (Matt 16:16–18). The effect of this was that the disciples must have recognized the unique God-consciousness within Jesus and the holiness of his life. There had to have been "a growing conviction among the disciples that God was in Christ in a unique way that had been unknown before and that had a momentous bearing on the religious future of Israel and the world."[48] Knudson went on to say there is no reason to draw a distinction between the Jesus of history and the Christ of faith because the New Testament teaching transcends this debate. The New Testament affirms a religion wherein Christ is the centrality of the faith, and this is in full keeping with Christ's relationship to God. Thus, the "Christ of faith" *is* the "Jesus of history."

In formulating the two-natures doctrine, what Chalcedon was to bring to light in contemporary thought was the essential elements of a doctrine of the person of Christ: "a perfect divine and a perfect human nature and one unified personality."[49] What Chalcedon did not do was define clearly the terms *nature* and *personality*[50] and how these two diverse natures could be combined in one person. Knudson stated that while Chalcedon pointed clearly to the two natures of Christ, it had no way of overcoming the dualism created, nor could it provide a basis for understanding the nature of person today. This becomes the modern task.[51]

The metaphysics of Chalcedon were Platonic in that it conceived of reality as both substance and a universal form of being. Personalistic metaphysics

---

46 Knudson, *Basic Issues*, 128. Here, "numinous" is in reference to Rudolf Otto's thought.

47 Knudson, 128.

48 Knudson, 129.

49 Knudson, 135.

50 While Knudson used the word *personality*, in light of our previous discussion we should interpret that as *person*.

51 Knudson, 136.

conceives of reality as active or dynamic on the one hand, and individual on the other. The Chalcedonian formulation led to an impression that there were two independent natures or substances that existed independently within Christ. This is not only an abstraction, but it is also a mistake. The two natures are not distinct independent substances. "They were simply different aspects of the one unique personality. And his personality is to be viewed, not as a substance, but as an agent."[52] Thus, the dualism of the two natures must be discarded and replaced with a doctrine that begins with the unity of Christ's personality.

The unity of Christ's being must be located within his own self-consciousness and self-activity. This unity is known to himself as an immediate experience. In Christ, God manifests Godself in the form of "a unique self-consciousness and a unique spiritual power."[53] The self-consciousness of Christ is grounded in the person and self-consciousness of God. In Christ's self-consciousness he has the experience of the awareness of his divine sonship, his sinlessness, his spiritual authority and his redemptive power. These unique characteristics are experienced in his self-consciousness, and it is to this self-consciousness and not to a dualistic nature that we must look to find evidence of his divinity. "The God-consciousness of Christ thus takes the place of the 'divine nature' in the traditional theory."[54] God's self-consciousness was in Christ not only as the immediate experience of his awareness of his divinity, but also as the metaphysical ground and source of Christ's spiritual uniqueness.

This spiritual uniqueness implies Christ's fundamental dependence upon God. We are all dependent upon God, but Christ was dependent in a unique way and to a unique degree. Christ was dependent upon God for the divine creative activity that was the work of his life. This unique work made Christ dependent upon God and the divine will to fulfill this work. This also means that the divine spirit was in Christ to an unprecedented

---

52 Knudson, *Basic Issues*, 137.

53 Knudson, 138.

54 Knudson, 138.

degree. The spirit was an agent of the divine activity; and in this, Knudson said that the spirit had no independent existence: "It was God in the act of communicating himself to Christ and establishing a direct personal relation with him, a relation to which Christ made his own contribution by his own free and personal response. There was thus a unique reciprocal interaction between him and the divine Spirit, and the constant potency of this interaction constituted 'a veritable existence of God in him.'"[55] In this unique way, Christ was both able to experience the God-consciousness within him and to fulfill the work of reconciling the world to God. Knudson concluded:

> We are to think of Christ as a man in whom God was present in a unique manner and to a unique degree. This presence consisted in a unique metaphysical dependence on God and in a unique reciprocal interaction with the divine Spirit. As a result of this twofold relation to God there emerged in Christ a unique and potent God-consciousness, in which God was both causally and consciously present and which expressed itself in qualities of mind and heart that have made him in the faith of the church the ideal man and perfect organ of divine revelation.[56]

L. Harold DeWolf did not use the language of self-consciousness but he did speak of Jesus as a person; and being a human person, Jesus had all of the limitations (of knowledge, power, ability, and so on) of any other human being. Yet, Jesus understood within himself the spirit and purpose of his calling; and to fulfill his calling, he had to subordinate all of his individual interests and desires to the will of God. It was in his subordination to God that he was able to fulfill God's purposes. Because he understood the will of God and was perfectly faithful in subjecting his will to God, "God was able to speak and act in mighty deeds through him as through no other."[57]

---

55   Knudson, *Basic Issues*, 139.

56   Knudson, 148.

57   L. Harold DeWolf, *A Theology of the Living Church* (New York: Harper & Brothers, 1953), 251.

Assessment

I find it interesting that in Thomas Oord's listing of why personalism is attractive to Wesleyans, he didn't list Christology.[58] Personalism has focused much attention on the person (within the discussion of the person there is also social ethics) and personality, epistemology and theism, but has not given as much attention to Christology. More attention needs to be given to Christology in order to bring personalism as a discipline forward and to make it accessible to more people of the Wesleyan persuasion. I have already identified the problems inherent in the definition of *person*, and revising this definition will aid in giving further clarification to the person of Jesus, both in Christology and in relation to the Trinity.[59] A more clarified definition of *person* and a fully appropriated Christology would bring personalism into a richer dialogue with the Wesleyan community.

---

58 See Oord, "Wesleyan Theology."

59 Knudson does have a discussion of the Trinity in his work, but it is hampered with the same problem of the meaning of person.

5

Christology "Human End Foremost": Albert Outler and John Deschner

Jerome Van Kuiken

J ohn Deschner (1923–2000) was an undergraduate when he first met Albert Outler (1908–1989) at a student conference in 1943. Of that meeting, Deschner reminisced:

> When he actually turned up—and especially afterward, when he consented to ride as far as Dallas with the University of Texas delegation, hunched up against a [cold wind] under a flapping tarp on the back of a truck—I decided that this Duke theologian *came human end foremost* [i.e., prioritized human relations and the shared human condition]. . . . I have always known that my truest perception of this man was my first.[1]

Outler soon moved to Yale, where Deschner studied under him, and then to Southern Methodist University's Perkins School of Theology in 1951, where Deschner joined him as a colleague in 1956 and both men remained until retirement. Both contributed significantly to the ecumenical

---

1 John Deschner, "Albert Cook Outler: A Biographical Memoir," in John Deschner, Leroy T. Howe, and Klaus Penzel, eds., *Our Common History as Christians: Essays in Honor of Albert C. Outler* (New York: Oxford University Press, 1975), ix (italics mine).

movement and the rehabilitation of John Wesley as a theologian. As professors, both "came human end foremost," befriending and counseling students and colleagues.[2]

Both men also paid ecumenically minded attention to Christology. Deschner's published dissertation, *Wesley's Christology: An Interpretation*, put its subject in dialogue with Lutheran and Reformed scholasticism to serve ecumenical exchange.[3] Outler viewed Christology as the crux of ecumenical theologizing.[4] In lectures at Perkins and beyond, he covered the doctrine's history and gave his own constructive interpretation.[5] Due to Outler's greater historical scope and doctrinal creativity, this chapter focuses on his contributions while adding Deschner's where appropriate. We shall see that for them both it was vital that Christ "came human end foremost."

Outler's Passion: Putting the Human Foremost

Outler's breadth of activity—spanning theology, churchmanship, history, pastoral care, and psychotherapy—made him admit that his *oeuvre* might be mistaken for "a jumble of interests and inquiries." Yet beneath the diversity lay a common concern: "the *humanum*—the nature of human nature. . . . Thus, I am and have been a theologian, first and last, using the methodologies of critical history and depth psychology as well as I

---

2 Deschner, "Albert Cook Outler," ix–xxi; Colleen Bradley-Sanders and Timothy S. G. Binkley, *A Guide to the Papers of Albert Cook Outler* (Dallas: Bridwell Library, Perkins School of Theology, Southern Methodist University, 2014), 13–15, https://www.smu.edu/Bridwell/Collections/SpecialCollectionsand Archives/~/media/Site/Bridwell/Archives/BA10514.pdf; "Theologian John W. Deschner dead at 76," United Methodist News Service, July 31, 2000, https://archive.wfn.org/2000/07/msg00216 .html; Lewis Howard Grimes, *A History of the Perkins School of Theology*, ed. Roger Loyd (Dallas: Southern Methodist University Press, 1993), 95–96, 99, 189, https://archive.org/stream /historyofperkins00grim/historyofperkins00grim_djvu.txt.

3 John Deschner, *Wesley's Christology: An Interpretation* (PhD diss., Dallas: Southern Methodist University Press, 1960, 1985; repr., Grand Rapids: Zondervan, 1988), xiv–xix, 5–7.

4 Albert Cook Outler, *Christology*, ed. Thomas C. Oden (Anderson, IN: Bristol House, 1996), 42–44, 208; cf. 210.

5 For a summary listing of Outler's Christological papers, see Oden's preface to Outler, *Christology*, 17. More details may be found in Bradley-Sanders and Binkley, *Guide*, 23, 47–48, 50–52, 55, 58, 67, 83, 143–44, 149.

could to illuminate the human possibility, the human tragedy, the human mystery."[6] This concern shaped his Christology, which Outler believed held the key to the *humanum*.[7] He used critical historical methods to describe the history of Christology and psychological concepts to prescribe its reconstruction. We shall survey his description and prescription before evaluating them.

For Outler, Christology's history begins with the historical Jesus. Our main sources, however, are the biblical Gospels, whose interest is not history per se but kerygma—the preaching of his spiritual meaning as resurrected Savior and Lord. History and kerygma differ but must not be set apart or at odds. While doubtful that the Gospels record everything just as Jesus said and did it, Outler was confident that the Evangelists' interpretations rest on historical facts.[8] The four Gospels' diversity signals that the early church accepted theological pluralism so long as it did not compromise one core conviction: in the man Jesus, God was uniquely present for salvation. Paul's letters, though, accent Christ's divine identity over his historical humanity. This tendency led later thinkers to Monophysitism, the absorption of Christ's human nature into his deity. Thankfully, the Hebrews epistle counterbalances Paul by stressing Jesus's humanity.[9] Outler

---

6 "Forty Years Later: Some Personal Reflections on Religion and Mental Health" (1972) and "Psychotherapy and the Christian Faith" (1968) in Leroy Howe, ed., *The Pastoral Psychology of Albert C. Outler* (Anderson, IN: Bristol House, 1997), 33–34, 262, respectively (quotations from pp. 33–34); cf. *Christology*, 228.

7 Outler, *Christology*, 206–8; Earl Lectures at Pacific School of Religion, Berkeley (1969) and "Psychotherapy and the Christian Faith" in Howe, *Pastoral Psychology of Albert C. Outler*, 42–92, 268–69, respectively.

8 Albert C. Outler, *The Christian Tradition and the Unity We Seek* (New York: Oxford University Press, 1957), 43–46, 71–72; *Christology*, 24–25, 60–65, 218–22, 285–87.

9 Outler, *Christology*, 26–36. Outler thinks this is why Hebrews was attributed to Paul (28).

often cited Hebrews' line that Christ was like us in everything except sin (Heb 4:15).[10]

Orthodoxy's "Monophysite Bias"

Following the apostles, the church's kerygma settled into a basic pattern, the "rule of faith." Theologians such as Origen and Augustine preserved the gospel's intelligibility amid the prevailing cultural influences (in their case, Platonism). Outler was no Platonist, but he saw patristic attempts to make the kerygma culturally comprehensible as good and necessary, albeit imperfect.[11] He would make the same effort in his prescriptive Christology. He especially resonated with Augustine. Outler's portraits of himself and the bishop of Hippo share the same profile: a self-aware theologian who uses history and psychology to grasp human need and its solution and who insists that reflection must end in pastoral practice.[12] Yet Outler faulted Augustine for focusing on God over Christ and on Christ's divinity over his humanity.[13] Outler detected this error throughout Christology's development and aimed to avoid it in his own doctrine of Christ.

Almost as soon as there was the kerygma of the divine-human Savior, there were distortions.[14] Ebionites (also known as adoptionists or psilan-

---

10 E.g., Outler, *Christology*, 30, 129, 139, 286, 314; cf. 296–98; Earl Lectures, 57, 59; "Psychotherapy and the Christian Faith," 268; *Christian Tradition*, 122; "'For Us Men and Our Salvation'" (1951) in Ted A. Campbell, ed., *Albert C. Outler as Historian and Interpreter of the Christian Tradition* (Anderson, IN: Bristol House, 2003), 154; "Through Jesus Christ, Our Lord" (1969) in Bob W. Parrott, ed., *Albert Outler the Preacher: Sermons on Several Occasions* (Nashville: Abingdon Press, 1988; Anderson, IN: Bristol House, 1995), 47.

11 Campbell, preface to *Albert C. Outler as Historian*, 9–10. Campbell's edited volume includes Outler's "Origen and the *Regulae Fidei*" (1939), "Introduction to Augustine of Hippo, *Confessions* and *Enchiridion*," and "The Person and Work of Jesus Christ in the Thought of Saint Augustine" (both 1955). Cf. "Psychotherapy and the Christian Faith," 262.

12 Compare Outler's self-description as quoted above with his description of Augustine in "Introduction to Augustine," 159, 161–62. Martin Marty has noted another commonality: both were hoarders! See Martin E. Marty, "Albert C. Outler: United Methodist Ecumenist," *Christian Century* 101, no. 7 (February 29, 1984): 218, https://www.religion-online.org/article/albert-c-outler-united-methodist-ecumenist/.

13 Outler, "Introduction to Augustine," 160; "The Person and Work of Jesus Christ," 183, 190, 192.

14 The remainder of this paragraph summarizes Outler, *Christology*, 69–148, 223–25.

thropists) were faithful to Jesus's manhood but diluted his deity to merely honorific status. Docetists did the opposite, denying Christ's humanity for his divinity's sake. Arians made the Son an intermediary being, greater than humans but less than God. In response, the church turned kerygma into dogma, defining its faith to exclude heresy. The Nicene Creed (381) secured half the kerygmatic confession of Christ by affirming that he shared completely the deity of God the Father. But it took the Definition of Chalcedon (451)—the "Mount Everest of Christology"[15]—to strike the right balance by teaching both the full deity and the full humanity of the one person Jesus Christ. The Chalcedonian Christ "was a whole and real person with a single identity, a single mission, an integrated self-understanding. And yet this single mission was acted out by two operations, two energy-systems, working so that they need not be *confused* with each other nor distinguished from each other too sharply."[16] The Jesus of history and the Christ of faith are the same person: a Galilean prophet yet simultaneously God acting in time and space to save.[17] Chalcedon rejected the heresies of Monophysitism, Apollinarianism (Christ as a hybrid of human body plus divine mind), and Nestorianism (Christ as a divine person and a human person in cooperation). Instead, the Chalcedonian Definition echoed Hebrews 4:15's claim that Christ's humanity was like ours in all but sin. Outler esteemed Chalcedon as the definitive dogmatic statement of the apostolic kerygma and the basis for contemporary ecumenical Christology.[18]

Outler narrates Christological history since Chalcedon as a tragedy of equal and opposite failures to maintain the Definition's balance. From the fifth through seventeenth centuries, Chalcedonian orthodoxy formally

---

15 Outler, *Christology*, 65.

16 Outler, 138 (italics his). Note Outler's understanding of Christ's two "natures" as two "operations" or "energy-systems," not two static entities. This, he insists, is what Chalcedon meant (134–35, 138–39). Protestant Scholasticism missed this point, garbling the dogma of two natures in one person as "how one thing can be two things" and so creating the conundrum that the Enlightenment rejected as nonsense (245).

17 Outler, 139, 145–46.

18 Outler, 136, 142–43, 288–89.

reigned.[19] But this formal orthodoxy suffered from "Monophysite bias," tending to compromise Christ's humanity in practice.[20] Outler cited several examples. First, later orthodoxy taught the doctrine of *anhypostasia*: the personhood (*hypostasis*) of Christ is divine; there is no human *hypostasis* in him, only an *anhypostatic* (impersonal) human nature. This formulation divides Christ from us since we humans are persons, not simply natures.[21] Second, Christian art forms changed the Gospels' humble Jesus into the cathedrals' heavenly *Pantokrator*,[22] the mystery plays' "wonderworking Christ,"[23] and the icons' slumbering Christ-child or deceased Jesus with eyes open to show his sleepless divinity.[24] Third, sacerdotalism and the cult of saints arose as stand-ins for the lost sympathetic human Jesus, while Gothic architecture thrust aloft to reach an aloof Lord.[25] Fourth, Christ as divine Savior partially eclipsed Christ as human ethical teacher and exemplar. The result was churchly "otherworldliness, asceticism, puritanism, the opposition of grace to nature, and the subordination of culture to the uses of piety."[26] Medieval society expected only monastics to imitate Christ's "heroic virtues." The Reformation demolished this expectation but buried Christ's ethical significance beneath a monumental concern for his atoning mediation.[27] Outler spotted a few candles amid Christendom's semi-Monophysitic gloom: Thomas Aquinas's Aristotelian view of Christ's human nature as individuated instead of impersonal; Francis of Assisi's and Bernard of Clairvaux's devotion to Christ's manhood and the ethics of love; and Reformed

---

19 Outler, *Christology*, 162–64.

20 Outler, *Christology*, 67, 127, 149–75, 191, 208, 255; *Christian Tradition*, 72 (cf. 122); "Through Jesus Christ, Our Lord," 45; "The Person and Work of Jesus Christ," 192.

21 Outler, *Christology*, 165–67.

22 Outler, 150; cf. "The Person and Work of Jesus Christ," 192.

23 Outler, *Christology*, 169.

24 Outler, 167.

25 Outler, *Christology*, 140; "Through Jesus Christ, Our Lord," 45; "The Person and Work of Jesus Christ," 192.

26 Outler, *Christology*, 165.

27 Outler, 140; cf. 164–65, 169, 212.

exegetes' refusal to spiritualize the historically conditioned significance of scripture and Christ's humanity.[28]

Modern Monophysitisms

Against orthodoxy's quasi-Monophysite, dogmatic Christology revolted the eighteenth-century Enlightenment and its outworking in nineteenth-century classical liberalism. This revolt dismissed dogma and even kerygma in the name of history—specifically, critical scholars' reconstructions of the historical Jesus behind the kerygmatic and dogmatic Christ. The pendulum swung from orthodoxy's "practical Monophysitism" to "a humanistic Monophysitism of the opposite sort": Jesus was fully human indeed, but his full deity fell into doubt. His primary value was as an ethicist, not a redeemer.[29] Long-dead psilanthropism revived.[30]

John Wesley lived just as the pendulum was swinging.[31] Against the Socinians' and deists' psilanthropism, he so stressed Christ's deity that Outler charged Wesley with the same "practical monophysitism" as the foregoing tradition.[32] Outler's assessment was influenced by pupil-turned-colleague Deschner's *Wesley's Christology*.[33] Deschner mined Wesley's Standard Sermons, *Explanatory Notes upon the New Testament*, and Methodist Articles

---

28 Outler, *Christology*, 170–75.

29 Outler, 191.

30 Outler, 100.

31 Outler, 180.

32 Outler, in *Works* 1:470 n. f (on Wesley's introduction to his discourses on the Sermon on the Mount); cf. Outler's comments on Wesley's sermon "On Knowing Christ after the Flesh" in *Works* 4:97–98, 99 n. 2.

33 Deschner published his dissertation in 1960. Four years later, Outler published his pioneering anthology *John Wesley* (Oxford: Oxford University Press, 1964). Outler cited Deschner's book in Albert C. Outler, "The Monophysite Bias of Orthodoxy and the Impact of Enlightenment" (audiocassette of Christology lecture, Southern Methodist University, February 25, 1965), end of Part 1. (The audiocassette itself carries the designation 949A III–153, but SMU's Special Collections webpage designates it 949A/4. See http://www.smu.edu/Bridwell/Collections /SpecialCollectionsandArchives/~/media/Site/Bridwell/Archives/BA10514.pdf, 143.) Outler's "John Wesley's Interests in the Early Fathers of the Church" (1983) in *Albert C. Outler as Historian*, 277–80, speaks of his "crusade toward altering the focus of Wesley studies" as starting ca. 1963 in response to the work of Deschner and others (p. 278).

of Religion for Christological material, organizing it according to the Protestant scholastic categories of Christ's single person (existing in two natures, divine and human), double state (humiliation and exaltation), and
triple office (prophet, priest, king). This procedure reveals that Wesley's
Christology is largely traditionally orthodox but that "Wesley betrays a decided emphasis on the divine nature and a corresponding underemphasis
on the human."[34]

Deschner himself rebuffed heretical labels: "It is too much to say that
Wesley's is a docetic Christology" when he regularly highlights the divine
nature over the human.[35] "There is no need to make a Nestorian of Wesley" when he occasionally treats one nature in isolation from the other.[36]
Deschner accepted Wesley's Chalcedonian pedigree,[37] also noting how
Wesley's comments on Christ's psychological states, physical age and appearance, and activities foreshadow nineteenth-century biographies of
the human Jesus.[38] Deschner's real concern was linking the lopsidedness
of Wesley's Christology with imbalances elsewhere in his theology—an
unsurprising concern since Deschner's *Doktorvater* was Karl Barth,[39] who
integrated all doctrines under Christology. Thus, Deschner detected in Wesley half-suppressed tendencies of abstracting divinity, holiness, and the
moral law from Christ and of ranking judgment, sanctification, and exaltation above mercy, justification, and humiliation as parallels to prioritizing
Christ's deity over his humanity.[40]

Returning to Outler, we find that he viewed the theologies of Barth
and fellow "neo-orthodox" scholars as another swing of the pendulum, an
overreaction from the Enlightenment's historical Jesus as moral genius to

34 Deschner, *Wesley's Christology*, 6. Specific evidence appears on pp. 17, 24–27, 30–36.
35 Deschner, 28.
36 Deschner, 30.
37 Deschner, 15, 28, 30.
38 Deschner, 26–27.
39 Deschner, xxi; cf. 82 n. 10 on Barth's crucial contribution to Deschner's dissertation.
40 Deschner, 30–31, 38, 48–49, 58, 102–8, 137–41, 154–57, 167, 182–86, 191–98.

the kerygmatic Christ as existential Savior.[41] Outler critiqued Rudolf Bult-
mann and Paul Tillich for continuing the liberal division between the human Jesus and the divine Christ (although, unlike their liberal forebears,
they favored the latter over the former).[42] Barth, on the other hand, re-
habilitated "orthodox Protestant Christology with typical Monophysite
leanings."[43] Emil Brunner broke new ground in his book *The Mediator* by
exploring Christ's historical personality, only to succumb in his *Dogmatics* to the traditional tug toward Monophysitism.[44] The need persisted for
someone to guide the erratic pendulum of Christology to an equipoise in
which both Christ's full Godhead and full manhood, both faith and history, both spiritual salvation and practical ethics receive their due.[45] This
task Outler set for himself as he shifted from historical survey to doctrinal
reconstruction.

Outler's Christological Method: "Human End Foremost"

Humanum—what it means to be human—was Outler's overarching interest. But he spurned modernity's "narcissism." We cannot unearth the truth
about ourselves by starting with self-examination or mysticism. Rather, we
must be turned out of ourselves toward God and others, and this turn to
the objective can only come in response to God's own initiative to reveal
in Christ our nature and destiny.[46] That revelation comes through the New

---

41 Outler, *Christology*, 230–32, 282–83.

42 Outler, 257–67, 270–80; cf. 203–204.

43 Outler, 255.

44 Outler, "Monophysite Bias," end of Part 1 and beginning of Part 2. Outler was referencing
    Brunner, *The Mediator: A Study of the Central Doctrine of the Christian Faith*, trans. Olive Wyon
    (Philadelphia: Westminster, 1947); see esp. pp. 265–71, 317–19, in which Brunner distinguishes
    between Christ's historical-psychological "personality," which is a feature of the human nature
    assumed in the Incarnation, and the underlying divine "Person." Brunner saw this distinction as
    faithfully translating the patristic *anhypostasia* doctrine in light of the modern understanding
    of personality. Cf. Brunner's *Dogmatics*, vol. 2, *The Christian Doctrine of Creation and Redemp-
    tion*, trans. Olive Wyon (London: Lutterworth Press, 1952), 360, in which (*pace* Outler) Brunner
    explicitly reaffirms his earlier stance. Cf. his nuanced discussion of Monophysitism (361–63).

45 Outler, *Christology*, 210.

46 Outler, 206–7; cf. 212.

Testament's merger of history and kerygma. Neither half of the merger should be slighted. Its historical witness may be critically investigated and established in basic profile, thus providing a "noetic preface to faith." Its kerygma invites faith in the divine identity and saving significance of the selfsame Jesus who lived in history. But because faith seeks understanding, dogma must supplement history and kerygma. Dogma is the church-sanctioned framework for explaining (insofar as possible) the mystery of Christ. For Outler, the Chalcedonian Definition remains Christology's crucial dogmatic touchstone. The product of previous Christians' reason and experience, it guides our reason and experience in faithfully interpreting the biblical testimony to Christ for our times.[47]

Outler's theological method thus recapitulates Christology's historical development: first history, then kerygma, then dogma. First-century history included a crucified Galilean named Jesus. The apostolic kerygma heralded his resurrection as Lord and Christ, the divine agent of reconciliation.[48] Chalcedon ruled that in Jesus Christ a single person shared a dual identity as human and God. How are today's believers to make sense of this dogma?

"The Man of God's Own Choosing"

Concerning Christology, if Outler's favorite verse was Hebrews 4:15; his favorite church council, Chalcedon; and his favorite heresy to hunt, Monophysitism; then his favorite hymn was Martin Luther's *Ein' Feste Berg* ("A Mighty Fortress") and its line that salvation comes by "the right man on our side, the man of God's own choosing."[49] Outler used this lyric to sum up his Christology. Christ is a "man on our side," fully sharing our *humanum*. But the philosophical and psychological models of human nature on which earlier Christians relied are obsolete. Gone is mind-body dualism,

---

47 Outler, *Christology*, 210–13, 217–34 (quotation from p. 233), 283–89. Note Outler's use on p. 213 of his Wesleyan Quadrilateral.

48 Outler, 295–97.

49 E.g., Outler, *Christology*, 35, 292–93, 296–97; "Through Jesus Christ, Our Lord," 44; Earl Lectures, 53, 61; addresses listed in Bradley-Sanders and Binkley, *Guide*, 48, 51, 58, 67 (twice).

with its notion that personhood is a discrete element of the human constitution, an immaterial, self-contained supplement to an otherwise anhypostatic human nature. Human nature is wholly physical yet marked by divinely initiated emergent self-consciousness. Personhood in the modern sense refers to the entirety of who we are as individuals, as selves. Outler distinguished three layers of selfhood: the "social self" (our sense of identity received from others); the "object self" (the sense of identity arising from our own self-reflection); and the "subject self" (the basic mystery of our personal being lying beyond examination and encompassing the totality of who we are). This subject self is God's direct creation and exists above space and time (hence in eternity). Moreover, to be a person is to be a project. As Outler put it, "To be a self is not to be self-possessed; it is, rather, to be an intentional activity process identified by God's specific intention and differentiated by God's specific purpose, these together constituting each [hu]man's uniqueness."[50] The human self is by nature open to God and capable of union with God and use by God without threatening its own identity and agency—hence the apostle Paul's "I live, and yet not I; Christ lives in me" (Gal. 2:20, Outler's paraphrase).[51]

Christ is just such a human, distinguished from us only by being "the right man . . . , the man of God's own choosing." God eternally chose to create a human whose subject self was identical with God-in-redemptive-action. This human's purpose was to model the fellowship with God for which humankind always was meant, thereby revealing God's saving love. This human is Christ.[52] Because God's choice is eternal, adoptionism and Arianism are excluded, Outler believed: "There was no moment in time when Jesus *became* the Christ. There was no moment when his sharing in the Father's *ousia* [being or nature], and in ours, was either less or more."[53] But because

---

50 Outler, *Christology*, 300–306; "Through Jesus Christ, Our Lord," 47–48; Earl Lectures, 49, 59–60 (quotation from latter page).

51 Outler, *Christology*, 295, 309 (quotation from this page); "Through Jesus Christ, Our Lord," 48–49.

52 Outler, *Christology*, 297–99.

53 Outler, 298; italics his; cf. 308–10; Earl Lectures, 61–62.

of the modern perception of personhood, Outler also believed that the old orthodox model of a divine person assuming an anhypostatic human nature is ruled out: "The 'Person' (i.e., the personal identity) of Jesus Christ is the Redeemer. This does not mean a divine person inserted into a human individual otherwise devoid of human personality. . . . It means rather that the divine project (the Divine Word) *is* the human personality. The identifying center of the human individual *is* the Word, or project, of God."[54] Consequently, the Son's personhood eternally depends on his humanity and redemptive mission: "In the very act of becoming a human person Jesus Christ became the person he was. . . . There was not any time when the Son was not. From the beginning he was, by the elect counsel of God, the Second Adam."[55]

Christ's *essential* uniqueness lies in his eternal election as the divine-human Redeemer. Yet he also has an *existential* uniqueness, for throughout his earthly life he was sinless.[56] Certainly he shared human finitude, passions, and frustrations, and with them, temptations and the potential to sin.[57] True indeed is the patristic slogan, "What he did not assume, that he did not heal."[58] But sinfulness is not essential to human nature—that is "the devil's illusion"[59]—and so Christ was perfectly human by being perfectly sinless. His trustful communion with God was unbroken; his obedience, un-

---

54 Outler, *Christology*, 297; italics his. Elsewhere he describes the Word impersonally as "God's meaning-giving activity in the world" (Earl Lectures, 57) and "God's ordering influence" ("Through Jesus Christ, Our Lord," 44).

55 Outler, *Christology*, 309–10; cf. 319; Earl Lectures, 62.

56 Outler, *Christology*, 296.

57 Outler, 33, 297, 307.

58 Outler, *Christology*, 300. Here and in his Earl Lectures, 65, Outler incorrectly attributes this slogan to Gregory of Nyssa; in fact, it is from Gregory of Nazianzus's *Epistle* 101.

59 Outler, *Christology*, 296; on p. 191 Outler refers without elaboration to two nineteenth-century "English" theologians, "Edwin" Irving and McLeod Campbell. *Pace* Outler, the former was named Edward and both were Scots. Both taught that Christ's human nature was "fallen," even "sinful." Barth adopted a modified version of this view. Outler confronted this Barthian version in a clash with Thomas F. Torrance at a World Council of Churches meeting. See E. Jerome Van Kuiken, *Christ's Humanity in Current and Ancient Controversy: Fallen or Not?* (London: Bloomsbury T&T Clark, 2017), 13–43, 166, 174.

stinting; his maturation in love, unobstructed. He embodies the perfected *imago Dei* for us to imitate.[60]

This Christology promotes human flourishing. Outler proposed a mutually heuristic relationship between philosophical, scientific, and theological anthropology on the one hand and Christology on the other. While modern understandings of personhood and psychosomatic non-dualism challenge the ancient doctrine of *anhypostasia*, theology may reciprocate by denying the reductionism of secular accounts of the human. Like Christ, we each have a transcendent origin, a unique purpose, and the potential to commune and cooperate with God in a lifestyle of perfect love.[61]

Christology in the Chalcedonian spirit likewise provides analogies to soteriology. Outler outlined an *ordo salutis* of five crises-in-processes: (1) the "first encounter with Jesus Christ"; (2) conviction of sin; (3) justification; (4) Christian perfection; and (5) the hope of resurrection. With each crisis comes a shift from the objective to the subjective: from Christ as a historical or creedal figure to a living, convicting presence; from biblical accounts of sinners' plight, Christ's career, and salvation's blessings to one's own experience of these as realities. The objective and subjective aspects of soteriology correspond to Christ's two natures (though which nature is associated with which aspect varies).[62] Outler offered other soteriological correspondences too. The Holy Spirit's activity in Christians' activity reflects the cooperation of Christ's divine and human natures.[63] The Reformation doctrines of salvation *sola fide, sola gratia*, and *sola gloria Dei* echo Christ's constant human reliance on God, not on his own (sinless!) efforts.[64]

Lastly, Outler applies the Chalcedonian analogy to the relationship of

---

60 Outler, *Christology*, 296–99, 307. Cf. pp. 30 and 33, in which Outler uses the Greek equivalent to *imago, ikon* (misspelled as *ikoy*; apparently the Greek letter *nu* was mistaken for an *upsilon*).

61 Outler, Earl Lectures, 42–80; "Christ in You, the Hope of Glory" (1969), in Parrott, ed., *Albert Outler the Preacher*, 57.

62 Outler, *Christology*, 315.

63 Outler, "Christ in You," 57.

64 Outler, "Psychotherapy and the Christian Faith," 269; *Christology*, 306.

soteriology and ethics, faith and works, so that salvation and faith relate to Christ's deity while ethics and works relate to his humanity. This analogy allows Outler to correlate the historic drift toward Monophysitism with neglect of ethics, for to the extent that Christ's virtues are divine, they cannot be imitated.[65] Contrariwise, the liberal reduction of salvation to ethics reflects a Christ whose humanity has dwarfed his divinity.[66] In both soteriology and ethics, dual-nature Christology supports synergism or reciprocal responsibility.[67]

Assessing a Legacy

Veritas liberabit vos is Southern Methodist University's motto—"The truth will set you free." Its source is the Johannine Jesus (John 8:32), speaking of the truth about his divine-human identity and authority (8:13–58). SMU colleagues Outler and Deschner sought to critically retrieve this liberating truth from the host of Christians past for the good of Christians present and future. After six decades Deschner's reading of Wesley's Christology remains authoritative. Scholars rarely challenge his claim that Wesley neglected Christ's humanity. Rather, beginning with Outler himself, they have further embellished his evidence and charged Wesley with Monophysitism, Apollinarianism, and even Docetism. Their evidence, however, is generally strained.[68] To take one oft-cited example: Wesley's *Explanatory Notes* on Luke 4:30 and John 8:59 suggest that Christ may have escaped a mob by becoming invisible. But Wesley's further notes, similar suggestions in contemporaries' commentaries, and scientific and popular interest in unseen things and people in Wesley's day together clarify that he believed Christ obstructed his enemies' vision, not docetically dematerialized. Charles Wesley even thought the same miracle had happened to his brother John during

---

65 Outler, *Christology*, 312–13; "Through Jesus Christ, Our Lord," 45. Outler's claim that God cannot be a moral exemplar would have surprised the biblical writers: see, e.g., Exod. 20:8-11; Deut. 10:17-19; Luke 6:32-36.

66 Outler, *Christology*, 179–80, 191; "Through Jesus Christ, Our Lord," 46.

67 Outler, *Christology*, 312–14; "For Us Men and Our Salvation," 147–49, 157; Earl Lectures, 53.

68 Jerome Van Kuiken, "Deschner's Wesley and the Monophysite Meme," *Wesleyan Theological Journal* 54, no. 2 (Fall 2019): 37–55, offers extensive documentation and rebuttal.

a riot![69] As another example, Wesley's *Notes* on Matthew 27:50 teach that Christ could have "quit His body as soon as it was fastened to the cross." Critics detect here an Apollinarian notion that the impassible divine Word was only loosely attached to vulnerable human flesh.[70] Yet these critics offer no counterinterpretation of Matthew 27:50 and John 10:18, on which Wesley based his affirmation that Christ had authority to lay down his life whenever he chose. They also overlook that what Wesley depicted as departing Jesus's body was not an impassible deity but his human spirit, which already had suffered unimaginable agonies.[71] Deschner's more positive contributions include his exposure of the theological possibilities inherent in Wesley's doctrine of Christ's triple office as prophet, priest, and king,[72] as well as Deschner's investment toward a Christologically normed ecumenical Wesleyan theology, which has begun to yield rich dividends.[73]

Outler's laudable commitment to Chalcedonianism in the service of ecumenism has advanced through the efforts of his appreciative former student Thomas Oden.[74] Oden commended Outler's Christology unreservedly.[75] If it is be appropriated, though, two imbalances require correction.

---

69 Van Kuiken, "Deschner's Wesley," 43–44.

70 Van Kuiken, 51–53.

71 Wesley's comment on Matthew 27:50 is specifically on Christ's dismissal of his *human* spirit. In his preceding comments on Matthew 26:37, 39, 41; 27:46, Wesley stressed the sufferings of Christ's soul/spirit. See John Wesley, *Explanatory Notes upon the New Testament* (repr. London: Epworth, 1948).

72 See William J. Abraham, "John Deschner on John Wesley's Christology," *Wesleyan Theological Journal* 54, no. 2 (Fall 2019): 26–36; Edgardo Colón-Emeric's chapter in this volume; and E. Jerome Van Kuiken, "All of Him for All of Us: Christ's Person and Offices in John Wesley and T. F. Torrance," *Participatio* supplemental vol. 4 (2018): 24–38, https://tftorrance.org/journal-s04.

73 Dennis F. Kinlaw, *Let's Start with Jesus: A New Way of Doing Theology* (Grand Rapids: Zondervan, 2005); Edgardo Colón-Emeric and Mark Gorman, *The Saving Mysteries of Jesus Christ: A Christology in the Wesleyan Tradition* (Wesleyan Doctrine Series 4; Eugene, OR: Cascade Books, 2019); Tom Greggs, *Dogmatic Ecclesiology*, vol. 1, *The Priestly Catholicity of the Church* (Grand Rapids: Baker Academic, 2019); Thomas A. Noble's systematic theology, forthcoming from The Foundry Publishing.

74 Thomas C. Oden, *Classic Christianity: A Systematic Theology* (New York: HarperOne, 2009), xxviii; preface to *Christology*, 18; cf. Jason E. Vickers, "Christology," in William J. Abraham and James E. Kirby, eds., *The Oxford Handbook of Methodist Studies* (Oxford: Oxford University Press, 2009; repr. 2013), 569.

75 Oden, preface to *Christology*, 14–17.

First is its sweeping judgment of "practical monophysitism" against pre-modern orthodoxy. Outler seemed to think that one cannot treat Christ as truly human apart from Western modernity's critical historical consciousness, naturalistic bias, and interest in interiority. But when we take on its own terms the worldview of other times and places, we find Christ's real humanity respected.[76] Theologians with abstract Christological theories like *anhypostasia* displayed "a passionate (some might even say excessive) devotion, not to God the Word, but to the human figure of Jesus."[77] Churches whose art portrayed Christ as *Pantokrator* in fidelity to the New Testament's apocalyptic visions also featured crucifixes, celebrated the Real Presence of Christ's flesh and blood in the Eucharist, and even housed purported relics of his humanity, such as his mother's milk, his foreskin and burial shroud, and bits of his cross and his crown of thorns.[78] The annual occasion of medieval mystery plays was the Feast of Corpus Christi ("*Body* of Christ"), the memorial of Christ's institution of the Eucharist. The plays themselves are as noteworthy for human realism as for religiosity. (For instance, in a Nativity scene, a shepherd hails the Christ-child as God yet gives him a ball as a baby toy! Clearly the Holy Infant is not too divine for playtime.)[79] By contrast, iconography eschews artistic realism.[80] The all-seeing eyes of the sleeping or dead Christ are not

---

76   See, e.g., the perceptive remarks of John J. O'Keefe, "The Persistence of Decay: Bodily Disintegration and Cyrillian Christology," in Peter W. Martens, ed., *In the Shadow of the Incarnation: Essays on* Jesus *Christ in the Early Church in Honor of Brian E. Daley, S. J.* (Notre Dame, IN: University of Notre Dame Press, 2008), 230, 232.

77   Richard Sturch, *The Word and the Christ: An Essay in Analytic Christology* (Oxford: Clarendon Press, 1991), 182.

78   Charles Freeman, *Holy Bones, Holy Dust: How Relics Shaped the History of Medieval Europe* (New Haven, CT: Yale University Press, 2011).

79   J. Ellen Gainor, Stanton B. Garner Jr., and Martin Puchner, eds., *The Norton Anthology of Drama*, 2nd ed. (New York: W. W. Norton, 2014), 539–70 (the ball appears on p. 569); cf. University of Chicago literary scholar David Bevington, "How Mystery Plays Got Started and Why They're Worth Reviving," *Chicago Tribune*, January 19, 1992, https://www.chicagotribune.com/news/ct-xpm-1992-01-19-9201060019-story.html.

80   Leonid Ouspensky, "Icon and Art," trans. Larissa Pavear, in Bernard McGinn, John Meyendorff, and Jean Leclercq, eds., *Christian Spirituality: Origins to the Twelfth Century* (New York: Crossroad, 1987), 382–93.

meant to be crudely photorealistic but symbolize his divine omniscience amid his human ignorance, a staple of traditional Christology.[81] Sacerdotalism, the cult of saints, monasticism, Gothic
architecture, and "the subordination of culture to the uses of piety"[82] reflect
not a denial but a different understanding of the *humanum*—one in which
hierarchy and holism are seen as natural and beneficial. This understanding
starkly contrasts with modernity's conviction that democracy, individuality, and the separation of sacred from secular and private from public are
more humane.[83] We moderns must beware confusing cultural difference
and political and philosophical disagreement with Christological heresy.

The second imbalance lurks in Outler's constructive Christology. As noted
earlier, he proposed that the divine Son's personhood derives from his humanity and redemptive mission. The unspoken implication is that God needs
the created world—indeed, a fallen world!—in order to be a Trinity. Outler's
proposal parallels Catholic scholar Piet Schoonenberg's, which Rome condemned.[84] As a contribution to ecumenical Christology, therefore, it seems a
nonstarter.[85] Additionally, Outler's strong comparisons between God's

---

81 Oden, *Classic Christianity*, 263–64.

82 Outler, *Christology*, 165.

83 Christopher Dawson, *Christianity and European Culture: Selections from the Work of Christopher Dawson*, ed. Gerald J. Russello (Washington, DC: The Catholic University of America Press,
1998); C. S. Lewis, *The Discarded Image: An Introduction to Medieval and Renaissance Literature*
(Cambridge: Cambridge University Press, 1964).

84 Sacred Congregation for the Doctrine of the Faith, *Mysterium Filii Dei* (1972), http://www
.vatican.va/roman_curia/congregations/cfaith/documents/rc_con_cfaith_doc_19720221_
mysterium-filii-dei_en.html, responding to Piet Schoonenberg, *The Christ: A Study of
the God-Man Relationship in the Whole of Creation and in Jesus Christ*, trans. Della Coul-
ing (New York: Seabury Press, 1971; Dutch original: 1969). On the incident, see Edward T.
Oakes, *Infinity Dwindled to Infancy: A Catholic and Evangelical Christology* (Grand Rapids:
William B. Eerdmans Publishing Company, 2011), 405–8; J. P. Galvin, "Schoonenberg, Piet"
New Catholic Encyclopedia, updated April 26, 2020, https://www.encyclopedia.com/religion
/encyclopedias-almanacs-transcripts-and-maps/schoonenberg-piet.

85 Cf. Catholic reactions to similar claims by post-Barthians in Bruce L. McCormack and Thomas
Joseph White, eds., *Karl Barth and Thomas Aquinas: An Unofficial Catholic-Protestant Dia-
logue* (Grand Rapids: Eerdmans, 2013); Paul D. Molnar, *Faith, Freedom and the Spirit: The
Economic Trinity in Barth, Torrance and Contemporary Theology* (Downers Grove, IL: Inter-
Varsity Press, 2015); Paul D. Molnar, *Divine Freedom and the Doctrine of the Immanent Trin-
ity: In Dialogue with Karl Barth and Contemporary Theology*, 2nd ed. (London: Bloomsbury
T&T Clark, 2017).

relationship to Christ and God's relationship to the rest of us recall Donald Baillie's *God Was in Christ* and fit a pattern of Methodist Christology
from Boston personalism to process thought, with concomitant charges of
a "degree Christology" and (despite Outler's protests) adoptionism.[86] Outler's difficulties arise from failing to balance *anhypostasia* with its comple-
ment, *enhypostasia*: together they teach that human nature in its impersonal
state (e.g., Mary's ovum) was united to the preexistent person of God the
Son and became truly humanly personalized.[87]

In the end, the Christological equipoise Outler sought eluded him. The
pendulum's momentum proved too powerful. His Christology reflects the
"divided mind" of scripture and tradition versus reason and experience that
he bequeathed the United Methodist Church.[88] Yet his—and Deschner's—
integrative theological vision, particularly for Christology, remains compelling.[89] Outler once wrote that his epitaph should "speak of one who was
sustained . . . by the vision of a Christian theology that gives history its full
due; that makes way for the future without having to murder the past; that
begins and ends with the self-manifestation of God's mystery in our flesh
and our history."[90] If that vision of the God who "came human end foremost" continues to inspire the church, both Outler and Deschner surely
would be pleased.

86 D. M. Baillie, *God Was in Christ: An Essay on Incarnation and Atonement* (New York: Charles
    Scribner's Sons, 1948). Outler, *Christology*, 328, 330, references Baillie, Boston personalist Al-
    bert C. Knudson, and process theologian Norman Pittenger. On Baillie's adoptionism, see J. H.
    Hick, "The Christology of D. M. Baillie," *Scottish Journal of Theology* 11, no. 1 (1958): 1–12; on
    the latter movements, see Vickers, "Christology," 562–67.

87 Oakes, *Infinity*, 157–60, 405; Molnar, *Faith, Freedom and the Spirit*, 216–17. Outler never men-
    tions *enhypostasia*.

88 Leicester R. Longden, "The Legacy of Albert Cook Outler: Nostalgia, Challenge, Prospect
    (Part 2)," *Catalyst* (March 23, 2015), http://www.catalystresources.org/the-legacy-of-albert
    -cook-outler-nostalgia-challenge-prospect-part-2/.

89 Leicester R. Longden, "The Legacy of Albert Cook Outler: Nostalgia, Challenge, Prospect
    (Part 3)," *Catalyst* (March 30, 2015), http://www.catalystresources.org/the-legacy-of-albert
    -cook-outler-nostalgia-challenge-prospect-part-3/.

90 "The Ordeal of a Happy Dilettante," *Christian Century* 77, no. 5 (1960), quoted in Bradley-Sand-
    ers and Binkley, *Guide*, 15.

6

The Christology of John B. Cobb Jr.

Michael Lodahl

From the publication of *Christ in a Pluralistic Age* in 1975 to *Jesus's Abba* in 2015, John B. Cobb Jr. has demonstrated a recurring deep and vested interest in Christology. With these two texts serving as bookends, we may appreciate Cobb's forty-year sojourning with the question of how the figure of Jesus continues to reverberate with power and relevance in our post-Darwinian, postmodern world.

Cobb is a United Methodist theologian whose teaching and writing influence is far from limited to his tenure as Ingraham Professor of Theology at Claremont School of Theology from 1958 until his retirement in 1990; he has continued tirelessly to write and to lecture worldwide. He is the single most important thinker in the process theological tradition, "fundamentally indebted to Alfred North Whitehead for [his] understanding" of "the terms 'God' and 'human being.'"[1] Thus, by Cobb's own admission, Whitehead's philosophy figures significantly in his interpretation of what it means "to speak of God as having become incarnated in a human being"[2]—certainly a central question in Christology.

The Divine Logos as Creative Transformation

In *Christ in a Pluralistic Age* (hereafter *CPA*) Cobb identified two critical and related factors that "played a dominant role in obscuring Christ" and

---

1 John B. Cobb Jr., *Christ in a Pluralistic Age* (Philadelphia: Westminster Press, 1975), 13.
2 Cobb, *CPA*, 13.

motivated his Christological venture: secularization and religious pluralism.[3] His response to these factors was to argue for a Logos Christology in which the divine Logos is "that process in which our imagination and life orientation can be transformed by lucidity of vision and openness to what we see"—"that process itself, and not that for which it calls at any moment, around which life can best be organized," which process Cobb famously named "creative transformation."[4] As exemplified in the concerns of feminist, liberation, and ecological modes of thought, "the drive toward redemption is universal, and Christ appears in the creative transformation of all life everywhere. . . . In the unending drive toward liberation, yesterday, today, and tomorrow, we discern Christ."[5] Creative transformation, in turn, implies and even demands a significant level of trust that in the historical development of Western secularization and in the growing recognition and appreciation of the great variety of religious traditions in the world—the two factors that Cobb identified as motivating his Christological project—the incarnate Logos, the Christ, is actively and dynamically present.

If the Logos is truly divine, and thus another way of naming God, one might ask how Cobb justifies identifying God with "creative transformation." Partly, of course, the answer lies in Cobb's immersion in process theology, especially in this case as adumbrated by Henry Nelson Wieman.[6] However, Cobb also (and more importantly) argued that "'Christ' names the divine reality as that reality is held to have been present and manifest in Jesus," and that it is therefore the ministry of Jesus as proclaimed in the Gospels that leads to an appreciation of God as the principle and power of creative transformation. This, Cobb believes, was relatively quickly suppressed in

---

3 Cobb, *CPA*, 18.

4 Cobb, 21.

5 Cobb, 57.

6 Wieman was a philosophical theologian who retired from the University of Chicago Divinity School just before Cobb's transfer into the divinity school from the MA program in the university's humanities division. In his *Theological Reminiscences* (Claremont, CA: Process Century Press, 2014) Cobb ambivalently discusses Wieman's role in his early theological development, particularly Wieman's *The Source of Human Good* (Chicago: University of Chicago Press, 1946), 33–35. In footnotes hereafter, *Theological Reminiscences* will be designated as *TR*.

the earliest generations of the church. "In fact, . . . the early Christian picture of God was controlled by the self-evident axiom, accepted by all, of
the absoluteness and the impassibility of the divine nature. . . .This meant
also that in the image of Christ the paradoxical power manifest in the cross
was replaced by the conventional power of compulsion and control manifest in worldly rule, now projected on the cosmos."[7]

This of course is an idea shared by many contemporary Christian theologians; the question in this case is, How does Cobb conceive of this incarnation
of the divine Logos in the person of Jesus? If indeed Jesus is the incarnation
of God in the world, why and how is this the case? It is in addressing this
question that Cobb's process commitments become more fully manifest.
"The Logos in its transcendence is timeless and infinite, but in its incarnation or immanence it is always a specific force for just that creative transformation which is possible and optimal for each situation."[8] The Logos is
everlastingly operative in the world in this way, and indeed "is but a special
case of causal efficacy in general."[9] That is, in every event of experience in
the world, the event or occasion comes into being by receiving, and thus
being informed by, the occasions that have preceded it; in this way, past occasions indwell what-is-happening-now, though Cobb insists that "the idea
of the presence or embodiment of one entity in another is impossible to
formulate clearly when the entities involved are thought of as substances"
rather than as dynamic, profoundly interrelated events of becoming.[10]

> As long as the basic model of reality in terms of which God and humans
> are conceived is derived from stones and tables, God cannot occupy at
> the same time the space occupied by a man or a woman. . . . [But in the
> process model of reality, where] the model is taken from experience in-
> stead of material objects, . . . every experience incarnates all the entities
> that it includes. The idea of genuine presence of one entity in another,

---

7 Cobb, *CPA*, 55.

8 Cobb, 72.

9 Cobb, 72.

10 Cobb, 72–73.

the lack of which has made many difficulties for theology, is fundamental and fully intelligible [in this model.][11]

In Cobb's Logos Christology, then, the term "Christ" refers to the Logos as incarnate in the world, "the process of creative transformation in and of the world."[12] Of course, this is a universal rather than particular presence—but this is nothing more or less than what we encounter in Logos Christologies of such early luminaries as Justin Martyr and Athanasius.[13] Most dramatically, the latter wrote that "the incorporeal and incorruptible and immaterial Word of God comes to our realm, although he was not far from us before. For no part of creation is left void of him; he has filled all things everywhere, [while] remaining present with his own Father."[14]

Two important questions emerge, however, from this sort of Christological claim: (1) If the Logos is truly present to and within every moment of experience throughout the universe, at all times and all places, is the presence of the Logos in the history of Jesus of Nazareth in any way distinctive or unique? and (2) If the answer to the first question is yes, can that answer be provided while at the same time affirming, and perhaps even protecting, the truly human nature and experience of Jesus? Cobb does attempt to answer these critical questions.

Jesus as the Christ, the Divine Logos Incarnate

Regarding the first question, it is important to keep in mind that the creatively transforming power of the Logos is never the only factor, or influence, in the becoming of an event. In the case of human experience, for example, there are the influences of other people, one's own past (both remembered and forgotten), larger social and historical currents—indeed, to one extent or another, every event that has ever occurred in the universe's

---

11   Cobb, *CPA*, 73, 74.

12   Cobb, 76.

13   In Justin, see *First Apology*, especially cc. 5 and 46; in Athanasius, *On the Incarnation of the Word*.

14   Athanasius, *On the Incarnation of the Word*, in The Library of Christian Classics, vol. 3, *Christology of the Later Fathers*, ed. Edward Rochie Hardy (Philadelphia: Westminster Press, 1954), 62.

history contributes its possibilities to the making of the present moment. Thus, "the Logos is now more, now less determinative in the constitution of occasions," Cobb wrote. "What people believe, to what they attend, and what they decide affect how the Logos is incarnate within them."[15] The attentive Wesleyan thinker should note that what Cobb described here is virtually indistinguishable from John Wesley's ideas about prevenient grace:

> [T]here is no man that is in a state of mere nature; there is no man, unless he has quenched the Spirit, that is wholly void of the grace of God. No man living is entirely destitute of what is vulgarly called *natural conscience*. But this is not natural: It is more properly termed *preventing* [or "prevenient"] *grace*. Every man has a greater or less measure of this, which waiteth not for the call of man. Everyone has, sooner or later, good desires; although the generality of men stifle them before they can strike deep root, or produce any considerable fruit. Everyone has some measure of that light, some faint glimmering ray, which, sooner or later, more or less, enlightens every man that cometh into the world.[16]

Similarly,

> If we [understand "salvation" to] its utmost extent, it will include all that is wrought in the soul by what is frequently termed "natural conscience," but [is,] more properly, "preventing [i.e., prevenient] grace": all the drawings of the Father; the desires after God, which, if we yield to them, increase more and more; all that light wherewith the Son of God "enlightens every one who comes into the world," showing every man "to do justly, to love mercy, and to walk humbly with his God"; all the convictions which God's Spirit, from time to time, works in every child of man—although it is true, the generality of men stifle them as soon as possible, and after a while forget, or at least deny, that they ever had them at all.[17]

---

15 Cobb, *CPA*, 138.

16 John Wesley, Sermon 85, "On Working Out Our Own Salvation," http://wesley.nnu.edu/john-wesley/the-sermons-of-john-wesley-1872-edition/sermon-85-on-working-out-our-own-salvation/, III.4.

17 Wesley, Sermon 43, "The Scripture Way of Salvation," http://wesley.nnu.edu/john-wesley/the-sermons-of-john-wesley-1872-edition/sermon-43-the-scripture-way-of-salvation/, I.2.

Interestingly, in *CPA* Cobb suggested that "'conscience,' in many of its uses, when not confused with the Freudian superego, refers to what Whitehead calls the 'initial aim,'" and that, further, the "designative reference of 'Christ' is also to this aim"[18]—without even the hint of a reference to Wesley's idea about "conscience" as a manifestation of prevenient grace in a person's life. Not that Cobb need feel so obligated. In any case, long before Cobb, Wesley also acknowledged that the divine presence is never solely constitutive of human conscience, for while it is "the Son of God, that is 'the true light, which enlighteneth every man that cometh into the world,'" the degree to which any human being, at any moment, experiences and internalizes that light "varies exceedingly, according to education and a thousand other circumstances."[19] Thus, to this initial extent at least, Cobb is employing a Logos Christology (or, to this point, anthropology) that is not at all unlike Wesley's understanding of the human as a thoroughly graced creature. Two decades after *CPA*, in fact, Cobb made the connection clear in his explicit turn to Wesley, *Grace and Responsibility: A Wesleyan Theology for Today*:

> Wesley is clear that grace . . . is the power for good. . . . It is the Holy Spirit which is the life of God within human beings. This means that concrete human beings are constituted in part by the presence of God within them. Human beings do not first exist in separation from God and then come into relation with God. Their very life is already God's presence within them. They exist by virtue of their inclusion of the divine life within them. . . . The relationship to God is constitutive of our being.[20]

But, again, the experienced quality of this relationship, in Wesley's memorable turn of phrase, "varies exceedingly, according to education and a thousand other circumstances"—to say nothing of a person's ongoing, dy-

---

18 Cobb, *CPA*, 83.

19 John Wesley, Sermon 105, "On Conscience," http://wesley.nnu.edu/john-wesley/the-sermons-of-john-wesley-1872-edition/sermon-105-on-conscience/, I.5, I.3.

20 Cobb, *Grace and Responsibility: A Wesleyan Theology for Today* (Nashville: Abingdon Press, 1995), 40.

namically interrelated responses to Christ's transformative presence in each present. Cobb, accordingly, can add that "the free and responsible human person [is] *partly* constituted by God's inbreathing moment by moment."[21]

How does all of this relate to Jesus's experience of God? If the divine presence as Logos is at least partially constitutive of every human's (to say nothing of every creature's) existence and experience, then in what way or ways was, or is, Jesus's "incarnation" of the Logos unique? This is still the question before us. "If Jesus is a paradigm case of incarnation, and if the structure of his existence as it incarnates the Logos is explanatory of his assurance and authority, the possibility of a distinctive mode of incarnation should be considered."[22]

Cobb suggests that "in the fullest incarnation of the Logos, its presence must constitute not only a necessary aspect of existence but the self as such,"[23] and that this is what occurred in Jesus. The reason *why* it occurred in this person would be, first and ultimately, a divine decision: a "structure of existence" in which "the presence of the Logos would share in constituting selfhood" would certainly seem to require that God's aim for Jesus be unique; indeed, "God gave to Jesus distinctive possibilities of actualizing himself around the immanent Logos."[24] In Jesus's case, then, "the 'I' in each moment is constituted as much in the subjective reception of the lure to self-actualization that is the call and presence of the Logos as it is in continuity with the personal past. This structure of existence would be the incarnation of the Logos in the fullest sense."[25] There is, to be sure, still the element of "subjective reception" such that Jesus's own volitional responses are required. Hence, Cobb continues, "we may assume that the distinctive structure of Jesus's existence did not characterize his infancy or remain constant through sleeping and waking states. When it emerged

---

21 Cobb, *Grace and Responsibility*, 41; italics mine.
22 Cobb, *CPA*, 138.
23 Cobb, 138.
24 Cobb, 173.
25 Cobb, 140.

and how steady it became are subjects on which we have little information."[26] What we do have, however, in general support of Cobb's scenario are statements such as this from Luke's Gospel, that "Jesus increased in wisdom and in years, and in divine and human favor" (2:52 NRSV). Cobb further suggests that the Gospel stories of Jesus's wilderness temptations, his struggling prayers in Gethsemane, and his cry of dereliction from the cross "witness to the belief on the part of his disciples that he was not continuously free from the tension between his 'I' and the Logos. To affirm today that he was fully human entails this same assumption."[27]

Thus, Jesus's capacity for faithful response to the creatively transformative presence of the divine Logos was not, and could not be, constant; creaturely existence is far too variable for this, even if we simply include only the most obvious factors, such as age, culture (e.g., Jesus was a first-century Jewish male from Galilee), religious instruction, family dynamics, and relations with others. In his *Theological Reminiscences*, Cobb straightforwardly reports that "Jesus began his mission focused on Jews and only Jews" until "a Syro-Phoenician woman taught him that this was inadequate" and then "Jesus's ministry and teaching became inclusive."[28] One may assume that, for Cobb, this was a moment in which the Logos as creative transformation was present to Jesus as a lure toward a more radically inclusive vision of God's redeeming love. One may also assume that Jesus had a meaningful choice before him in this moment: respond positively to the divine wisdom challenging him in this woman's witty reply about dogs waiting for scraps, or retreat to the more comfortable, less challenging parameters of ministering only to "the lost sheep of the house of Israel"—or very likely any number of other possibilities in the moment.

We will return to this point later, but let us briefly acknowledge that Wesley would have had little to no patience for the role of truly human agency and responsibility in Jesus's existence, especially vis-à-vis God, as

---

26 Cobb, *CPA*, 142.

27 Cobb, 142.

28 Cobb, *TR*, 280.

described by Cobb. For the moment, having seen that for Cobb Jesus must have been offered a distinctive aim by God to become the Christ, i.e., the Logos incarnate, as his identity, we must still wonder how and why it was that Jesus responded so faithfully. Granted, in Cobb's view we need not assume that Jesus was thoroughly, entirely, and unfailingly faithful to the divine call; "we not only assume that he was tempted, but that he yielded to temptation."[29] Even so, and even in acknowledging the stark role that the New Testament assigns to Jesus's struggles with temptation and doubt, it is remarkable that this person, "at least at important times in his life . . . freely chose to constitute his own selfhood as one with this presence of God within him."[30] How, and why, did he do so? This is the heart of Christology.

Certainly it would be important to acknowledge the formative role of the history and traditions of Israel in the development of Jesus, a role that, to be sure, is adumbrated in the Gospel genealogies. Matthew's genealogy in particular suggests that Jesus is the fruition of a long historical tradition that prepared the way for him through Israel's own halting responsiveness to God's aims presented through the Torah and the prophets.[31] Indeed, it would be a legitimate question whether Jesus could have functioned as he did—or for that matter, functioned at all—without the precedent of Moses and particularly the prophets (cf. Matt. 9:13, 12:6). In his more recent *Jesus' Abba: The God Who Has Not Failed*, Cobb wrote that "Jesus stood in the tradition of the prophets. . . . That Jesus' spiritual Abba is the God of the prophets is clear in all his deeds and sayings. . . . Jesus' Abba is the God of the prophets qualified as love."[32] While none of this can *explain* how and why Jesus was such a faithful human in responding to God's distinctive calling upon his life, perhaps it at least provides a social, religious, and historical context for considering the possibility of such faithfulness.

---

29 Cobb, *CPA*, 130.

30 Cobb, 173.

31 See Michael Lodahl, *Shekhinah/Spirit: Divine Presence in Jewish and Christian Religion* (Mahwah, NJ: Paulist Press, 1992), 160–63.

32 Cobb, *Jesus' Abba: The God Who Has Not Failed* (Minneapolis: Fortress Press, 2016), 10, 11.

Jesus as Truly Human, Free, and Responsible

In *CPA* Cobb devotes considerable attention to the tensions between the Antiochene and Alexandrian streams of Christological reflection. At its most basic, this tension may be described as Cobb does: "One could begin with Jesus as a man and ask whether and how he was related to God. One could begin with God and ask in what way he became man."[33] There should be no question regarding where Cobb's sympathies lie, though he holds that both traditions were handicapped by an inadequate substantialist metaphysic.

> Incarnation for the Antiochenes could be understood only as the closest imaginable proximity and harmony of the divine and the human substances, which still retained their mutual externality. Incarnation for the Alexandrians could be understood only as the substance of God clothing itself in aspects of humanity without being affected by that act. . . . But both struggled to show that God was present in Jesus in the fullest sense without destroying the distinction between God and Jesus or denying Jesus's full humanity. . . . New conceptualities are now available that abandon the idea of substance and make possible a fuller and less paradoxical expression of the creative and valid intentions behind the Chalcedonian creed.[34]

It is clear that the "new conceptualities," derived essentially from Whiteheadian philosophy, will recognize and even celebrate the fully human nature of Jesus—even as we remember that human nature (like all created nature) "includes in some measure the immanent Logos, which is the lure to the fullest possible . . . realization in each moment."[35] In Whitehead's scheme, of course, this divine lure is typically named "initial aim." Since all creaturely existents, including human beings, are to some degree constituted in each moment by the divine presence experienced as "initial aim," it is no denial of Jesus's full and creaturely humanity to affirm

---

33 Cobb, *CPA*, 156.

34 Cobb, 168.

35 Cobb, 171.

also the divine nature present and active within his life. Indeed, "the more fully the [divine] lure is responded to, the more fully the human potential is actualized. The optimum realization would occur when human existence constituted itself in unity with the lure, as in the case of Jesus. This perfect incarnation of the Logos is at the same time the highest embodiment of humanity."[36]

Such notions are of course not unique to Cobb, but perhaps we can dwell here a little longer. Think of Mark's Gethsemane scene, in which Jesus said to his inner circle of disciples, "'I am deeply grieved, even to death; remain here, and keep awake.' And going a little farther, he threw himself on the ground and prayed . . . 'Abba, Father, for you all things are possible; remove this cup from me; yet, not what I want, but what you want'" (14:34–36 NRSV). In the very midst of this profound struggle we encounter "the highest embodiment of humanity"—an utter opening of himself to God's presence as *Abba*—intimate, tender, and compassionate Love.[37] In such complete receptivity to the divine Logos, Jesus's life as witnessed to by the Gospels becomes revelatory of God. "If it is in Jesus that we perceive what God's immanence is and does, then it is from Jesus that we should learn what God is like. We can and must reverse the long history of retaining ideas of God uncongenial to what is apparent in Jesus."[38] Such a move certainly would ameliorate the difficulty often associated with affirming that in him "all the fullness of God was pleased to dwell" (Col. 1:19 NRSV), since that divine fullness will tend now to be characterized as humble, compassionate love, a Love "who calls people beyond every established structure and principle for the sake of creative new possibilities."[39] Certainly this Johannine characterization of God as love (1 Jn. 4:8, 16), itself so beloved of John Wesley, provides the perfect segue to the considerations to follow.

---

36 Cobb, *CPA*, 171.

37 Cobb, *Jesus' Abba*, 11–14.

38 Cobb, *CPA*, 168.

39 Cobb, 168.

Cobb's Christology and Methodist Theological Developments

I believe Cobb is correct to have noted the deep resonance between his Whiteheadian anthropology and Wesley's interpretation of human beings as thoroughly and deeply graced creatures.[40] Just as for Cobb the Logos as creative transformation is universally immanent, so for Wesley divine grace—which is nothing other than the Holy Spirit—"is free in all to whom it is given. It does not depend on any power or merit in man; no, not in any degree, neither in whole, nor in part. . . . Whatsoever good is in man, or is done by man, God is the author and doer of it. Thus is his grace free in all; . . . [and] it is free for ALL, as well as IN ALL."[41] Similarly, for neither Wesley nor Cobb does this imply at all that human agency is unimportant; indeed, for both of them it is the presence of God at work within us that evokes and empowers our free response.

Process categories may in fact make more explicit many of Wesley's largely undeveloped themes in theological anthropology. Late twentieth-century Nazarene theologian Mildred Bangs Wynkoop certainly seemed to think so, writing in the introduction to her *A Theology of Love: The Dynamic of Wesleyanism*, "'Process Theology' makes a much needed correction to the dualisms of a former day. It is my considered opinion that, though the metaphysical foundation of process thought is not the only solution to theological problems, its insights are inescapable in a biblical theology."[42] Many of those dualisms would hinge on a substantialist metaphysic that Wynkoop, admittedly drawing more deeply upon Buber than upon Whitehead, eschewed.

Wynkoop seemed to be suggesting (to a conservative theological

---

40 In one of my very earliest interactions with Cobb, as we discussed this particular theme, he summarized: "Whitehead and Wesley were both Arminian."

41 John Wesley, Sermon 128, "Free Grace," http://wesley.nnu.edu/john-wesley/the-sermons-of -john-wesley-1872-edition/sermon-128-free-grace/, 3–4.

42 Mildred Bangs Wynkoop, *A Theology of Love: The Dynamic of Wesleyanism* (Kansas City, MO: Beacon Hill Press of Kansas City, 1972), 11.

audience) that Wesley's theological insights gesture and grope toward a certain kind of metaphysic, rather than having been derived from one. Perhaps hedging her bets, she continued:

> John Wesley's understanding of love can be supported only by an underlying "metaphysic" which is dynamic in nature. His theological position was not, however, derived from a metaphysical point of view. Rather, his religious and biblical insights lead to a metaphysic which, it is believed, commends itself to modern man's new understanding of nature and furnishes a ground for the Christian meaning of life.[43]

Wynkoop, it seems, was hinting that Wesley's pastoral and theological genius was highly suggestive of, and amenable to, a processive metaphysical description of the universe. Though she framed her basic idea carefully and unobtrusively, we can extract her point: a faithfully Wesleyan approach to Christian faith and practice is suggestive of a metaphysic that "commends itself to modern man's new understanding of nature"—and it seems highly unlikely that she meant anything other than an evolutionary understanding of nature (though she expressed herself gingerly in the early 1970s). And while of course theological reflection within the assumptions of evolutionary theory is hardly the unique province of process theologians, let alone solely of Cobb, it is eminently arguable that no other theological tradition has so thoroughly and consistently tried to proceed on that basis.[44] To the extent that Methodist theologians perceive this to be a virtue, then Cobb's Christology, or at least something similar in a process vein, may be deemed helpful.

Note, though, that Wynkoop's book offers nothing by way of explicit Christology; indeed, in terms of the doctrines both of Christ and of the Trinity, her theology is exceedingly sparse. Similarly, in the one recommendation of Cobb's theology written by a Wesleyan scholar for a specifically

---

43 Wynkoop, *A Theology of Love*, 11.

44 I have argued this elsewhere in "Divine Sovereignty in the Process Theological Tradition (with a Little Help from John Wesley)," in *The Sovereignty of God Debate*, ed. D. Stephen Long and George Kalantzis (Eugene, OR: Cascade Books, 2009), 75–96.

Wesleyan audience, there is no mention of Christology whatsoever.[45] So how does, or might, Cobb's Christology fare among self-consciously and serious Methodist theologians?

Part of an answer lies in the question of how important is some degree of faithfulness to Wesley's Christology for contemporary and future Methodist reflection. Another part lies in the question of the relative adequacy of Wesley's Christology itself. Earlier in this essay I mentioned my judgment that Wesley would not have had much sympathy for Cobb's deep concern for Jesus's fully and truly human existence and experiences. A few examples should quickly illustrate this. In his comments on Jesus's escape from his fellow Nazarenes in the hometown synagogue (Luke 4:30), Wesley suggested that Jesus eluded them "perhaps invisibly";[46] when commenting on a comparable story in John (8:59), he mused, "Probably by becoming invisible."[47] It is striking that Wesley so quickly appealed to a "disappearing act" that seems strongly to imply that he had no issue with the notion that Jesus's human body could become invisible at will. In other words, this is not a body as we know and experience bodies.

Likewise, in commenting on Calvary, Wesley cavalierly suggested that Jesus "could have continued alive, even in the greatest tortures, as long as He pleased, or have retired from the body whenever He had thought fit," that in fact he showed the extent of his love "inasmuch as He did not use His power to quit His body as soon as it was fastened to the cross, leaving only an insensible corpse to the cruelty of His murderers; but continued His abode in it, with a steady resolution, as long as it was proper."[48] What Wesley here was attempting to describe is not the

---

45 John Culp, "A Dialog with the Process Theology of John B. Cobb, Jr.," *Wesleyan Theological Journal* 15, no. 2 (Fall 1980): 33–44.

46 Wesley, *Explanatory Notes upon the New Testament* (London: Epworth Press, 1977), 217, note on v. 30. To his credit, he then added, "or perhaps they were overawed; so that, though they saw, they could not touch him."

47 Wesley, 342, note on v. 59.

48 Wesley, 134, note on v. 50.

THE CHRISTOLOGY OF JOHN B. COBB JR.

Word that *became flesh*; no, this begins to seem docetically as though the Word *slipped inside some skin for a while*, "as long as it was proper." This is Alexandrian Christology to an extreme, which Cobb properly identified as the heresy of Apollinaris.[49] This Jesus that Wesley described is not a body—frail, vulnerable, passive, passioned, ruptured, broken, or bleeding. This is the Logos in his "abode," and of course a temporary abode at that.[50] It is difficult to conceive of a contemporary or future Methodist theologian having much interest in defending Wesley's Christology, at least concerning these matters. I think Christologies of the foreseeable future (and hopefully into the indefinite future) will continue to be governed by Donald Baillie's impassioned dictum in the mid-twentieth century, "No more Docetism!"[51] Even if somehow Wesley were cleared of

---

49 Cobb, *CPA*, 157. It is not difficult to find strong Apollinarian accents in the Christology of H. Orton Wiley, the twentieth-century dean of Nazarene theologians who was deeply beholden to such nineteenth-century Methodist giants as John Miley (1813–1894) and William Burt Pope (1822–1903). Indeed, even within the small confines of mid-twentieth century Nazarene theology, a hot debate arose between the crypto-Apollinarian Wiley and Stephen S. White, the first professor of theology at the then-new Nazarene Theological Seminary. In his *Essential Christian Beliefs* (Kansas City, MO: Beacon Hill Press, n.d.), White wrote, "Jesus Christ, as the Incarnate One, faced temptation as human beings face it. . . . Could the God-man have sinned? Of course He could have. Either this was the case or else His temptation was a farce. There can be no genuine temptation where there is no possibility of sin. A Christ who went through this earthly life without sin could not be any inspiration to me if He failed to sin because He could not. He did not sin because He would not sin. He chose not to yield to temptation. In the realm of moral acts there are no musts or cannots; there are only wills or will nots" (48). Wiley begged strongly to differ; Jesus could not have committed sin; indeed, the question can even be raised only within the context of the Nestorian heresy. *Christian Theology*, (Kansas City, MO: Beacon Hill Press, 1952), 2:153. We have already noted that Cobb quite offhandedly assumes that Jesus did yield to temptation—and that indeed our contemporary assumptions regarding Jesus as "altogether one of us . . . and what [this] means for Christian faith is a creative transformation in which we can discern Christ" (*CPA*, 130). We can safely assume that Wesley, Wiley, and White would all have been dismayed by news of such a creative transformation.

50 For a treatment of other dramatic instances of Wesley's strong reservations about Jesus as a truly human body, see Matthew Hambrick and Michael Lodahl, "Responsible Grace in Christology? John Wesley's Rendering of Jesus in the Epistle of Hebrews," *Wesleyan Theological Journal* 43, no. 1 (Spring 2008): 86–103. Of course, as explored elsewhere in this volume, John Deschner got the ball rolling in his doctoral dissertation, written under Karl Barth's tutelage, published as *Wesley's Christology: An Interpretation* (Dallas: Southern Methodist University Press, 1960, 1985).

51 See the opening pages—and then all the rest of the pages—of D. M. Baillie's classic *God Was in Christ: An Essay on Incarnation and Atonement* (New York: Charles Scribner's Sons, 1948).

this charge, he flirted far too often, and easily, with its implications. No Methodist should want to do Christology in a Wesleyan way if it meant having to defend Wesley's decidedly paltry portraits of Jesus's human nature.

Clearly, for Wesley Jesus's human nature was quite unlike other human beings who lived in the presence and power of prevenient grace. For Wesley, Jesus would have had no need for this gracious empowering of the Logos/Spirit.[52] Instead, he understood Jesus to be the *appearing* of the Word in human flesh, even *appearing* to be one of us—but ultimately an alien to human existence and experience. He is the embodying of divine grace, the incarnation of divine grace—but not the embodying of its reception as a truly human response. In Randy Maddox's words, "Wesley's consuming emphasis on the deity of Christ was an expression of his conviction that *God is the one who takes initiative in our salvation* . . . By emphasizing Christ as the pardoning Initiative of God in salvation, Wesley has underlined the prevenience of *grace* to our *response.*"[53] But Maddox is too forgiving here, particularly in a book whose title and perduring theme is *responsible* grace. A critical aspect in any adequate Christology must be the affirmation of full human nature and experience in the life of Jesus. One cannot dismiss or ignore the crucial importance of human *response* to God in the life and ministry of Jesus, even as one cannot dismiss or ignore the divine initiative of grace in Jesus. An adequate Christology will strive to maintain and uphold both of these emphases; certainly this is, and should remain, a critical "orienting concern"[54] of Methodist theologians.

My argument, then, is that Cobb offers an improvement over Wesley in regard to Christology—at least as it pertains to an appreciation and even celebration of Jesus's truly human nature, existence, and experience. In doing so, Cobb also offers a metaphysical picture of reality that can make

---

52 Cobb demonstrates understandable willingness to use these terms interchangeably in *Can Christ Become Good News Again?* (St. Louis: Chalice Press, 1991), 37.

53 Randy L. Maddox, *Responsible Grace: John Wesley's Practical Theology* (Nashville: Kingswood Books, 1994), 117, 118.

54 To employ Maddox's useful phrase. *Responsible Grace*, 18–19, 38–39, 44.

good sense of Jesus's (and everyone else's) deeply relational existence and can also suggest a way to envision the actual and effective presence of God within his (and everyone else's) living experience, decisions, and words. This metaphysic does take seriously, at its very basis, the evolutionary portrait of the universe. These are all virtues of Cobb's Christology, in my estimation.

The
Futures of Methodist
Christology

7

The Image of God Is a Black Woman: Feminist and Womanist Christologies

Christina M. Smerick

> The power of woman is her dependence, flowing
> from the consciousness of that weakness which
> God has given her for her protection.
>
> **—The General Association of Massachusetts (Orthodox), 1837**

> For women, nothing short of a shaking of the male universal foundation
> of theology is required to construct an adequate feminist Christology.
>
> **— Jacquelyn Grant, *White Women's Christ***

In 2009, Jane Craske opened her chapter titled "Methodism and Feminism" with "Feminism is a contentious word."[1] It is now more than a decade later and that remains the case. What that says about our openness to the experience of women as a church and as a society is fairly depressing. And yet I press on, treading some of the same ground in hopes that my male counterparts will not skip this chapter because it "has nothing to do with" them. Women make up more than 50 percent of the *imago Dei* in the world, after all, and therefore their experiences of God-in-Christ should be more than mere footnotes to male-dominated theology.

But writing a chapter on the topic of feminism and Christology is also fraught with peril. The dangers abound: one can get pedantic and overexplain

---

1   Jane Craske, "Methodism and Feminism," *The Oxford Handbook of Methodist Studies*, ed. William J. Abraham and James E. Kirby (Oxford: Oxford University Press, 2009), 662.

the history of Christology (Personhood! Works! Offices!); one can get defensive and overexplain the history of feminism (The vote! Domestic violence! Inequality! Pat Robertson!). One can end up being repetitive, covering the same ground that has been covered very well already. Therefore, I am focusing on what I think is the real question for this new volume in the first place: *What is new?* What has changed since 2009, when Dr. Craske wrote her essay? What more needs to be said about Methodism, Christology, and feminism?

Well. Quite a lot.

As I write this, we are nearing the third decade of the new millennium. Who knows what the world is like in the far future after 2020 when this will be published? At this point, it is anyone's guess. But right now, we (in the US, but also in Great Britain, and indeed in many areas of Europe) are in what might be called interesting times. It does no good to write an essay on Christology and feminism while pretending that context does not matter—because if anything matters for feminist theology, it is *context*. And our context is this: we live in an era where the chickens are coming home to roost, where both nations and (white) Christianity in general are being called to task for unconfessed, unrepentant sins. As the United States fights not to acknowledge its roots—and branches, and fruit—in profound racism and genocide, as the Catholic Church fights not to hold predators accountable for heinous acts against children, and as Protestant churches fight not to hold their male pastors accountable for sexual assault, rape, pedophilia, and sexual harassment, the pressure is mounting, the center cannot hold, and it is well past time for the (white, male) church to *listen* to other voices, voices that bring judgment but also redemption.

Historical work on Christology has been amply explored by scholars in the broadly Methodist tradition. Most of those historical examinations have emphasized or problematized John Wesley's "high" Christology, which emphasized the divinity of Christ over against the trends of his day. However, when we approach the history of the twentieth century—and it is now, friends, definitely "history"—the trend in scholarship is to provide a paragraph or two on womanist theology, feminist theology, liberation theology, as if these are mere footnotes to the great discussions of the well-educated white men of the past. Feminist theologians, however, would and do argue that the inherited tradition of Christology in *all* Christian traditions is at best a calcification, a statue formed in our image (or rather, the image of a white man), one that stultifies the Spirit and imprisons (to use Jacqueline Grant's term) both Jesus himself and the church. This essay, therefore, is a small step in rectifying that problem.

A feminist Christology in the 2020s and beyond cannot be a Christology divorced from issues of race, class, and gender. A feminist Christology emerging out of or informing a Methodist tradition cannot ignore the very real fissures in our churches and communities. A feminist Christology cannot be anything less than prophetic in these times. A mere survey is insufficient.

What is at stake here is an understanding of and relationship with Christ that is not oppressive, that does not exclude any part of who a person is. A feminist Christology may require some shifting of perspective for those who are not female, and yet should be inclusive of difference and embrace the diversity of humanity. A feminist Christology above all should point to the kingdom.

Feminist Christology unapologetically focuses on the kenotic humanity of the person of Christ. While many debates rage in tiny circles regarding whether and why Wesley would emphasize the divinity of Christ over the humanity, nevertheless again, in the twenty-first century, the God of love who lowered Godself in the Incarnation is the central beginning point for feminism. But why? Why not focus on the divinity of Christ, on the salvation that divinity inevitably brings? Why risk reducing Christ to the merely human?

For a number of good reasons.

First, as historical theology professor Diane Leclerc puts it, "The true God's essential characteristic is love . . . is also *essentially* humble, as revealed in the humanity of Jesus the Christ."[2] We cannot understand God without the incarnation of God in Jesus, and this act is not one of domination

---

2 Diane Leclerc, "The Humility of God: The Humanity of Jesus as Wesleyan Ecclesiologic," *Didache: Faithful Teaching* 17, no. 2 (2018): 1.

and authority, not one of judgment, but one of self-sacrificing love. This framework allows the marginalized to draw close to a person who otherwise would be out of reach. People at the margins cannot access the foot of the King; but they can access the creche. God's very nature, Leclerc wrote, is humility—and this is a far cry from, and a tremendous contrast to, the systems we have subsequently built in the name of Christ, systems that oppress and abuse without consequence. Frankly, women and other marginalized people do not need another authority figure to literally lord over them; they need love, and they need a way to understand their humanity as precious and redeemed, not condemned. The world condemns enough.

Second, much of Christology seems to focus, intentionally or not, on either Power or Reason for its support structures. (See Boston personalism.) Both of these concepts are fundamentally white, European, and male in creation and concept. They are tainted, if you will, with the very structure of oppression. As feminist and civil rights activist Audre Lorde wrote, one cannot dismantle the master's house with the master's tools, and relying on philosophical-rational or powerful-authority models of Christology just ends up reifying the patriarchal structures that feminist Christology seeks to avoid. Not to mention that one has to ignore the Gospels almost entirely if one wants to build a philosophical-rational and/or power/masculine version of Christology. Feminist Christologies offer a means of recovering the suffering of Jesus; the Incarnation; the "with-us" of Immanuel. They also offer what we say Jesus offers most: comfort and rest. Methodism has had in the roots of its various traditions a focus on the marginalized. We may have lost that focus as we have gained economic and social power, but our origins are in walking with, living life with, those whom society has marked as inferior or unimportant. Recovering that call—that our salvation is not just tied to but dependent upon our solidarity with the poor and outcast—may allow the Spirit some breathing room.

However, as I have intimated, feminist Christology focuses almost entirely on issues of sexism and patriarchy. These are indeed systems of oppression, and historically women have been marginalized and disempowered in the church. However, this is not the sum total of "oppressions" people have suffered, often at the hands of the body of Christ. A merely feminist Christology, therefore, is insufficient. So, after providing a brief history of feminist theology and a more thorough overview of feminist Christology, I turn to African-American theology professors Jacquelyn Grant and Eboni Marshall Turman for *womanist* Christology.[3] Womanist Christology addresses the trifecta of oppressions as lenses through which we may better understand Jesus: it addresses not merely patriarchy, but racism and classism as well. The history of the United States in particular is a history of those three systemic sins, those rotting fruits, and a Christology that is worth its weight in the twenty-first century is one that acknowledges and addresses those experiences forthrightly.

Also: Womanist theology is *good theology*. We have heard enough of abstract debates concerning the person/works/offices of Christ, debates that seem quite removed from the real life of the church and of Christ. We have been fed a steady diet of white male theology and have taken it as the norm, the neutral, the objective, when in fact it is a theology formed in the image of its creators. We do not escape or leave behind our social situations when we write theological discourses. This reification is what has created the dead statues of theology. Womanist Christology, and womanist theology more broadly, does not deny the situatedness of its authors— it embraces and uses that. As one of my students said in class, "It seems that if we are all made in the image of God, but we only read white male theology, we are only getting a small percentage of a vision of who God is." We all bear the image of God, but for thousands of years we have refused to see God's face in women, and in the US, we have *particularly avoided seeing the image of God* in black women. The image black women bear is crucial. It is life- and spirit-giving. And it is time, past time, *long* past time, that we gazed upon it and listened to the voices of its bearer.

---

3   As I will mention later in the essay, the term "womanist" was coined by Alice Walker as a way to distinguish the work of black feminists from white feminists. White feminism, particularly second-wave feminism, excluded tacitly or explicitly black women's experiences and perspectives. As such, black women did for themselves. "Womanist is to feminism what purple is to lavender," Walker is famous for saying. Womanism is a richer method of analysis, because it does not isolate patriarchal sin from its co-sins, racism and classism.

History of Feminist Theology in Four Paragraphs

Feminists ask what can be said about a religious expression [the Chalcedonian Definition] which make[s] its supreme deity *totally* represented in *one male figure* through whom everyone must pass in order to be saved?
— **Jacquelyn Grant**, *White Women's Christ*

First, it is helpful to provide some sort of working definition of "feminism," recognizing that the singular use of the term is problematic. There are indeed multiple "feminisms," both historically (first–fourth-wave) and in terms of goals (liberal, radical, socialist, etc.). Generally speaking, however, what all feminisms have in common is that they advocate for the full equality of women under law and in practice. However, when we move into feminist theological discourse, the categories shift quite a bit. None of the "goal" categories mentioned above map simply onto feminist theologies. Carol Christ, a "champion of women's issues and diversity on college campuses,"[4] divides feminist theology into two main camps: reformists and revolutionaries.[5] Simply put, reformists remain within the Christian tradition and seek to destabilize patriarchal adherences, while revolutionaries think that the whole Christian structure is rotten to the core regarding its view of women. Divinity professor Elisabeth Schüssler Fiorenza, however, divides feminist theologies differently: a complementary approach, which seeks to argue that women's very femininity is needed by the church; a critical approach, which both criticizes the obvious patriarchal inheritances in both scripture and tradition and recovers liberating aspects of that same inheritance; and what Jacquelyn Grant calls the "rejectionist" approach, which claims, like the "revolutionaries," that Christianity is patriarchal to the core and must be abandoned.

The intersection of theology and feminism can be traced back to a variety of historical moments, but a key one for US feminism was the creation

---

4   "Biography," Berkeley Office of the Chancellor, UC Berkeley website, accessed May 28, 2020, https://chancellor.berkeley.edu/chancellor-christ/biography.

5   Carol P. Christ, "The New Feminist Theology: A Review of the Literature," *Religious Studies Review* 3, no. 4 (1977): 203–12.

in 1895 of *The Woman's Bible* by Elizabeth Cady Stanton, one of the key suffragists in the fight for the vote. She formed a committee of twenty-six interested women to provide a correction to the Revised Version of the Bible that had been published by the Church of England. She viewed the translation—and indeed all translations—as being needlessly biased against women, something she believed God was *not*. The work, which comprised two volumes (one on Torah, the other on the rest of Christian scripture), was of course decried from the pulpit as a work of Satan—but it was also a bestseller. The work stood as a commentary on Scripture, rather than a translation of it. It pushed against the notion of woman (Eve) as the originator of sin, introduced a feminine element into the Trinity, *and* argued that rationally, Jesus could have had an earthly father (since he had an earthly mother) *or* a heavenly Mother (since he had a heavenly Father). One could understand the controversy! And the result was that no one really raised these issues again until 1964. Yes. 1964, when Margaret Brackenberry Crook's book *Women and Religion* was published. Reception of this work was cool, and it took another two *decades* before it was taken seriously in academia. I hope you can sense from this brief history how resistant both academics and the church were to women's theological viewpoints.

If we wish to set a date during which feminist theology really hit the scene, we would probably need to go with Mary Daly's *The Church and the Second Sex* in 1968. Daly famously argued for a Goddess as a necessary corrective to the inherited tradition of understanding God as male, and eventually abandoned Christianity altogether. Later writers, such as feminist scholar Rosemary Radford Ruether and Schüssler Fiorenza worked more constructively, yet critically, within the received tradition to recover interpretations of scripture, the creeds, and Christ that did not isolate, separate, or ignore women's experience. This is a key element of all feminist theology: the centering of experience as an appropriate lens through which to approach Scripture. If this seems too human-centric, these authors would remind you that white males have been doing exactly that: centering the white male lens as the *only* appropriate way to understand scripture. They reify the lens, however, and claim it to be "universal," applicable to all human beings. This is simply not the case, as half of all human beings can tell you. The key difference between feminist theology and "traditional" theology is that feminist theology does not insist that its lens is the *only correct one*. Have no fear, for most feminist theologians, the goal is not to topple patriarchy only to establish matriarchy in its place!

Key to feminist theology is the person of Christ—his maleness, his suffering, his humanity. Therefore, we turn now to a more focused summation of feminist Christology in the twentieth century.

Feminist Christology

Key goals for feminist Christology, according to Jacquelyn Grant, are (a) to "develop a wholistic theology"—current classic theological texts and traditions only reflect half of the human experience, and must be broadened to include women's experience; (b) to eliminate dualism in theological thought, particularly the dualism of patriarchy, which assigns clear behavioral "norms" as "natural" and aligned essentially to biological sex; and finally, in a constructive sense, (c) to provide "new and positive images of women."[6] An additional element is the subsequent examination and critique of received doctrines, which carry the taint of patriarchy and must be reexamined.

The latter element—doctrine—and a key issue for feminist Christology has to do with the maleness of Christ. Most feminist Christologies ask the key question, Can a *male* Christ truly offer salvation to *women*, whose experiences are excruciatingly different? Ruether wrote, "Theologically speaking, we might say that the maleness of Jesus has no ultimate significance. It has social symbolic significance in the framework of societies of patriarchal privilege."[7] In other words, the maleness of Christ may not have direct soteriological significance, but given that we all receive the message of salvation via the social structure of the church, which is patriarchal, it can be a stumbling block for women.

---

6   Jacquelyn Grant, *White Women's Christ, Black Women's Jesus: Feminist Christology and Womanist Response* (Atlanta: Scholars Press, 1989), 45–46.

7   Rosemary Radford Ruether, *Sexism and God-Talk: Toward a Feminist Theology* (Boston: Beacon Press, 1993), 137.

A vital question, then, for feminist Christology in general is whether the Incarnation itself is radical enough to break the paradigm of patriarchal dominance. Jesus experienced this world as a man; and that is a very different experience from that of a woman, especially in his culture. We have evidenced this by, in the Catholic tradition, refusing women the authority to administer the Eucharist; in the Protestant tradition, by reifying and reinforcing a few lines from Timothy to keep women out of the pulpit. The notion that women cannot be priests *because they are women* is a key exclusion, one that many theologians justify by gesturing toward Jesus's masculinity.

However, patriarchy is not totalizing—deconstructive elements break through. In Julia Baudzej's "Re-telling the Story of Jesus," she gives an account of medieval texts and representations that "treat the body of Christ as female."[8] His wounds were understood as nutritive, like breasts. Julian of Norwich referred to "Jesus our Mother," and Jesus's body both bleeding and feeding us via the Eucharist are elements of motherhood. Medieval Christology was less gender binary because the gender-binary method of understanding bodies was not as prevalent. The body was understood not as "sexual" primarily, but as "fecund and decaying."[9]

Baudzej turns then to current theologians, primarily Eleanor McLaughlin and Catherine Bynam, both of whom attempt to read Christ's incarnation as an overthrow of all orders and systems, including patriarchy. They rely on Jürgen Moltmann's understanding that "God's Fatherhood dies *with* the Son," thus undermining the gender binary and annihilating the domination of maleness. However, these moves, though necessary and helpful, do not free women in actual lived experience—they remain abstract in the domain of theology rather than exploding it.[10]

Several feminist theologians argue that "Jesus did not fit in with patriarchal

---

8   Julia Baudzej, "Re-telling the Story of Jesus: The Concept of Embodiment and Recent Feminist Reflections on the Maleness of Christ," *Feminist Theology* 17, no. 1 (2008): 79.

9   Baudzej, "Re-telling the Story of Jesus," 80.

10   Baudzej, 79.

gender," but rather engaged in what Baudzej calls "relational kenosis," and that the church—male and female—is the continuation of Jesus's body in the world, and is the "completion of the Incarnation," a completion that undermines patriarchy at its root. In every case, these authors perceive the Incarnation as not just a breaking of the divine/human binary, but of all binaries, all orders and constructions accrued since the fall. That the church has doubled down on fallen structures and systems is a testament to our *failure* to be the body of Christ.[11]

It seems, then, that feminist Christologies do an excellent job of dismantling patriarchal interpretations of Christ and help problematize both the practices and theology of the church. We should be done, then, yes?

Well.

Feminist Christologies do well to dismantle patriarchy—but they leave racism and classism intact. One cannot end oppression by ignoring some of its key manifestations. White feminist Christology tends to ignore black women's experiences; it also tends to ignore poor women's experiences, and indeed women's experiences around the globe. As Jacquelyn Grant wrote, "white feminists do not transcend their own criticisms of other Christologies."[12] But the problem goes deeper.

Feminist theology and Christology start in the middle of the problem. Without accounting for, confessing, and atoning for the deep, prevalent racism that white women have had toward black women, particularly in the United States, any theology or Christology that emerges from the feminist tradition is still bad fruit. As Grant has pointed out, black women were not "sisters" to white women for centuries—they were *property*. Even after emancipation, black women were not free: they continued to labor as domestic servants without hope for advancement. "It was a caste system that reproduced slavery's structures of brutality, oppression, and dehumanization."[13] White feminism in general assumes the white experience is

---

11 Baudzej, "Re-telling the Story of Jesus," 80.

12 Grant, *White Women's Christ*, 5.

13 Grant, 198.

the norm, the universal. As such, white feminist theology leaves much systemic sin in place in its constructions.

Womanist Christology

An antidote has been the rise of black womanist theology and Christology. The term "womanist" was first coined by Alice Walker to mean "a strong Black woman who has sometimes been mislabeled as a domineering, castrating matriarch."[14] Black women's experience is a trifecta of sexism AND racism AND, for a good portion of modern history, classism. This intersection frames their experience of Christ. As such, they understand Jesus to be a co-sufferer with them, one who comes to bring liberation to the oppressed—and in American history, there has been no one more systemically and consistently oppressed than black women. Unlike feminist Christologists, Womanist theologians are not worked up about Jesus's maleness, for it is his *humanity,* not his gender, that is crucial.

Womanist theology borrows from black liberation theology, most famously put forward by James Cone (RIP). One of Cone's more controversial claims regarding Jesus was that Jesus is black. As you can imagine, this produced, among the few white theologians who read it, some consternation along the lines of "You've criticized us for making Jesus white! No fair!" Of course, Cone is not making an ethnic argument about Jesus's heritage, but rather interpreting the ongoing presence and life of Jesus in the context of modern-day oppression. Jesus was Jewish—an occupied people, once slaves themselves, who were oppressed by an external government. In our modern context, who are the slaves? Who are the systemically oppressed? In the United States, that group has been, by and large, black people. As such, if Jesus truly comes to liberate the oppressed, to set the captive free, to side with the poor and lowly so much so that he becomes the poor and lowly, then in our imaginative context, Jesus would be a black man.

Likewise, however, black liberation theology has often valorized suffering,

---

14 Grant, *White Women's Christ,* 205.

and historically the black church has been as blind to misogyny and patriarchy as white feminists are to racism. Eboni Marshall Turman wrote, referencing Christian ethics professor Marcia Y. Riggs, that "the black church's concern for liberation and justice is nullified by the 'male power' that perpetrates sexual-gender injustice upon the bodies, minds, and spirits of Black women."[15] In order to ever escape the constant brokenness of the body of Christ in the world, Turman calls for "the oppressed to not only seek to overcome their own oppressions, but to . . . resist . . . re-inscrib[ing] injustice in the lives of others" by insisting on a Christology that claims a "'just is' inconceivable element of Jesus's identity" before any secondary identity as a historical person. Jesus always-already is embodied difference, always-already is human-divine, and thus does not operate on a binary the way the church often wants to suggest.[16] Chalcedon solved the binary by arguing that "incarnate identity is rooted in an activity of God that is beyond how social and historical realities act upon bodies."[17] This binary is the "bad fruit" of poor Christology, one that manifests in the either/ors of sexism, racism, classism, and so on. If the church is the body of Christ in the world, it must work to overcome the false binaries, and instead seek justice for all bodies, for all bodies are part of the body of Christ. In short, the church must, according to Turman, "displac[e] the primacy of the sociohistorical, and its appealing to its God-image in order to better understand how the image of God manifests in the world."[18]

But womanist theology and Christology is not merely critical of received structures; it is also constructive itself in its focus on both the person and the works of Christ. Aligning with black liberation theology, womanist Christology is *liberative*: Jesus's work in the world and in our hearts is one of liberation, of freedom. "Freedom" has quite a different ring to it, however,

---

15 Eboni Marshall Turman, *Toward a Womanist Ethic of Incarnation: Black Bodies, the Black Church, and the Council of Chalcedon* (New York: Palgrave Macmillan, 2013), 137.

16 Turman, *Toward a Womanist Ethic*, 158.

17 Turman, 164.

18 Turman, 164.

when one's people have been literally enslaved; when womanist theology discusses the freedom of Christ, they mean it as a literal social and political phenomenon, not as merely an abstract idea.

Second, the person of Jesus is primarily understood as a "co-sufferer"— as a person who knows suffering and anguish intimately. Again, while this is a part of many Christologies (albeit not all), for womanist theology, the person of Jesus is salvific because he understands and stands with black women in their suffering. Jacquelyn Grant goes so far as to say that Jesus, in our context, is a black woman—he identifies with those at the bottom of the pecking order.

Finally, Jesus, in womanist Christology, *overcomes*. His very being as the God-man is one of both/and, not either/or. Turman explores this thoroughly in her aforementioned work. The very nature of Christ, since before the beginning of the world, was both/and—therefore, binary divisions and hierarchies are already undone in the person of Christ. It is only when our churches and our theologies mistake fallenness for the Way of the Kingdom that we end up with systems that oppress, denigrate, and dehumanize others.

Conclusion

The history of Christology is rich and complex; even the past three hundred years of Methodist Christology contain heresies and accusations of heresy; an attempt to analyze Christ into categories; and finally, in the last century, diverse perspectives on the person and body of Christ. In crucial ways, Western Wesleyan theology is at a crossroads. We have been edging down the path of diverse scholarship but have tried to have it both ways: to both incorporate women's and people of color's voices into our lexicon while remaining essentially the same. This is a fool's game, and I would argue sin's game as well. We have been faced with choices for seventy-five years now. If the Wesleyan tradition would like to continue, it is past time to embrace feminist and womanist (and liberationist) theologies.

We are lucky that we have a rich Christology, provided by Dr. Diane Leclerc, from which to engage womanist Christology. Leclerc's emphasis on the humility of Christ, Jesus's "scandal of particularity," and the responsibility of the church to "suffer on behalf of others" all echo and reinforce the emphases of womanist Christology upon liberation, suffering, and overcoming. In other words, it is no great stretch to recognize Jesus in the face of womanist Christologies—provided we *read them.*

I began this essay with a challenge and, frankly, a bit of pessimism. I can say that for many Christian women, the cry "How long, Lord?" echoes in our hearts, as we wait for our male brethren to wake up, catch up, read up, on *our* experiences. We have read yours. This call, however, is weak sauce compared to the frustrated shouts of black women, who address their exhaustion and outrage to not only their male brethren, but their white ones as well. How long? How long before our undergraduate courses treat women and black theologians with the same reverence we hold for Brueggemann and Wesley? How long before seminaries prioritize the marginalized voices rather than simply reifying white male (mostly dead) theological viewpoints? How long before men admit that white male theology is not universal, but written from a white, male perspective—and that therefore other perspectives from others who also bear the *imago Dei* are *equally important, if not more so*?

Who is Jesus? Who is our Savior, and whom does he save? As with every aspect of theology, it matters how you answer those questions. Your theology, your Christology, is not abstract and without consequence. It literally frames the way you interact with your siblings in Christ. It may influence your salvation. If you seek Jesus, we welcome you to seek him among those who haven't been taken seriously. You may find him there in new and fresh ways. Thanks be to God.

8

Jesús Was Born in Guatemala: Toward a Latinx Wesleyan Christology

Edgardo Colón-Emeric

In the spring of 2019, the Central American Methodist Course of Study, where I regularly teach, hosted a concert in Ahuachapán with the Salvadoran composer Guillermo Cuéllar. The students sang along as he played music from the Salvadoran Popular Mass, but the song that elicited the most vigorous response was one by the Nicaraguan composer Carlos Mejía Godoy.[1]

Cristo ya nació en Palacagüina,	Christ was born in Palacagüina,
De Chepe Pavón Pavón	From Chepe Pavón Pavón
Y una tal María.	And a so-called Mary.
Ella va a planchar muy humildemente	She is going to iron very humbly
La ropa que goza la mujer hermosa	The clothes worn by the beautiful wife
Del terrateniente.	Of the Land Owner.

The final decades of the twentieth century were a fruitful time in Latin American Christianity. New theologies, such as the theologies of liberation, were written from contexts where previous generations had only yielded translations and adaptations of European works. New expressions of Christian

---

1 The Spanish text of this song is found in Carmen José Alejos Grau and Josep Ignasi Saranyana, *Teología en América Latina*, vol. 3: *El Siglo de las Teologías Latinoamericanistas (1899–2001)* (Madrid: Vervuert, 2002), 358. English translation mine.

life, like the base ecclesial communities, sprang up across the landscape. New songs, including "The Christ of Palacagüina," set to music these new theologies and forms of life. Christology is always embedded in a web of cultural practices. "The Christ of Palacagüina" is not simply a Latin American Christological song; it is Nicaraguan. The language and imagery of its refrain and verses is situated in a land groaning under the dictatorship of Anastasio Somoza. For Mejía Godoy, the Christological titles commonly sung of Jesus in church were honey-flavored poison pills handed out by those in power.[2] This is a Christology that is born in a context of civil unrest, church protest, and the struggle for dignity. The Christ of Palacagüina dreams of growing up to be not a carpenter, like his father, but a guerrilla fighter.

Why did my Central American Methodist friends resonate strongly with a Nicaraguan Catholic's protest song? The answer, I suggest, is that because it affirms faith in a Christ incarnate in their own history. In this essay, I want to trace the contours of a Latinx Wesleyan Christology. To accomplish this goal, I will begin by reviewing Wesley's Christology with the help of John Deschner's magisterial work on this topic. Next, I will consider images and faces of Christ from Latin American and Hispanic perspectives. The overlapping of these two lenses will yield a Latinx Wesleyan Christology that finds confirmation in a Methodist pastor's witness that Jesus was born in Guatemala.

Wesley's Christology

John Deschner's work on Wesley's Christology is the most significant exploration of Wesley's understanding of Christ written to date.[3] His book draws

---

2 For this abuse of Christology, see Paul in Romans 16:18, "For such people do not serve our Lord Christ, but their own appetites, and by smooth talk [*chrēstologia*] and flattery [*eulogia*] they deceive the hearts of the simple-minded" (NRSV). When Cyril of Jerusalem read Paul's letter, he interpreted the apostle to mean that "the heretics do this by coating over their poison pills of godless doctrines with the honey of the name of Christ." *Catechetical Lectures* 4.2, Ancient Christian Commentary on Romans (Downers Grove, IL: InterVarsity, 1998), 377. The usage of the term *Christology* to name the church's teaching of Christ is relatively recent. Cf. Rafael Ramis-Barceló, "En Torno al Surgimiento de la Noción Moderna de 'Cristología,'" *Gregorianum* 100, no. 1 (2019): 27–47.

3 John Deschner, *Wesley's Christology: An Interpretation* (Dallas: Southern Methodist University Press, 1985).

on Wesley's standard sermons and *Notes on the New Testament* and displays the results in the categories of Barthian theology. Deschner identified two distinctive aspects of Wesley's Christology.

First, there is in John Wesley's theology a valorization of the "whole Christ." This means, wrote Deschner, "Christ in all his offices, not only atoning for our sins, but also guiding and empowering our recovery of the image of God."[4] Wesley believed that Jesus of Nazareth was "a Prophet, revealing to us the whole will of God; that He was a Priest who gave Himself a sacrifice for sin, and still makes intercession for transgressors; that He is a King, who has all power in heaven and in earth, and will reign till He has subdued all things to Himself."[5] As the hymns for Ascension Sunday make clear, the return of Jesus to his Father entails the exaltation of the true Elijah, the consecration of the true Aaron, and coronation of the true David.[6] Jesus super-fulfills the roles of prophet, priest, and king because he is truly God. He is the holy one of God; "His divine righteousness belongs to his divine nature, as he is ὁ ὢν, 'He that existeth, over all, God, blessed for ever;' the supreme, the eternal, 'equal with the Father as touch his godhead, though inferior to the Father as touching his manhood.'"[7] Christ teaches us who God is, enables us to participate in the divine nature, and guides us into the communion of the Father, the Son, and the Holy Spirit.

The centrality of the "whole Christ" is consistent with Wesley's holistic soteriology. Christ is both the justifier and the sanctifier; he forgives and heals; he is for us and in us. Wesley warns, "We are not ourselves clear before God, unless we proclaim him in all his offices."[8] The whole Christ must

---

4   Deschner, *Wesley's Christology*, xvi.

5   John Wesley, "A Letter to a Roman Catholic," in *John Wesley*, ed. Albert C. Outler (New York: Oxford University Press, 1980), 494.

6   Cf. Charles Wesley, *Resurrection Hymns* (1746), hymn 16, and *Ascension Hymns* (1746), particularly hymns 2 and 4. These can be accessed in https://divinity.duke.edu/initiatives/cswt /charles-published-verse.

7   John Wesley, *The Works of John Wesley*, vol. 1, *Sermons* (Nashville: Abingdon Press, 1984), 452. Henceforth referred to as WJW.

8   John Wesley, Sermon 36, in Wesley, *The Works of the Reverend John Wesley, A. M.*, ed. John Emory (New York: J. Emory and B. Waugh, for the Methodist Episcopal Church, 1831), 325.

be preached and sung. Thus, on the anniversary of his conversion Charles Wesley sings:

> O for a thousand tongues to sing
> My great redeemer's praise,
> The glories of my God and King,
> The triumphs of his grace.[9]

Second, Wesley taught his fellow Methodists to focus their attention on the "present Christ." Wesley did not neglect the cosmic Christ or the coming Christ. However, Deschner noted that Wesley emphasized "the Christ whose cross is the present ground of a divine forgiveness which underlies everything, whom one encounters 'now' in the means of grace, and whose 'mind' takes form today in the renewed 'affections' of the believer's heart."[10] Methodists take Paul's words in 2 Corinthians 6:2 to heart: "See, now is the acceptable time; see, now is the day of salvation!" (NRSV). In the present Christ, we "anticipate our heaven below."[11] In Christ we see what it means to be truly human—holiness of heart and life, internally and externally righteous—and receive the power to become like him.

Christ is holy of heart. Said Wesley:

> His internal righteousness is the image of God, stamped on every power and faculty of his soul. It is a copy of his divine righteousness, as far as it can be imparted to a human spirit. It is a transcript of the divine purity, the divine justice, mercy, and truth. It includes love, reverence, resignation to his Father; humility, meekness, gentleness; love to lost mankind, and every other holy and heavenly temper; and all these in the highest degree, without any defect, or mixture of unholiness.[12]

Christ is holy in life. "It was the least part of his *external righteousness*,

---

9   *The United Methodist Hymnal* (Nashville: The United Methodist Publishing House, 1989), Hymn 57.

10 Deschner, *Wesley's Christology*, xvi–xvii.

11 *The United Methodist Hymnal*, Hymn 57.

12 WJW 1:452–53.

that he did nothing amiss; that he knew no outward sin of any kind, 'neither was guile found in his mouth;' that he never spoke one improper word, nor did one improper action."[13] Moreover, "'He did all things well.' In every word of his tongue, in every work of his hands, he did precisely the 'will of Him that sent him.' In the whole course of his life, he did the will of God on earth, as the angels do it in heaven. All he acted and spoke was exactly right in every circumstance. The whole and every part of his obedience was complete. 'He fulfilled all righteousness.'"[14]

There is a clear correspondence between the human righteousness of Christ and the Methodist General Rules: avoid evil, do good, and attend to all the ordinances of God. The correspondence is not accidental, for everything in Wesley's Methodism was oriented toward the renewal of the image of God in the human being. By participating in the means of grace, humans are empowered to avoid evil, do good, and thus grow into the stature of Christ. The transformation of the sinner into a saint depended on Christ's graceful presence today. Faith will fail "unless we be endued with power from on high; and that continually, from hour to hour, or rather from moment to moment."[15] The "now" is all-important because our justification and sanctification depend on a continual indwelling of the whole Christ.

Deschner's interpretation of Wesley's Christology is respectful and appreciative. At the same time, Deschner worried that the clarity of Wesley's Christological vision is impaired by an inadequate account of the humanity of Christ. Deschner offered two pieces of evidence to substantiate his suspicion. First, Wesley's translation of 1 John 4:2 relegates the Christ's human nature to a subordinate clause. Second, Wesley omitted the phrase "of her substance" from the edited version of the Articles of Religion that he sent to the Methodist Episcopal Church. For Deschner, Wesley's "lack of

---

13   WJW 1:453.

14   WJW 1:453.

15   John Wesley, *The Works of John Wesley*, ed. Thomas Jackson, vol. 12 (Grand Rapids: Baker Book House, 1978), 397.

precision with respect to Mary as mother of Christ in both natures, taken together with the reserve about the human nature" raises the specter of Nestorianism in Wesley's Christology.[16]

The anti-Chalcedonian specter raised by Deschner haunts the agenda of interpreters of Wesley's Christology. For example, Edward Oakes wrote, "Wesley's account of the sufferings of Christ in the passion carries a whiff of Apollinarian Logos-Sarx Christology."[17] Clearly, these interpreters agree that there is a problem with Wesley's Christology, but they do not agree with the exact nature of the problem. Does Wesley's Christology lean toward Apollinarianism or Nestorianism? Geoffrey Wainwright offered a helpful alternative to Deschner's reading. What we find in Wesley is not Apollinarianism, Nestorianism, or Monophysitism, but "a healthily Alexandrian view of Christ's person."[18]

Deschner's interpretation of Wesley's Christology is not simply retrospective but also prospective. He looked ahead to how this Christology could benefit from entering into the theological conversation with ecumenical and liberation theologians. It is important for Wesleyan theology to engage ecumenical theology precisely on the point of Christology. Deschner stated, "We have learned with Outler's help how limiting it can be to understand Wesley simply as a Protestant, and how insistent he himself was upon the ecumenical tradition as the foundation and interpretive context for the Methodist message of salvation."[19] Deschner believes that engaging ecumenical theology deepens the Chalcedonian moorings of Wesley's Christology. He also believes that engaging liberation theology would strengthen the practical dimension of Wesley's theology. According to Deschner, Wesley's theology can be read at different levels: the "articulated" theology of his sermons and treatises, the "presupposed" theology of these

---

16 Deschner, *Wesley's Christology*, 30.

17 Edward Oakes, *Infinity Dwindled to Infancy: A Catholic and Evangelical Christology* (Grand Rapids: Eerdmans, 2011), locs. 3205–6, Kindle.

18 Geoffrey Wainwright, review of *Wesley's Christology: An Interpretation*, Perkins Journal 39, no. 2 (1986): 55–56 (55).

19 Deschner, ix.

writings, and the "enacted" theology of his ministry. "That enacted theology asks for much more reflection from students of Wesley's theology than it has yet received, and it may be that a liberation theology schooled in praxis-reflection methodologies will have the insight and will to undertake it."[20] It is to the Latin American and Latino/a versions of these theologies that we next turn.

Latin American and Latinx Christology

Two of the most important collections of essays on Christology from Latin American and Latinx perspectives were directed by Methodists. In 1977, José Míguez Bonino published the book *Jesús, Ni Vencido Ni Monarca Celestial*. It was published in English in 1984 as *The Faces of Jesus in Latin America*.[21] In 2009, Harold Recinos and Hugo Magallanes published *Jesus in the Hispanic Community*.[22] Both books are ecumenical in scope, making ample room for Protestant and Catholic voices. In this sense, they embody well the Wesleyan Catholic spirit. John Deschner was familiar with Míguez Bonino's theology. Indeed, it is quite possible that the faces of Christ represented in this work are precisely those that Deschner thought needed to be considered carefully by Wesleyan theologians.[23] At the same time, the Wesleyan heritage is not particularly evident in these works. Indeed, the terms *Wesley* and *Methodism* do not appear in either book. Despite these lacunae, the books are extremely helpful guides to the images of Christ at work in shaping the Christian imagination of Latin American and Latino/a people. The purpose of identifying these images is to point out their

---

20 Deschner, *Wesley's Christology*, xiii.

21 José Míguez Bonino, ed., *Jesús: Ni Vencido Ni Monarca Celestial* (Buenos Aires: Editorial Tierra Nueva, 1977); English translation: *Faces of Jesus: Latin American Christologies*, trans. Robert R. Barr (Maryknoll, NY: Orbis Books, 1984).

22 Harold J. Recinos and Hugo Magallanes, eds., *Jesus in the Hispanic Community: Images of Christ from Theology to Popular Religion* (Louisville: Westminster John Knox Press, 2009).

23 For Deschner's engagement with Míguez Bonino, see "More Than Inclusiveness: The New Christian Majority and the Shift in the Ecumenical Conversation about Church Unity," *The Ecumenical Review* 43, no. 1 (1991): 57–67 (62–63); "The Changing Shape of the Church Unity Question," *Mid-Stream* 29, no. 1 (1990): 26.

cultural captivity in order to be freed of them for more biblical, life-giving images of Jesus Christ as liberator and mestizo.

Jesus the Liberator

Embedded in Latin American Christologies is a distinction between the "historical Jesus" and the "Christ of faith." The former is the source; the latter is the interpretation. The history of interpretation has bequeathed images of Christ that have normalized oppression in Latin America. The title of Míguez Bonino's book accurately names two dominant images: *vencido* (beaten victim), *monarca celestial* (heavenly monarch). In churches throughout Latin America, images of Christ's crucified, bleeding, tortured, nearly naked body can be found in close proximity to images of Christ clothed in a splendid, gold- and silver-embroidered gown, wearing a jeweled crown and looking imperiously detached from the troubles of the world. The colonial Jesus was a Janus-like figure who looked like a dying Atahualpa or like the apotheosis of King Ferdinand I.[24] By starting with the historical Jesus, Latin American theologians seek to unmask the Spanish Christ that came to the Americas, in order to discover a new, more hopeful face.

The path followed by Wesley's Alexandrian, Johannine Christology yields precedence to an Antiochene, synoptic Christology from below. Jesus is fully human. Latin American theologians call attention to Jesus's prayer life, his radical openness and surrender to God, and his solidarity with the marginalized. In *Jesus the Liberator*, Jesuit theologian Jon Sobrino speaks of Jesus as one who "belongs, then, to the current of those who hope in history, in the midst of oppression, who again and again formulate a utopia, who believe justice is possible. And in this way we can say that Jesus's humanity is true humanity."[25] Jesus's life and ministry reveal true humanity as oriented toward the kingdom of God. The kingdom is a utopia that fulfills the dreams of a people caught up in suffering; it is a liberating reality that

---

24 Cf. George Casalis, "Jesús," in Míguez Bonino, ed., *Faces of Jesus*, 72–76.

25 Jon Sobrino, *Jesus the Liberator* (Maryknoll, NY: Orbis Books, 1993), 75.

comes in the midst of the oppression and resistance of the anti-kingdom.[26] The anti-kingdom is in force wherever true humanity is being denied, even in the visible church, for example, in its oppressive Christologies. In this Christological vision, salvation is the integral liberation of the oppressed and sanctification can only be attained in joining the struggle with the poor for the sake of the poor.

Jesus is the liberator. This is the chief title for Jesus in the Latin American Christologies of the 1970s and '80s. It is also a theme present in Latin American Methodist hymnody. The translation of "O for a thousand tongues to sing my great redeemer's praise" reads *"Mil voces para celebrar a mi libertador"* ("A thousand voices to celebrate my liberator"). The theme of liberation is developed more fully in another Methodist hymn *"Tenemos Esperanza"* ("We Have Hope").[27]

"Tenemos Esperanza"	"We Have Hope"
Porque El entró en el mundo y en la historia;	Because he entered the world and history;
porque El quebró el silencio y la agonía;	Because he broke the silence and the anguish;
porque llenó la tierra de su gloria;	Because he filled the earth with his glory;
porque fue luz en nuestra noche fría.	Because he was light in our cold night;
Porque nació en un pesebre oscuro;	Because he was born in a dark manger;
porque vivió sembrando amor y vida;	Because he lived sowing love and life;
porque partió los corazones duros	Because he broke the hard hearts;

---

26 Sobrino, *Jesus the Liberator*, 72.

27 *Mil Voces para Celebrar* (Nashville: The United Methodist Publishing House, 1996), Hymn 129. English translation mine.

"Tenemos Esperanza" (continued)	*"We Have Hope"* (continued)
y levantó las almas abatidas.	And raised the crushed souls.
Por eso es que hoy tenemos esperanza;	This is why today we have hope;
por eso es que hoy luchamos con porfía;	This is why today we fight with boldness;
por eso es que hoy miramos con confianza,	This is why today we look with confidence
el porvenir en esta tierra mía.	To the future in this land of ours.
Por eso es que hoy tenemos esperanza;	This is why today we have hope;
por eso es que hoy luchamos con porfía;	This is why today we fight with boldness;
por eso es que hoy miramos con confianza,	This is why today we look with confidence
el porvenir.	To the future.

In this hymn, Bishop Federico Pagura looks at the national crisis and widespread human rights violations during Argentina's dirty war and anchors his hope on a Christ who sides with the oppressed against the oppressor. Two Wesleyan notes stand out in this hymn. First, the hymn emphasizes today. The hope that Christ makes possible is not just for life in glory but for life in history. We hope for today and it is hope for today that gives us confidence to look to the future. Second, the hymn emphasizes human participation. Hope in Christ encourages Christians to join the struggle to make this hope real today. The vision of life revealed by Christ becomes a commission for the Christian.

Jesus the Mestizo

Despite the many connections between them, the Latinx context significantly differs from the Latin American one. Hispanics are marginalized in distinctive ways. The experience of hyphenation and hybridity renders them too Latin for Americans and too American for Latins. The faces of Jesus in the Hispanic communities envisioned by Recinos and Magallenes are more fluid than those in Latin America because in the United States Jesús is a *sato*, a mongrel, a mutt. In the words of Loida Martell Otero, to call Jesus a *sato* "underscores the experience of being relegated to the bottom rung of society precisely as one who is perceived to be nonhuman, impure, and of no intrinsic value—*sobraja*."[28]

The Latinx Christological vision of cultural hybridity has been strongly influenced by the work of Mexican American theologian Virgilio Elizondo.[29] Latin American history is marked by *mestizaje*, a term used to denote the mixing of Spanish and indigenous cultures that followed the conquest. The ambiguities and tensions that accompany *mestizaje* have characterized Latin American and Hispanic identity. Elizondo owes his renown as the father of Latino theology to being the first to bring this experience into a theological register. According to Elizondo, "The human scandal of God's way does not begin with the cross, but with the historic-cultural incarnation of his Son in Galilee."[30] Jesus of Nazareth in Galilee is a mestizo. As Elizondo understands it, "Galilee was the home of the simple people—that is, of the people of the land, a hardworking people, marginated and oppressed regardless of who was in power or what system of power was in effect. They were the ones who were left out and exploited by everyone else. They shared the fate of other peoples living on the margins of 'better' civilizations."[31] The borderland status of Galilee justified Nathanael's question to Jesus in John 1:46: "Can anything good come out of Nazareth?" (NRSV). Elizondo explained, "Nobody looks for leadership from or has high expectations of those who live

---

28 Loida I. Martell-Otero, *"Encuentro con el Jesús Sato*: An *Evangélica Soter*-ology," in Recinos and Magallanes, eds., *Jesus in the Hispanic Community*, 74–91, 77.

29 Virgilio Elizondo, *Galilean Journey: The Mexican-American Promise* (Maryknoll, NY: Orbis Books, 1983).

30 Elizondo, *Galilean Journey*, 53.

31 Elizondo, 52.

in the sticks, the *barrios*, the *ranchitos*, or inner-city slums."[32] There is a Galilean principle at work in God's salvation history. "It is in the unsuspected places and situations of the world and through 'unlikely' persons that God continues to work today." [33] God chooses the borderlands as the setting for his drama of redemption and border crossers as his privileged audience. Elizondo's Galilean principle coincides with the theological vision of a hymn by the Cuban American Methodist theologian Justo González.[34]

> From all four of earth's faraway corners,
> flows together the blood of all races
> in this people who sing of their trials,
> in this people who cry of their faith;
> hardy blood that was brought by the Spanish,
> noble blood of the suffering Indian,
> blood of slaves who stood heavy oppression,
> all the blood that was bought on the cross.

González sees in the history of the Americas the tortuous path of God's ministry of reconciliation. From the diversity of ethnicities in these lands, God is creating a new people, a mestizo people who point to a tomorrow without borders where all dwell together in peace and love. Through the blood of the cross of Christ, God is dismantling the walls of separation and reconciling all peoples, Jews and Gentiles, Africans, Indians, Europeans, and Asians. Jesus makes possible a new humanity, a new way of being ethnic. He is, in the words of González's *Credo Hispano*, "God made flesh in a person for all humanity, God made flesh in an age for all the ages, God made flesh in one culture for all cultures."[35] González's harmonization of Antiochene and Alexandrian approaches, of a historical Jesus and a cosmic

32 Elizondo, *Galilean Journey*, 52.

33 Elizondo, 92.

34 *Mil Voces para Celebrar*, Hymn 378.

35 Justo L. González, *Credo Hispano* (Hispanic Creed), in *Mil Voces para Celebrar*, 70.

Christ, is an example of the direction for Wesleyan Christology proposed by Deschner.

Toward a Latinx Wesleyan Christology

In his book on Wesley's Christology, John Deschner hoped that engagement with the methodologies of theologies from the Global South would bring to the fore the practical theological orientation of Wesley's ministry. In effect, Deschner longed for a Christology that is classically Chalcedonian and contextually concrete. In this final section, I overlap the focal points of Wesleyan, Latin American, and Hispanic Christology with a view toward a Latinx Wesleyan Christology. The resulting image can be expressed in two axioms: the whole Christ liberates, and the present Christ is mestizo today.

The Whole Christ Liberates

Wesley rightly insists that Christ is to be preached in all his offices, but his heirs have not always been faithful in discharging this responsibility. The emphasis has been on Christ as priest and mediator of forgiveness. The Latin American and Hispanic voices considered here would encourage the Wesleyan to preach Christ as prophet and king also. At the same time, looking at the whole Christ through the overlapping of Wesleyan and Latino/a lenses brings two other significant features to the fore.

First, the whole Christ is human and divine. The Alexandrian and Antiochene approaches need to be held together. Followers of the Antiochene way must be ever mindful of the inherent ambiguity in all the "historical" works of Jesus. Indeed, his disciples frequently misunderstood his signs and sayings. Followers of the Alexandrian way can never forget the limitations inherent in all knowledge of God. Both paths converge on the second person of the Trinity, the Son of God. The Latinx Wesleyan Christology that I envision here would resist a hard distinction between the Jesus of history and the Christ of faith. Failure to keep these united results in the Christological dead ends described by Míguez Bonino. "We seem to have both a Christ who is the Second Person of the Trinity but historically inoperative, and localized 'Christs' from whom actions (magical, perhaps) are looked for in the natural, human world."[36] It is through the witness of the church in the power of the Holy Spirit that we know Jesus Christ today. The whole Christ includes Christ as head and his body.

Second, the whole Christ is the liberator. There is no need to play off the roles of Christ against each other, as if being a prophet were connected to the struggles for liberation and being a priest to the maintenance of the status quo. The threefold office of Christ as a whole is oriented to the liberation of humanity and creation from bondage to sin and to leading it on to perfection in the kingdom of God. The development of a Latinx Wesleyan Christology calls for a rereading of the *munus triplex* of the whole Christ from the periphery. Liberation theologian Elsa Támez explained, "What is novel for us is the consideration of justification and liberation from a historical perspective of oppression, poverty, and struggle."[37] The significance of a historical perspective leads us to the second Christological feature.

The Present Christ Is Mestizo Today

The presence of Jesus, Immanuel, is central to a Latinx Wesleyan Christology. At the end of his life's journey, John Wesley's deathbed declaration says it well: "The best of all is, God is with us."[38] Jesus is "God incarnate, and dwells by his Spirit in the hearts of his people."[39] Pablo Andiñach was being a good Wesleyan biblical scholar in titling his theology of the Old Testament *"El Dios Que Está"* (The God Who Is Present). He wrote, "The God who is present is no mere spectator in the drama of creation. The scriptures highlight a God who is committed to human life and who, far from being

---

36 José Míguez Bonino, "¿Quién Es Jesucristo Hoy en América Latina?" in Míguez Bonino, ed., *Faces of Jesus*, 6.

37 Elsa Támez, *The Amnesty of Grace: Justification by Faith from a Latin American Perspective*, tr. Sharon H. Ringe (Eugene, OR: Wipf & Stock, 2002), 36.

38 John Whitehead, *The Life of the Rev. John Wesley* (Auburn: J. E. Beardsley, 1793), 542. Accessed from https://catalog.hathitrust.org/Record/007683665.

39 Wesley, *Notes on the New Testament*, Matt 1:23.

isolated, inserts himself into the ways of humanity and follows closely the destiny of human beings."[40]

A Latinx Wesleyan emphasis on the present Christ calls for a double concretion of that present. First, the present becomes concrete in everyday life. Jesus inserted himself into ordinary life. Echoing the thought of Irenaeus of Lyons, Wesley wrote, "So our Lord passed through and sanctified every stage of human life."[41] Jesus hallows infancy, childhood, youth, and adulthood. Since these stages are not lived in the abstract but in the concrete, Jesus's sanctification of the stages of human life has implications for the conditions of human life. Elsa Támez wrote, "The first sign of life is the recovery of the image of God in humanity choked by sin, where death lies in ambush in hunger and insignificance. It is a matter of feeling the pulse of God 'in the depths of hell,' and of experiencing grace on the garbage dump."[42] God in Christ is most immanent in the places of exclusion. Támez stated it accurately: "Though all human beings manifest a broken image of God (the victimizers as well as the victims), God chooses a meeting place so that God's image might be reproduced in every living being. God makes this choice not in order to exclude some people, but precisely in order to negate exclusion by including all people, beginning among those presently excluded."[43]

---

40 Pablo R. Andiñach, *El Dios Que Está* (Pamplona, ES: Editorial Verbo Divino, 2014), 25.

41 Wesley, *Notes on the New Testament*, Luke 2:43. Wesley did not follow Irenaeus in the latter's positive assessment of old age. Wesley added, "Old age only did not become him." By contrast, Irenaeus wrote of Christ, "He was an old man for old men, that He might be a perfect Master for all, not merely as respects the setting forth of the truth, but also as regards age, sanctifying at the same time the aged also, and becoming an example to them likewise. Then, at last, He came on to death itself, that He might be 'the first-born from the dead, that in all things He might have the pre-eminence,' [Col 1:18] the Prince of life [Acts 3:15], existing before all, and going before all." (*Against Heresies* 2.22.4). Wesley's judgment on this point follows a strand of Christian tradition that is picked up by Hans Urs von Balthasar, who wrote, "Jesus appears before the world at thirty, at the age of full maturity, beyond which no essential development could humanly be expected," Balthasar, *Man in History* (London: Sheed & Ward, 1968), 268. More positively, and perhaps by way of a synthesis, Balthasar also observed, "There are no 'old' saints. All of them are youthful even in advanced age." "Young until Death," *Explorations in Theology, V: Man Is Created* (San Francisco: Ignatius Press, 2014), 223.

42 Támez, *The Amnesty of Grace*, 132.

43 Támez, 132.

Second, the present becomes concrete in history. Thus, discerning the present Christ calls for reading of the signs of the times. For Wesley, the signs of the times are Christologically centered and soteriologically oriented.[44] A Latinx Wesleyan reading of the signs of the times would look for tokens of Christ's advent within the violent, mestizo-making history of Latin America and the United States because Christ entered into our history. The present Christ is mestizo because the body of Christ in history is mestizo. Jesus ended the hostility between Jews and Gentiles and made them into a new humanity through his crucified flesh (cf. Eph 2:13–16). This Ephesian Moment, as missiologist Andrew Walls terms it, is relived throughout the church's long history of mestizo-bearing encounters yielding Latin American and Hispanic Christs.[45]

A Latinx Wesleyan Christology starts from the mystery of the conception and birth of Jesus but does not stop there. A Christology centered on the mystery of the Incarnation to the exclusion of the transfiguration underappreciates the possibility of the status quo being swept up by the Holy Spirit into the history of salvation. All cultures, historical ages, and peoples bear the marks of sin. We can profess faith with González in the "God made flesh in one culture for all cultures," only if we read the "for" missiologically. Latinx Wesleyan theologians would benefit from engaging the theological vision of Saint Óscar Romero, whose Christological thought centers on the transfigured Christ who transfigures the people of God and the land of El Salvador.[46] God is "for all cultures" in that he promises the healing and transfiguration of all nations. Commenting on the mountain to which Jesus led his disciples in Matthew 28:18, Wesley says "this was probably Mount

---

44 Sermon 66 in WJW 2:523: "What times were those concerning which our Lord is here speaking? It is easy to answer; the times of the Messiah; the times ordained before the foundation of the world, wherein it pleased God to give his only begotten Son, to take our nature upon him, to be 'found in fashion as a man,' to live a life of sorrow and pain, and, at length, to be 'obedient unto death, even the death of the cross,' to the end that 'whosoever believeth on him should not perish, but have everlasting life.'"

45 Cf. Andrew F. Walls, *The Cross-Cultural Process in Christian History* (Maryknoll, NY: Orbis Books, 2002), 72–84.

46 Cf. Edgardo Colón-Emeric, *Óscar Romero's Theological Vision: Liberation and the Transfiguration of the Poor* (Notre Dame, IN: University of Notre Dame Press, 2018), 115–68.

Tabor, where (it is commonly supposed) he had been before transfigured. It seems to have been here also, that he appeared to above five hundred brethren at once."[47] Tabor is the starting point for the Great Commission and its goal. Christ sends his church to make disciples for the transfiguration of the world.

Conclusion

What keeps Christology from becoming an exercise in biblical eisegesis and cultural affirmation? Do Nicaraguans sing of a Christ born in Palacagüina simply because they are Nicaraguans? Míguez Bonino warned us of the risk of this kind of Feuerbachian approach to Christ. "In that case christology would be either nothing but a manner of speaking, or a form of the projection of such conditions and ideologies . . . Christology could serve only to justify an already existing historical praxis."[48] Míguez Bonino's solution to this conundrum is hermeneutical, namely "a hermeneutics that respects not only the original historicity of the text but also the singularity of the reader's locus."[49] This is wise counsel, to which Charles Wesley would recommend adding a doxological coda.

> Furnished with intellectual light,
> In vain I speak of thee aright,
> While unrevealed thou art:
> That only can suffice for me,
> The whole mysterious Trinity
> Inhabiting my heart.[50]

A few years ago, I was teaching theology at Duke's Pastoral Program in Guatemala. Because the native language of a number of my students was

---

47 Wesley, *Notes on the New Testament*, Matt 28:18.

48 Míguez Bonino, "¿Quién Es Jesucristo Hoy en América Latina?" 3.

49 Míguez Bonino, 4.

50 Charles Wesley, *Hymns on the Trinity* (1767), Hymn 19; https://divinity.duke.edu/initiatives/cswt/charles-published-verse.

K'iche, one of the Mayan tongues, I required the assistance of a translator, and because it was an oral culture, I dispensed with written examinations. Instead, I tested my students by asking a series of true or false questions, like, "Marcion loved the Old Testament, true or false?" My students had never taken this kind of test before, so I offered a sample question. "Jesus was born in Guatemala, true or false?" Most students caught on quickly.

Then it was Juan's turn. He paused, then said, "True."

I assumed that Juan had misunderstood me, so I asked again. "Jesus of Nazareth, not Jesús your cousin, was born in Guatemala. True or false?"

Again, he paused, thought hard, and answered, "True."

I admit that I became a little flustered. If he was having trouble with this question, what would happen when we turned to questions about Irenaeus? So, I asked him, "Why do you say that Jesus was born in Guatemala? The Bible says that he was born in Bethlehem."

"Yes," he said, "but he was born in my heart."

Marvin, my translator, tried to help, but Juan remained resolute. Jesus was born in Guatemala.

Later, as I reflected on this experience, I remembered reading that Atticus of Constantinople, the predecessor of Nestorius, instructed the empress and her sisters that "if they imitated the virginity and chastity of Mary, they would give birth to God mystically in their souls."[51] Juan was a good Wesleyan theologian; he was no Nestorian. By the power of the Holy, the whole Christ had become present in his life. Yes. Jesús was born in Guatemala.

---

51 Maxwell Johnson, *"Sub Tuum Praesidium:* The *Theotokos* in Christian Life and Worship before Ephesus," *Pro Ecclesia* 17, no. 1 (2008): 52–75, 69.

9

Essential Kenosis Christology

Thomas Jay Oord

Traditional views of God's omnipotence present obstacles to a plausible Christology. Traditional views of God's love also present obstacles. In this essay, I argue that Christology based on essential kenosis overcomes those obstacles. I do so by arguing we ought to understand God's power as uncontrolling love, and I say God's love is analogous with creaturely love.

Before making these arguments, a disclaimer seems appropriate: What is most plausible to some may not be so to others. A high degree of plausibility avoids logical contradictions and seeks rational coherence. It accounts for the broadest array of experience and fits our deepest intuitions. But among limited creatures like ourselves, accounts of experience differ and intuitions vary. Consequently, what is most plausible to one may not be to another. Those whose intuitions are shaped by the priority of love, however, should find essential kenosis Christology highly plausible.

Kenosis

Nearly all Christians wonder how to make sense of the revelation of God in Jesus Christ. Some Christians find kenosis Christologies attractive in this making-sense endeavor. Key statements for kenosis Christology come from a hymn the apostle Paul included in his letter to the church in Philippi.

Paul prefaced this hymn by saying readers ought to regard the good of others before their own. To illustrate this principle, he cited the kenosis hymn. Its lyrics say Jesus expressed *kenosis*—variously translated "self-emptied," "self-gave," and more[1]—as a servant.[2] Jesus acting for the good of others was especially evident when he humbled himself and when he endured death on a cross. After citing the hymn, Paul argued that God made this kind of love possible for his Philippian readers. Christians today believe God acts to empower them to "will and to work" for good.

Jesus's kenotic life and death, say many theologians, reveal that God engages in self-giving, others-regarding love. Jesus re-presents God. And God's empowering love enables creatures to promote good as they work out their own salvation.

For much of Christian history, kenosis Christologies focused on creedal claims about Jesus being both human and divine. Jesus had two natures, said early Christians, and these natures were communicated to one person. As human, Jesus did not possess every divine attribute. For instance, he was not omnipotent, omnipresent, immutable, omniscient, and so on.[3] Most kenosis Christologies assume Christ voluntarily set aside some attributes to become specially incarnate in Jesus of Nazareth.

In recent decades, discussions of kenosis Christology have shifted.[4] Instead of pondering which divine attributes were communicated to Jesus and which were set aside, theologians today appeal to kenosis to talk about how Jesus *reveals* God's nature. Instead of imagining how Christ relinquished attributes when becoming incarnate in the Nazarene, many now think Jesus's kenosis tells us about who God is and how God acts. Rather than metaphysical divestment, a great deal of kenosis theology today speculates about divine attributes.[5]

---

1 *Kenosis* translated as self-giving love corresponds well with passages found throughout Scripture. I defend this claim in Thomas Jay Oord, *The Uncontrolling Love of God: An Open and Relational Account of Providence* (Downers Grove, IL: InterVarsity Press, 2015), chap. 7.

2 For an analysis on the philosophical and theological implications of these *kenosis* translations, see Oord, chap. 7.

3 On the historical debate of kenosis and Jesus's two natures, see David Brown, *Divine Humanity: Kenosis and the Construction of a Christian Theology* (Waco, TX: Baylor University Press, 2011).

4 Among recent helpful texts on kenosis, see John Polkinghorne, ed., *The Work of Love: Creation as Kenosis* (Grand Rapids: William B. Eerdmans Publishing Company, 2001).

5 For a collection of writings along these lines, see essays in Polkinghorne, ed., *The Work of Love*.

I believe this contemporary view of kenosis fits well with Jesus's own witness and the Bible's broad themes.[6] The cross of Christ especially reveals divine power as noncoercive and God as suffering with creation.[7] Although Jesus is not God, his revelation of divine love makes him the "exact representation of [God's] nature" (Heb. 1:3 NASB). Just as Jesus self-gave for the good of others, God self-gives for our good. In fact, God's moment-by-moment self-giving is an essential aspect of divine providence. God's self-giving is persuasive and empowering rather than self-oriented and overpowering.

My interpretation of kenosis focuses on understanding God's power in light of God's love. I believe we should think of God first and foremost as one who loves, and divine power ought to be considered in light of love. Jesus's kenosis gives us grounds to speculate that God necessarily expresses self-giving and others-empowering love.

I use the word "necessarily" in my claim that God's love is self-giving and others-empowering. Scripture does not tell us whether God necessarily or contingently expresses self-giving, others-empowering love. The modal question of God's love—necessary or contingent—aligns with questions philosophers have about divine voluntarism versus essentialism.

Philosophers attracted to voluntarism believe God voluntarily decides who to be and what attributes to express. Will comes logically first in God. God could decide to be and act otherwise. For voluntarists, God's sovereign will comes logically first among divine attributes. God could choose to know or not know, to control or not, even to exist or not. And so on. Duns Scotus and William of Ockham are often associated with this view.

By contrast, essentialists claim God cannot voluntarily decide who to be or which attributes to express. At least some of God's attributes are eternally fixed. This means who God is and what God does is fixed, at least to

---

6 See, for instance, 1 Cor. 1:18–25. On this, see the work of biblical scholars James D. G. Dunn, *Christology in the Making*, 2nd ed. (London: SCM, 1989), 116; Gordon D. Fee, "The New Testament and Kenosis Christology," in *Exploring Kenotic Christology: The Self-Emptying of God*, ed. C. Stephen Evans (Vancouver, BC: Regent College, 2006), 29.

7 A number of theologians claim God's activity is cruciform. For an example, see Gregory A. Boyd, *The Crucifixion of the Warrior God*, vols. 1 and 2 (Philadelphia: Fortress Press, 2017).

some extent. Essentialists say God necessarily exists, for instance, and God cannot decide to stop existing. God necessarily knows all that is knowable, and God cannot voluntarily choose to be ignorant. And so on. Thomas Aquinas and Jacob Arminius are typically associated with this view.

When it comes to God's love, essential kenosis sides with the essentialist tradition. The essential kenosis view claims love comes logically before the divine will and logically first among attributes of God's nature. Consequently, God necessarily loves, and God cannot fail to do so. Furthermore, God's love extends to everyone and everything. While God freely chooses *how* to love in each moment, God necessarily loves all creatures and entities in every moment.[8]

Essential kenosis stands in contrast to theologies based on volitional divine self-limitation, whereby God chooses to restrict the divine self.[9] According to essential kenosis, self-giving and others-empowering love comes logically first in the divine nature. Consequently, God does not voluntarily self-limit. God necessarily loves others.

Some theologians appeal to voluntary self-limitation to answer questions of God's power. These theologians typically say God chooses not to control others, at least most of the time, although God theoretically could control. Some follow Jürgen Moltmann in saying God voluntarily withdraws for the sake of creation, allowing space for creatures. Roger Olson speaks of self-limitation in terms of God "permitting" creatures to act. "Nothing can happen that God does not *permit*," says Olson, "but that is not the same as saying he *causes* or renders certain everything and certainly not evil, sin, or innocent suffering."[10] The idea that God allows but does not cause

---

8 Open theism provides a key to understanding that God necessarily loves but contingently chooses how to love. Because the future is open and undetermined, God cannot know with certainty which actions will promote overall well-being best. So, God freely chooses among best options. See my explanation in *The Uncontrolling Love of God*, chap. 7.

9 For an advocate of this view, see Jeff B. Pool, *God's Wounds: Hermeneutic of the Christian Symbol of Divine Suffering*, vol. 1, *Divine Vulnerability and Creation* (Cambridge, UK: James Clarke & Co., 2009), 139.

10 Roger E. Olson, "What's Wrong with Calvinism?", March 22, 2013, http://www.patheos.com /blogs/rogereolson/2013/03/whats-wrong-with-calvinism/.

evil is common among Christian theologians in the Wesleyan tradition.

John Polkinghorne expresses well the voluntary self-limitation view in relation to evil. God allows "the created other to be and to act, so that, while all that happens is permitted by God's general providence, not all that happens is in accordance with God's will or brought about by divine special providence," says Polkinghorne. "Such an understanding is basic to theodicy's disclaimer that God does not will the act of a murderer or the destructive force of an earthquake, but allows both to happen in a world in which divine power is deliberately self-limited to allow causal space for creatures."[11]

As the quotes above indicate, voluntary divine self-limitation cannot solve the problem of evil. The view says God permits or allows evil rather than preventing it. The voluntary self-limitation view implies God does not always use power for good—e.g., preventing evil—God essentially possesses. Consequently, victims, survivors, and the abused cannot trust a God who, as Polkinghorne puts it, "is deliberately self-limited to allow causal space for creatures." A wholly good God would occasionally become un-self-limited, in the name of love, to prevent preventable evil.

The "permitting evil" problem is easily illustrated. Imagine a father who chooses not to constrain one of his children from killing the other, when constraining was possible. We would not call this father perfectly loving. Imagine a mother who chooses not to stop a heavy bar from falling on her child and killing it. Mothers who don't prevent death when preventing it is possible are not loving. Imagine the police officer who voluntarily self-limits and allows a rapist to do his dastardly deeds. That officer would not be doing her job, let alone expressing love. In sum, loving individuals do not allow the genuine evil they could prevent.

In sum, kenosis understood as voluntarily self-limitation leaves God culpable for failing to prevent genuine evil. I have explored this problem in detail in various books, so I will not rehearse it here.[12]

---

11   John Polkinghorne, "Kenotic Creation and Divine Action," in *The Work of Love*, 102.

12   See my books *The Nature of Love: A Theology* (St. Louis: Chalice Press, 2010); *The Uncontrolling Love of God* (2015); and *God Can't: How to Believe in God and Love after Tragedy, Abuse, and Other Evils* (Grasmere, ID: SacraSage, 2019).

Essential kenosis, by contrast, claims that God necessarily expresses self-giving, others-empowering, and therefore uncontrolling love. God always acts to love but never controls. And because God loves everyone and everything, God cannot control anyone or anything. God's nature is to be uncontrolling, because love is uncontrolling.

For instance, God necessarily gives freedom to complex creatures. God gives agency and self-organization to less complex entities. God provides the power to be to the smallest entities of existence. And God's necessary love makes possible both lawlike regularities and random events. All of these divine actions express God's providential love for all.

When creatures use their God-given gifts wrongly, God should not be blamed. Because divine love is necessarily uncontrolling, God is not morally responsible for failing to prevent genuine evil. God neither causes evil nor allows it. God is not culpable.

To summarize this section, we might say Jesus reveals God's love to be self-giving, others-empowering, and uncontrolling. This is *kenosis* as understood by many contemporary theologians. Essential kenosis is based on the additional metaphysical speculation that this love is logically first among divine attributes and a necessary aspect of God's nature. God cannot control others, because divine love is inherently self-giving, others-empowering, and uncontrolling.

Jesus's Incarnation, Miracles, and Resurrection

My essential kenosis Christological argument begins with the claim I explored above: Jesus reveals God as one who expresses uncontrolling love. This argument builds from various biblical statements, but I especially note the kenosis passage in Philippians. Essential kenosis makes a metaphysical claim that God's love is necessarily uncontrolling.

The implications of essential kenosis for Christology have not been explored much. In this section, I address three issues some might think at odds with the uncontrolling love perspective: (1) the Holy Spirit conception of Jesus ("the virgin birth"); (2) the miracles Jesus enacted; and (3) God resurrecting Jesus from the dead. I will argue essential kenosis accounts for these issues without claiming God acting in a controlling way. I will not appeal to mystery.

Common explanations for the Holy Spirit conception of Jesus, various miracles, and the resurrection assume the traditional view of divine omnipotence. This view says God sometimes acts supernaturally to do miracles single-handedly. To put it another way, God acts as a sufficient cause to bring about miracles, either breaking the laws of nature or overriding creaturely actors and factors. I find the traditional explanation of miracles problematic.

As I have noted, this view of God's power generates the problem of evil. But it creates other problems too. The traditional view makes it difficult to understand why the Bible would have errors, why divine communication today would be ambiguous, why God would create through a long and painful evolutionary process, why diverse Christianities and religions exist, why God doesn't single-handedly end the climate crisis, and so on.

Most Christologies assume God supernaturally intervened to become incarnate in Jesus. They assume God controls creatures or circumstances when enacting miracles in general and resurrecting Jesus in particular. Essential kenosis Christology affirms biblical and contemporary miracles. But this theology says miracles occur as God works *alongside* or *with* actors, circumstances, and factors in creation.

Miracles are never events single-handedly determined by God; they always occur as God acts in tandem with others or circumstances. They never require the breaking of natural laws. Miracles are good and unusual events that occur as God works in relation to creation.[13]

Consider what is commonly called "the virgin birth" but is better called "the Holy Spirit conception" of Jesus. Mary's cooperation with the angelic messenger—she said, "be it unto me"—is often missed or underemphasized by Christologies that assume God single-handedly controls others. To many traditional Christologies, the Holy Spirit conception was a unilateral event.

---

13 I explain and defend this definition of a miracle in *The Uncontrolling Love of God,* chap. 8. I explain why God can't heal single-handedly in *God Can't,* chap. 3.

CHAPTER 9

Of course, one can read the annunciation as mythical or metaphorical and thereby sidestep questions of divine action. But if one thinks the conception story tells us something true about divine causation, Mary's cooperative response should play an essential part of an adequate explanation.

The biblical witness to Mary's cooperation aligns nicely with essential kenosis Christology. This miracle occurred when a creature—Mary—cooperated with God's action. In addition, essential kenosis overcomes the worry we have with traditional Christologies that God, the Spirit, or an angel forced Mary to be the mother of Jesus. In other words, essential kenosis provides a framework to denounce the idea that Mary was raped or the subject to nonconsensual impregnation. Essential kenosis Christology says this special incarnation was a consensual arrangement between God and Mary.

The cooperative nature of miracles is evident in the one whom Mary birthed. When doing miracles, Jesus often said to those healed, "Your faith has made you well." The healed play a role in their own recovery. At other times, the biblical text tells us that factors and actors in the environment played a vital role in miracles. Even dramatic miracles such as Jesus saying "Come forth" to Lazarus can be interpreted as involving both divine and creaturely action.

Unfortunately, some interpret "Your faith has made you well" as meaning the healed person's cooperation *alone* brought healing. In other words, some think healing can be explained without reference to *any* divine action. Maybe it was luck, maybe the placebo effect, perhaps natural causes. By contrast, essential kenosis says *all* healing involves both divine and creaturely causation.

Others interpret "Your faith has made you well" as implying those not healed lacked faith. This interpretation blames the victim, only furthering injury. By contrast, essential kenosis says those not healed may have consciously cooperated and had plenty of faith. But uncooperative actors and factors in their body and environment prevented the healing. In other words, agents and factors in one's body can play a cooperative or uncooperative role in the healing God wants to occur. With this explanation, essential kenosis overcomes problems other Christologies face related to victim-blaming.

The cooperative nature of miracles is especially evident when Jesus cannot perform miracles. The classic case is Nazareth. "He could not do many miracles there because of their unbelief," says Matthew (13:58, paraphrased; Mark 6:6 is even stronger). Jesus cannot heal a blind man completely on his first attempt, according to Mark (8:24–25). Jesus heals many in need of a physician, says Mark, but not all (1:34). Often overlooked, in other words, are biblical accounts of those whom Jesus could not heal fully or at all.

The miracle many Christians believe most important is Jesus's resurrection. God raised Jesus from the dead, said the apostles Paul (Gal. 1:1; Rom. 8:11) and Peter (Acts 2:32; 1 Pet. 1:21). Most Christologies seem to affirm this miracle is an example of God acting as a sufficient cause. God must have single-handedly resurrected Jesus, they say, controlling to raise him to life.

One might think Jesus's resurrection offers a case of God alone bringing about results. But we must ask, Do biblical texts say God *single-handedly* resurrected Jesus? No. Do biblical accounts say *NO* other factors or actors were involved? No.

We have no information on *how* God raised Jesus from the dead. While many theologians assume God did it unilaterally, the texts don't say this. Of course, the texts also don't say Jesus cooperated with God's resurrecting. Consequently, the resurrection is open to multiple causal explanations, so long as those explanations involve a primary role for divine action.

The essential kenosis explanation of Jesus's resurrection says God was the primary actor in Jesus's resurrection. But Jesus's mind/spirit and bodily members also played a role. It's not hard to imagine cooperative factors and actors in Jesus's resurrection. For instance, it's not hard to imagine Jesus's mind/spirit cooperating with God's efforts. Those like me, who affirm continued subjective experience beyond bodily death (e.g., "life after death"), will think Jesus's mind/spirit could cooperate with God. Someone so in tune with God ("I and the Father are one," John 10:30) would naturally cooperate.

We can also imagine the elements of Jesus's body cooperating or being rightly aligned, despite their damaged state. After all, Jesus's body didn't disappear into nothingness. We know from other resurrection accounts—in the past and present—that dead bodies can be revived without the aid of sufficient causes. The near-death experience literature offers numerous examples. Besides, a body dead thirty-six or so hours has not decomposed.

We find other intriguing factors and actors in the resurrection stories. For instance, Matthew speaks of an angel rolling the stone from the entrance. If God can single-handedly raise Jesus, why send an angel to open the door? Or consider the ambiguity of Jesus's post-resurrection sightings. The women who came to the tomb mistook Jesus for a gardener. Those on the road to Emmaus didn't recognize Jesus until he broke bread. And so on. A God who can single-handedly raise Jesus and who thinks witnesses to the resurrection are important ought to be able to make recognition of the risen one unambiguous.

The most important argument for thinking God's raising of Jesus was a cooperative venture comes from the logic of love itself. To many, it is an a priori truth that love is uncontrolling. Love does not override or occur in a vacuum. Love is not a solitary activity. To those who affirm uncontrolling love as an a priori truth, the logic of love itself leads to thinking God's loving resurrection of Jesus was not single-handed. God always acts in loving ways. If the resurrection had been unilateral, it would not have been loving.

Others find the a posteriori case more plausible for thinking God's resurrecting Jesus was an endeavor between deity and humanity. The a posteriori case looks at the evidence and arguments I noted earlier. It looks at other questions of existence, including the biblical witness. It then builds a case that says God's resurrecting Jesus must not have been a unilateral act. I earlier mentioned several elements of this case, not the least of which are the implications of uncontrolling love for solving the problem of evil.

But the a posteriori case builds from the Bible. It asks, "How does the Bible talk about divine action?" A careful examination of scripture reveals that *no* biblical passage explicitly says God single-handedly controlled others. To put it another way, no passage in Scripture explicitly says God was the *only* actor in an event and no creaturely actors, factors, or causes contributed. None.

The a posteriori case notes that the vast majority of biblical passages explicitly or implicitly speak of both divine and creaturely activity when describing how events occurred. Admittedly, a small number of passages are silent about creaturely action. And a small number are silent about divine action. But these minority voices never *explicitly* deny divine or creaturely action. The idea that God single-handedly creates, performs miracles, redeems, sanctifies, and even resurrects has no explicit biblical support.

Of course, many Christians read biblical statements that only mention divine action and then *assume* creatures were uninvolved. But the biblical text does not explicitly endorse this assumption. And if one thinks a priori or a posteriori God's love is uncontrolling, it won't come as a great surprise to discover biblical authors never explicitly say God controls others in the sense of single-handedly determining them.

This discussion leads to a final obstacle most traditional Christologies and their assumption of traditional omnipotence face. I call it the problem of selective miracles. We might put the problem as a question: "If God can single-handedly resurrect, cure illnesses, heal, protect, and more, why do *so few* miracles occur?"

The vast majority of our prayers for healing do not produce miraculous results. Christians offer reasons for so few miracles, but these reasons often cause psychological distress in those not healed, not to mention theological conundrums. Does God fail to answer prayers because God is aloof and uninvolved? Do the hurt and sick need to earn God's miraculous action by praying more? Do miracles fail to occur because they are not part of some divinely preordained plan? Does God not care about every problem, at least not enough to do something about it? Is God punishing those who are not healed? Questions abound.

Essential kenosis solves the problem of selective miracles. It says God always works to heal. Always. But God can't heal single-handedly, so our prayers do not always bring about miraculous results. For miracles to occur, animate creatures must cooperate, or the inanimate conditions of creation must be aligned.[14] The God of essential kenosis can only enact miracles when creatures, organisms, cells, or other entities cooperate, or

---

14 For a full explanation of these ideas, see *God Can't*, chap. 3, and *The Uncontrolling Love of God*, chap. 8.

the inanimate conditions of creation are conducive. God is not aloof, uncaring, punishing, or waiting for us to earn a miracle.

We might summarize this section by saying the miracles associated with Jesus—from the Holy Spirit conception, to miracles Jesus performed, to God raising him from the dead—involved God working in relation with creation. While other Christologies claim or assume God exerted supernatural control, essential kenosis says God did not single-handedly cause these miracles. This view overcomes the problem of selective miracles using the logic of God's uncontrolling love.

Jesus Reveals God's Love

The biblical witness claims that Jesus reveals or re-presents God's love.[15] We best know what God's love is like through the witness of Jesus. Although numerous Old Testament writings point to God's covenantal and steadfast love, we see divine love clearest in Jesus the Christ.

Unfortunately, Christologies built from the thought of influential theologians cannot claim Jesus reveals God's love. In this section, I explore some well-known theologians and their mistaken views of divine love. Had they taken the revelation of God in Jesus as their primary methodological touchstone, they may have radically rethought their views of divine love. In contrast to them, essential kenosis Christology takes Jesus's love as the best witness to what God's love is like.

The Analogy of Divine and Creaturely Love

Augustine's theology of love is a prime example of traditional theologies creating problems for Christology. His thought creates various obstacles to thinking Jesus reveals God as one who loves in any sense!

Augustine's most extensive writing on love comes from a book he called *Teaching Christianity (De Doctrina Christiana)*.[16] At the outset, Augustine

---

15 See John 17, 1 John 3, and other New Testament passages.

16 I use the New City Press translation: Augustine, *Teaching Christianity (De Doctrina Christiana)* (Hyde Park, NY: New City Press, 1996).

made a distinction between two ways of relating to others: using them and enjoying them.[17] This distinction proves central to what he believed about love. "Enjoyment consists in clinging to something lovingly for its own sake," he said, "while use consists in referring what has come your way to what your love aims at obtaining, provided, that is, it deserves to be loved."[18]

Only God can provide true satisfaction, said Augustine. Therefore, God should be the only one we love for his own sake.[19] This means, of course, Augustine thought we ought to use people rather than enjoy them for themselves.[20] Those upset by this idea, he said, "must not take offense" that we "love them for God's sake and not their own."[21] We should not love our fellow creatures, because they have no value of their own and, therefore, cannot satisfy.

Does the revelation of love we find in Jesus Christ say we ought to use our fellow creatures? No. Does it say they have no value? No.

In a section titled "God Does Not Enjoy Us, but Makes Use of Us," Augustine explored divine love. He acknowledged that Jesus says God loves creatures for their own sakes. Given his two categories of love—enjoy and use—he posed a question for himself: "How does [God] love us?" In other words, does God use us or enjoy us?

If God enjoys us, said Augustine, "it means he is in need of some good of ours, which nobody in his right mind could possibly say. Every good of ours, after all, is either God himself, or derived from him."[22] God has no desires we could possibly satisfy. We do not contribute to a God, who has all value eternally. So, God can't enjoy us.

The only way God can love us, according to Augustine, is to use us. "He does not enjoy us, but makes use of us," he stated bluntly. "Because if he

---

17 Augustine, *Teaching Christianity*, bk. 1, par. 3.

18 Augustine, bk. 1, par. 4.

19 Augustine, bk. 1, par. 4.

20 Augustine, bk. 1, par. 20.

21 Augustine, bk. 1, par. 21.

22 Augustine, bk. 1, par. 21.

neither enjoys us nor makes use of us, I cannot find any way in which he can love us."[23] Despite Jesus saying God loves the world so much he gave the begotten Son so that we might have abundant life, Augustine thought God uses the world. Despite God creating us and all creation and calling us "very good" (Gen. 1:31 KJV), Augustine believed God doesn't enjoy us for our own sakes.

Does Jesus's revelation of love say God uses and does not enjoy us? No.

Even the claim God loves by using us presented Augustine with a problem. And he realized it. His notion of use implied that God desires something other than himself. But according to Augustine's view, this cannot be. God is the only valuable one. So, Augustine taught that God actually "does not make use of us either. Our making use of things is directed to the end of enjoying God's goodness," he said. But "God's making use of us is directed to his goodness."[24] So God cannot love us at all; God can only love himself.

Does Jesus's revelation of love sound anything like this? No. Does Jesus reveal a God only oriented toward himself? No.

What's going on? Why did Augustine describe God's love differently from the way Jesus described it? The problem is Augustine consistently used "love" to mean something different from what Jesus and most biblical writers meant by the word. Augustine thought of love as desire. "Love is a kind of craving," he explained.[25] To love someone or something is to desire that someone or something.

Jesus spoke of love primarily as promoting blessedness, *shalom*, abundant life, goodness, salvation. "For God so loved the world, that he gave his only begotten Son," begins perhaps the best-known verse in the Bible (John 3:16 KJV). This verse tells us God expressed love by giving the Son so the world might benefit: have eternal life. "Love your enemies," said Jesus. "Do good to those who hate you" (Luke 6:27). I could quote dozens of quotes from Jesus that link love with well-being.

---

23 Augustine, *Teaching Christianity*, bk. 1, par. 32.

24 Augustine, bk. 1, par. 32.

25 Augustine, *Eighty-Three Different Questions*, 35, 2.

Other biblical writers spoke of love not primarily as desire but as compassion, caring, being kind, offering salvation, or promoting some other form of well-being. The apostle John wrote, "How does God's love abide in anyone who has the world's goods and sees a brother or sister in need and yet refuses to help?" (1 John 3:17 NRSV). I could list many other passages that assume love is primarily about promoting well-being in some form.

Instead of taking the words and actions of Jesus as his basis for understanding God's love, Augustine portrayed God in ways that make divine love utterly different from Jesus's love. According to Augustine's view, we cannot draw analogies between God's love and Jesus's love. But the language Jesus and biblical writers used to talk about God often explicitly or implicitly affirmed similarities between Creator and creatures.

When we begin with Christ and scripture, we find bidirectional analogies between God's love and creaturely love. That is, we get a sense of what our love should be by looking at God as revealed in Jesus. That's one direction. And we get a sense of what divine love is like by looking at love we express. That's the other direction. Jesus's words and life serve as a bridge in this bidirectional analogy, because he portrayed divine love as similar to creaturely love. We see this bidirectional analogy, for instance, when Jesus says, "If you who are evil know how to give good gifts to your children, how much more will your heavenly Father give good things to those who ask him" (Matt. 7:11).

To say creaturely love is analogous to divine love does not mean divine and human loves are identical in all ways. God's love, according to analogy, would be different in degree from human love, but not altogether different in kind. God everlastingly gives and receives love, for instance, whereas each creature has not always been a giver and receiver. God never fails to love; creatures sometimes fail to love and thereby sin (see the point about us being "evil" in the previous paragraph). God loves from complete social awareness, because God is omnipresent. Humans love from limited awareness, because they are localized. These differences and more, however, do not contradict the argument that godly and creaturely love are similar in other ways. In fact, these similarities make theologies of love meaningful.

Analogies of love are the basis for making sense of biblical passages about imitating divine love. If God's love is entirely different in kind from ours, Jesus's command to "be merciful, just as your Father is merciful" (Luke 6:36 NRSV) becomes absurd. Jesus revealed that God acts in love to promote the well-being of others. We should emulate God by expressing this love.

The Relationality Inherent in Love

Other ideas about God's love present obstacles to a plausible Christology. Especially problematic is the ancient view that God is in all ways impassable/nonrelational. Although the biblical witness reveals Jesus's love as relational, these theologians claimed God is not relational. God gives but does not receive; God is in all ways unaffected by others. God not being relational creates huge problems for understanding God as loving.

Thomas Aquinas said God is not in loving relationship with creation. "A relation of God to creatures is not a reality in God," he wrote. In his view, God knows creatures as ideas without being causally affected by them.[26] Influencing relations with creation "are not really in Him," Aquinas said. Such love relations "are ascribed to him only in our understanding."[27] In other words, we only *imagine* God expresses giving-and-receiving love. But God doesn't *actually* express this love.

Anselm also said God does not love creation in giving-and-receiving relationships. He recognized that God's non-relationality—which is required for passions and sympathy—means God cannot express compassionate love. "How are you compassionate, and at the same time passionless?" Anselm prayed. "For if you are passionless, you do not feel sympathy. And if you do not feel sympathy, your heart is not wretched from sympathy for the wretched. But this it is to be compassionate."

In response to his own question, Anselm said, "When you behold us in our wretchedness, we experience the effect of compassion, but you do not

---

26   Thomas Aquinas, *Summa Theologica,* I (Westminster, MD: Christian Classics, 1981), q.6, a.2, ad 1.

27   Thomas Aquinas, *Summa Contra Gentiles* II (Notre Dame, IN: University of Notre Dame Press, 1981), 13–14.

experience the feeling. Therefore . . . [you are] not compassionate, because you are affected by no sympathy for wretchedness."[28] Anselm was right that a nonrelational God cannot be compassionate. And yet he thought affirming God's non-relationality is more important.

The love of Jesus involved relational response. Jesus's love was both giving and receiving. And the love we see expressed in our own lives involves relational response. Love is inherently relational, in the sense of being affected by others and affecting them.[29]

If God cannot be affected by others, it makes little sense to say God loves others. Christologies that say or imply God is not relational cannot claim Jesus reveals God as one who loves. To put it starkly: if Jesus reveals love as including relational receiving, the God who cannot receive in relationship cannot love.

Essential kenosis Christology overcomes this obstacle. It says the definition of love that applies to Jesus (and us) also applies to God. While God's love differs in degree (is relentless, expressed toward all others, most influential, etc.), God's love does not differ in kind. Our love is analogous to God's.

Essential kenosis Christology claims that just as Jesus loved in relation with others, God loves in relation with others. Just as Jesus was affected by others, God is also affected. Just as Jesus was moved with compassion, God is also moved with compassion. Because God is omniresponsive when acting to love, God is the most moved mover rather than the unmoved mover.[30]

Essential kenosis Christology makes an additional speculative move about the necessity of God's relational love. This move stands alongside God's uncontrolling love as necessary, which we explored in the previous section. It says God is essentially relational. That is, relational love is a

---

28 St. Anselm, *Proslogium*, trans. Sidney Norton Deane (La Salle, IL: Open Court, 1951), 13–14.

29 Love is best defined as acting intentionally, in relational response to others, to promote overall well-being. I have explained and defended this definition in various publications, including *Defining Love: A Philosophical, Scientific, and Theological Engagement* (Grand Rapids: Brazos Press, 2010).

30 Both Abraham Heschel and Clark H. Pinnock call God the most moved mover. For Pinnock's reference, see *Most Moved Mover: A Theology of God's Openness* (Grand Rapids: Baker, 2001).

necessary attribute of God. God everlastingly relates in love with others, either in Trinity, with creation, or both.

Claiming God is necessarily relational is essential if one wants to claim God is necessarily loving. If love is inherently relational and God's nature is love, God must be loving in relation to others everlastingly. I have written about this in many other publications, so I will not rehearse the arguments here.[31]

Conclusion

I have argued that both the traditional view of God's power and traditional views of God's love present obstacles to plausible Christologies. Essential kenosis overcomes those major obstacles, however. It does so by saying Jesus reveals God's love and power. The kenosis of Jesus tells us that God's love is self-giving, others-empowering, and uncontrolling. Essential kenosis says this love is essential to God, which means God cannot control others. The idea that God cannot control others solves the problem of evil and a host of other questions traditional Christologies cannot solve.

Essential kenosis also fits well with what Jesus revealed God's love to be like. Rather than altogether different in kind, God's love is analogous to love as expressed by Jesus and by us. The relational element central to love itself plays a central role to an essential kenosis Christology.

31 In addition to *The Nature of Love,* see my essays "Strong Possibility," and "My Response," in *Divine Impassibility: Four Views of God's Emotions and Suffering,* ed. Robert J. Matz and A. Chadwick Thornhill (Downers Grove, IL: IVP Academic, 2019).

10

Why Did God Become a Man of the Spirit? Toward a Wesleyan Pentecostal Spirit-Christology

Chris E. W. Green

Introduction: The Problem with (Some) Spirit-Christologies

Spirit-Christologies, at least those developed by Pentecostals, including Wesleyan Pentecostals,[1] often assume a basic metaphysical competition or contrast between the human and the divine, both in terms of God's relation to us and in terms of the communion of Christ's two natures. God, in these contrastive/competitive accounts, must limit his power in order for creation to exist freely and integrally. Creation can be itself only in independence from the Creator. That is why the divine nature in Christ had to "go quiet" for his humanity to have its own voice.[2] Ken Archer made the point sharply: "Such limitation creates the necessary space which enables God and humanity (as well as creation) to enjoy authentic interpersonal relationships."[3] And Andrew Gabriel said more or less

---

1 For the difference between Wesleyan and Finished-Work Pentecostals, see Kimberly E. Alexander, *Pentecostal Healing: Models in Theology and Practice* (Dorset, UK: Deo Publishing, 2006).

2 Ralph Del Colle, *Christ and the Spirit: Spirit-Christology in Trinitarian Perspective* (Oxford: Oxford University Press, 1994), is a notable exception to this rule, as is Frank Macchia, whose work I will take up later in this chapter.

3 Kenneth J. Archer, *The Gospel Revisited* (Eugene, OR: Wipf & Stock, 2011), 103.

the same thing, although he was focused on the doctrine of the Spirit:

> With respect to divine omnipotence, the Spirit acts kenotically as the Spirit makes room for creaturely freedom, even to the point of allowing creatures to resist him. In this sense, the Spirit "surrenders" or "empties himself" as he exercises his power within created reality. This is a divine self-limitation (kenosis) of the exercise of divine power. . . . The powerful "fire" of the Spirit can even be quenched and restrained. Even the church sometimes resists the Spirit and, therefore, it is in continuous need of reform. One can resist the Spirit. The kenotic Spirit generally does not force. Rather, believers are invited to "walk by the Spirit" and to be "led by the Spirit" (Gal. 5.16, 18).[4]

Amos Yong, perhaps the best-known theologian in the global Pentecostal movement, draws on a version of this competitive/contrastive model in his theology of disability: "A world that is contingent, that includes spontaneity, and that features free creatures is possible precisely because God 'withdraws' himself in order to create 'space' for others (the world and its various creatures)." For Yong, it is because God withdraws that the world is possible—and why it immediately and necessarily also finds itself at risk. "In such a world, genetic mutations have evolved creatures and whole species that have perished because of inability to adapt to their environment, have resulted mostly in spontaneous abortions, and have produced congenital disabilities (e.g. Down Syndrome); this same world has also allowed accident to happen (e.g. head injuries), and disabilities caused by the irresponsibility of free creatures (e.g., fetal alcohol syndrome)."[5] God "distances"

---

4 Andrew Gabriel, *The Lord Is the Spirit* (Eugene, OR: Pickwick, 2010), 190. Notice, for Gabriel, kenosis is, by definition, divine self-limitation. This view is not limited to Pentecostals, of course. David Law's view (see "Kenotic Theology" in I. A. McFarland, D. A. S. Fergusson, and K. Kilby, eds., *The Cambridge Dictionary of Christian Theology* [Cambridge: Cambridge University Press, 2014], 262) seems to be typical: "Despite its problems, however, some version of kenosis is arguably necessary if Christianity is to hold fast to the doctrine of the incarnation, for only if Christ lays aside or scales down some aspect of his divine nature is it possible to conceive of him being divine and yet able to live a genuinely human life. Furthermore, kenosis is central not only to Christology, but to Christian life and discipleship as such. The notions of self-giving, self-sacrifice, service, and love of others which it denotes are essential for Christian existence."

5 Amos Yong, *Theology and Down Syndrome* (Waco, TX: Baylor University Press, 2007), 180.

himself from creation, and so creation is vulnerable to evil and evils. But if God were not "distant," creation would not be itself at all.

Earlier, in his *The Spirit Poured Out on All Flesh*, Yong argued that Pentecostals can and should retrieve and reappropriate Spirit-Christology for a number of reasons, all of which point to metaphysical concerns. Spirit-Christology, unlike Logos-Christology, better appreciates Jesus's humanity, frees us from the unnecessary restrictions of ancient Hellenistic ontologies, and therefore reframes the Oneness-Trinitarian debates. Most important, Yong argues, Spirit-Christology, unlike traditional Christological accounts, highlights Jesus's life as a model for our Spirit-anointed lives.[6] And the imitation of Christ is essential to Pentecostal being-in-the-world.

In a more recent work, Yong makes it clear that he, like the Catholic charismatic Ralph Del Colle, does not want to reject "high Christology" out of hand. He does, however, want to emphasize the Spirit-empowered humanity of Jesus, because this is the best way for contemporary believers to grasp the nature and purpose of the Spirit-filled life. What Jesus did, he did humanly and in the power of the Spirit. Therefore, we, filled with the same Spirit, can and should expect to do the same.[7]

Sammy Alfaro's approach is perhaps more radical than Yong's. His approach privileges the insights of early Pentecostals, many of whom were Wesleyans, shaped in the Holiness traditions. And as a result, Alfaro is more willing to bracket out the categories and concerns of traditional Christian orthodoxy. Like Yong, Alfaro holds that Pentecostal spirituality is focused on Jesus's *humanity*—and just in this way on his *utter dependence* on the Spirit. But Alfaro goes further than Yong in insisting that this "utter dependence" is possible only if the divine nature is willingly given up. "In becoming dependent, *the Son surrendered the independent use of his divine attributes*

---

6 Amos Yong, *The Spirit Poured Out on All Flesh* (Grand Rapids: Baker Academic, 2005), 110.

7 In his own words, "Understandings of Jesus of Nazareth as anointed by the Spirit to accomplish the works of God provide a more conducive framework for seeing Jesus's solidarity with human beings and project a springboard for envisioning missional discipleship in his footsteps." Amos Yong, *Renewing Christian Theology* (Waco, TX: Baylor University Press, 2014), 241.

in incarnation. The Word became flesh and exercised power through the Spirit, *not on its own.*"[8]

Alfaro finds this kenotic Spirit-Christology everywhere in early Pentecostal teaching: "Jesus became the Captain of our salvation on account of his complete dependence on the Spirit on his way to Calvary. He lived and died as a man, but a man guided by the power of the Holy Spirit. During his earthly existence, Jesus *relinquished his divine powers and relied on the Spirit* in order to become God's perfect and spotless sacrificial Lamb."[9] He believes that the view of charismatic Anglican vicar A. A. Boddy is representative: "at no time did Jesus exercise his divine powers independently but was always relying on the Spirit to accomplish his mission."[10]

Alfaro is right: many early Pentecostals did suggest that Jesus could be the exemplar only if he denied the use of his divinity. They did not want to say that Jesus was not God, of course. On the contrary, they believed that his death and resurrection were salvific precisely because he was God. But they *did* want to say that Jesus, as God, had the power to give up his powers, and that he did so for our sakes, revealing in his kenotic ministry what it means to live in radical dependence on the Holy Spirit.

In an early editorial on divine healing, A. A. Boddy stated it clearly: Christ's life was "the representative human life *lived under our conditions,*" as opposed to God's conditions, precisely because he "accepted conditionally the Holy Ghost *as we may accept Him* to be the indwelling Divine Life."[11] Around the same time, an unnamed contributor to the *Weekly Evangel* claimed that "the Lord of glory emptied Himself and took the place of absolute dependence upon His Father. The place of 'Nothing' that God might be 'All.'"[12] And Elizabeth Sisson, a formidable figure in the early movement, contended

---

8 Sammy Alfaro, *Divine Compañero: Toward a Hispanic Pentecostal Christology* (Eugene, OR: Wipf & Stock, 2010), 84. Emphasis added.

9 Alfaro, *Divine Compañero*, 84. Emphasis added.

10 Alfaro, 35.

11 A. A. Boddy, "Health in Christ," *Confidence* 3, no. 8 (August 1910): 175. Emphasis added.

12 "Nothing," *Weekly Evangel* 215 (November 17, 1917): 8.

that what Christ did in giving up his rights, all Christians must do: "As the Father wanted none of the living of Christ's humanity, when He was here in His human life, wanted only His emptiness, as a human shell in which God could express Himself in word and action, so Christ wants over again our perpetual self-emptied lives, in which to live, in the glory of the Father. As Faith appropriates such ideal Divine Provision, the supply comes forth."[13]

Spirit-Christology and Classical Metaphysics

Other examples—and counterexamples, no doubt—could be given, but the point is clear: many Pentecostals looked and continue to look to Jesus as the exemplary man of the Spirit.[14] And the same is true for some Wesleyans, as well,[15] in part because some suspect Wesley's Christology undermines the integrity of Christ's humanness.[16] In all of these accounts, the overriding assumption is that Jesus can be exemplary only if he does not by any means draw on the resources of his divine nature. But where does this assumption come from? And is it necessarily true?

As I have already suggested, it comes from the underlying metaphysical conviction that the divine and the human exist in radical competition with one another. Insofar as God is fully God, we cannot be fully ourselves. Insofar as we are fully ourselves, God is not fully God. But this conviction is wrong from the start. If we allow a more traditional metaphysics to shape our understanding of incarnation,[17] we see that Jesus could not have

---

13 Elizabeth Sisson, "The Goal: The Mark," *Weekly Evangel*, April 20, 1918, 4.

14 See Christopher Stephenson, *Types of Pentecostal Theology: Method, System, Spirit* (Oxford: Oxford University Press, 2013).

15 See, for example, George Bailey, "Wesleyan Spirit-Christology: Inspiration from the Theology of Samuel Chadwick," paper presented at Oxford Institute of Methodist Theological Studies (August 2018). Bailey begins with the assumption that "for the divinity of Christ to so assume human flesh in the birth of Jesus Christ demanded much to be given up."

16 See John Deschner, *Wesley's Christology: An Interpretation*, 2nd ed. (Dallas: Southern Methodist University Press, 1985); Randy Maddox, *Responsible Grace: John Wesley's Practical Theology* (Nashville: Kingswood Books, 1994); and Richard M. Riss, "John Wesley's Christology in Recent Literature," *Wesleyan Theological Journal* 45, no. 1 (2010): 108–29.

17 See Kathryn Tanner, *God and Creation in Christian Theology: Tyranny or Empowerment* (New York: Blackwell, 1988), 40–48.

surrendered "the independent use of his divine attributes" for at least two reasons: first, because the divine attributes are not a set of powers or potentials that the divine persons choose to employ now and again; second, because God is three subsisting relations, which means the "persons" simply cannot act independently from each other, as affirmed in the doctrine of inseparable operations.

Better understood, the doctrine of God makes it clear that we cannot meaningfully say God "withdraws" or denies his own being in order to create, or that he denies his own will in order to save. Creation is not itself in independence from God, but in absolute dependence upon him. God does not distance himself from us in order for us to be free, but frees us by being the inmost source and ultimate end of our existence. This is why Paul again and again pointed forward to the eschaton: creation is fully itself just because God is "all in all."[18]

All to say, creation does not need the diminishment or withdrawal of God, but God's nearness, God's fulfilling fullness. And it is that very nearness, that same fulfilling fullness, that Christ embodied. He did not give up his intimacy with the Father in order to become human or to depend upon the Spirit.[19] It was his intimacy with the Father, his filial communion, that constituted his humanity and was revealed at his baptism. The Spirit rested upon Christ as the sign that his humanity was fully opened up, absolutely available, to the divine life.

If we are Christians, this is how we know that there is no competition, no duality, between God and creatures. What is true in Christ is true of the relation of God to all creation. In becoming finite, taking finitude up as his own, "the infinite Word shows once and for all equally the non-*duality* of God and the world and the non-*identity* of God and the world."[20]

---

18   See Robert Sokolowski, *The God of Faith and Reason: Foundations of Christian Theology* (Notre Dame, IN: University of Notre Dame Press, 1982), 1–52.

19   In terms of his creatureliness, Jesus is no less dependent on the Father than he is on the Spirit: "The Son can do nothing on his own, but only what he sees the Father doing; for whatever the Father does, the Son does likewise" (Jn 5:19 NRSV).

20   Rowan Williams, *Christ the Heart of Creation* (London: Bloomsbury, 2018), 227.

The divine is not an "other" to the human in Christ, and God is not an "other" to creation.[21] God's transcendence is more radical than that. "God differs to the point of being the non-other."[22] Or, in the words of fifteenth-century German philosopher Nicolaus Cusanus, God is *non aliud*— not a thing at all—and therefore is not affected or effected as things must be. It is just for this reason that God can be one with the creature without confusion or violation of any kind, either to God or to the creature. That is to say, the creation is in the creator and the creator is in the creation in such a way that the creator is always creator and the creation is always creation.[23]

Emptiness and Fullness, Christ and The Spirit

So, how should we speak about Christ's relation to the Spirit? Is a non-competitive, non-contrastive Spirit-Christology possible? Is it possible for Wesleyans, including Wesleyan Pentecostals? I believe it is, and I think that Cyril of Alexandria showed how it might be done. Cyril could at times talk about Christ surrendering his glory, or of his descending to "human humiliation."[24] But he regularly insisted that when Christ was "emptied" this did not at all mean that his divine nature was eliminated or changed in any way. Instead, the Word shared with his flesh his divine glory.[25] Cyril does not think Christ had to rid himself of his divine powers in order to be truly human. The opposite is true: he was truly human precisely because his

---

21 So Tyler Wittman: "God's relation to creation must be 'non-contrastive' and characterized by 'non-duality.' This means that God is not a thing alongside other things, and so God's agency in and among creatures does not crowd out or frustrate created agency in the way that two creatures may displace one another." Wittman, *God and Creation in the Theology of Thomas Aquinas and Karl Barth* (Cambridge: Cambridge University Press, 2019), 17.

22 Jean-Yves Lacoste, *La Phénoménalité de Dieu: Neuf Etudes* (Paris: Éditions du Cerf, 2008), back cover.

23 David B. Burrell, *Faith and Freedom: An Interfaith Perspective* (Oxford: Blackwell, 2004), 129–42, 217–33.

24 Cyril of Alexandria, *Commentary on John*, vol. 2 (Downers Grove, IL: InterVarsity Press, 2015), 201.

25 Cyril of Alexandria, *Scholia on the Incarnation of the Only-Begotten*, in John McGuckin, *Saint Cyril of Alexandria and the Christological Controversy* (Crestwood, NY: Saint Vladimir's Seminary Press, 2010), 5.

humanity was brought into absolute and abiding communion with his divinity. In him, the emptiness of sinful human existence is filled to overflowing with the fullness of the life of God.

In John's Gospel, Jesus prays to be restored to his former glory, the glory he had with the Father in the beginning (John 17:5). Yet at the very beginning of the Gospel it is said, "The Word became flesh and lived among us, *and we have seen his glory*" (John 1:14 NRSV). Cyril held these truths together: if in one sense God's glory is hidden or veiled in the Incarnation, in another sense it is revealed. God, being God, is always inherently glorious. But God, being a living God and a gracious God, can be differently glorious according to our needs. In Christ, that glory simply is the full humanity fully alive.

This seems to be what Cyril had in mind when he described Christ's humanity as a coal glowing with divine fire.[26] The flesh of God bears the glory of God, makes the divine glory humanly experienceable: "the Word of God [is] united with the manhood, and not as having cast aside what he is, but rather as having transformed what he assumed into his own glory and power."[27] Taking up human nature as his own, the transcendent Christ was not changed or limited but changed it by his unlimited changelessness.[28] He became what it is only so that it might become what he is.

At the beginning of the *Scholia,* Cyril says the fall stripped humanity of the Spirit, ruining our nature, making it unworthy of intimacy with God. Christ, in giving/receiving the Spirit, restores the Spirit to us, "re-rooting" the Spirit in our nature.[29] "He received the Spirit for our sakes in order to sanctify our entire nature. He did not come to help himself but to become for all of us the door, the beginning, and the way to heavenly blessings."[30]

---

26 Cyril, *Scholia on the Incarnation,* 9.

27 Cyril, 9.

28 Cyril, 12.

29 Frances Young, "*Theotokos:* Mary and the Pattern of Fall and Redemption in the Theology of Cyril of Alexandria," in Thomas Weinandy and Daniel A. Keating, eds., *The Theology of St. Cyril of Alexandria: A Critical Appreciation* (London: T&T Clark, 2003), 67.

30 Cyril of Alexandria, *Commentary on John,* vol. 1 (Downers Grove, IL: InterVarsity Press, 2013), 82.

God the Word is "full" in regard to his own nature, and perfect in every respect. From his own fulness he gives out his benefits to all creatures, as he said, "I will pour out my spirit upon on all flesh" (Isa. 44:3). When we say that he was "emptied out" it has no derogatory reference to the Word's own nature nor, as might be thought, was he changed or made inferior in any respect. For he himself, just like his Begetter, is unalterable and immutable, and was never capable of any passibility. But when he became flesh, that is became man, he appropriated the poverty of humanity to himself.[31]

Here, Cyril identified the incarnation with Pentecost. Christ, at one with the Spirit, both receives (humanly) and gives (divinely) the Spirit. As Cyril said in his commentary on the Gospel of John, Jesus "receives the Spirit through himself for us." [32] Humanity, because of sin, is by nature "empty," just as God, by nature, is full, fulfilling, overflowing. "He was emptied in this way, by reason of our likeness, being full, as God."[33] Christ has taken our humanity as his own, and in this way has laid claim to our emptiness. At his baptism, he shared his communion with the Spirit with us, filling our emptiness with his fullness, the divine nature he and the Spirit share with the Father. Importantly, Cyril did not think that Christ had to limit or negate his divinity in order to "make room" for the Spirit. Human being itself, as Christ made it his own, was itself the room the infinite Spirit filled up beyond all measure.

The Divine Exaltation of Humanity

Cyril's theology harmonizes perfectly with the Christ hymn in Philippians 2. Of course, I know that this passage can be and often is read to mean that to be found in human form Christ had to *give up* the form of God. But I am convinced it should be read differently. God made obedience and suffering his own by taking on human nature and did so by "remaining

---

31 Cyril, *Scholia on the Incarnation*, 5.

32 Cyril, *Commentary on John*, 1:82.

33 Cyril, *Scholia on the Incarnation*, 12.

what he was." "He was made like us, not losing His own nature, for He is unchangeable as God."[34] Christ's kenosis, his pouring out of his fullness into the emptiness of human nature, not only unveiled God; it also exalts humanity—and in particular the humanity of those treated most inhumanely.

Jesus did not have to surrender his divine privileges in order to come and live a human life. In fact, it is a mistake to think of God as privileged in the first place. He is not *philanthropic*, condescending to help those who are beneath him. He is *love*, drawing his creatures into full equality with him. It follows, then, that the Incarnation was not a humiliation for God, although it certainly reveals that God is humble. As Anselm said, "In the incarnation of God it is understood that no humiliation of God came about: rather it is believed that human nature was exalted."[35]

In becoming "obedient to the point of death, even death on a cross" (Phil. 2:8), Christ did not alter himself, did not become less or other than he was and is and shall be. Said differently, taking on humanity, Christ was not stripped of his dignity; instead, he dignified our nature, and in the process revealed that a slave, even a criminal slave, is no less human, no less worthy, than a lord. Better, in a world such as ours—a world corrupted by the powers of sin and death, a world of injustice and tragedy—it is only in the form of a slave that Christ could perform his humanity fully. That is to say, God's "form," when expressed humanly, was necessarily given in the "form of a slave." It is not the becoming human that was humbling for Christ; it was the becoming "obedient to the point of death" (Phil 2:8). Christ became human and then humbled himself—and even this did not make him less God-like. His *kenosis* in its entirety simply disclosed what God is like. God exalts himself in humanity. All to say, in spite of what we have come to think, kenosis is not *emptying* (in the sense of the divine becoming less itself) but *filling* (in the sense of making humanity more itself by giving it a share in divine life). In Cyril's words, God the Word does not

---

34 Cyril, *Scholia on the Incarnation*, 7.

35 Anselm of Canterbury, *The Major Works* (Oxford: Oxford University Press, 1998), 275.

empty himself of his fullness but in his fullness descends *into* emptiness and fills it with himself.[36]

Anselm, commenting on this passage, made a claim every bit as startling as Cyril's:

> For it is not meant that he could not have attained his exaltation in any other way but by obedience unto death; nor is it meant that his exaltation was conferred on him, only as a reward of his obedience (for he himself said before he suffered, that all things had been committed to him by the Father, and that all things belonging to the Father were his); but the expression is used because he had agreed with the Father and the Holy Spirit, that there was no other way to reveal to the world the height of his omnipotence, than by his death.[37]

That last line is right to the point. In the death of Jesus, a death Jesus freely suffered, interceding for us and warring against the devil,[38] God made himself fully known just as the sheer emptiness of death was overwhelmed by the inexhaustible fullness of life.

The Fullness of Pentecost

Sergei Bulgakov distinguished two modes or movements within the one hypostatic "descent" of the Spirit that marks the beginning of the New Creation. At the Annunciation, which is *Mary's* Pentecost, the Spirit rested upon and so was revealed in the humanity of the *Theotokos*. At the baptism, Christ's Pentecost, the Spirit rested upon and so was revealed in the humanity of the God-man. "Only in the Baptism does the Holy Spirit descend hypostatically, 'like a dove' (Matt. 3:16), thus accomplishing the adoption by the Father of the entire God-Man, not only in the Divine but also in the human essence. This is a new and as if second descent of the Holy Spirit from heaven."[39]

---

36   Cyril, *Scholia on the Incarnation*, 17.

37   Anselm, *The Major Works*, 278.

38   Anselm, 252.

39   Sergius Bulgakov, *The Comforter*, trans. Boris Jakim (Grand Rapids: Eerdmans, 2004), 265.

"This is a new . . . descent," and it entails a new relationship for Jesus to the Spirit. "Jesus becomes Christ, i.e., the Anointed by the Spirit, the Spirit-bearer."[40] And by "virtue of His anointment in His personal Pentecost which is His baptism, the anoinment becomes accessible in Him to the entire world."[41] In his descent of the incarnation, Christ took our emptiness as his own. In the Spirit's descent at Christ's baptism, the beginning of Pentecost, that emptiness was filled once and for all.

This is precisely the theme of Frank Macchia's recent *Jesus the Spirit Baptizer*. Pentecost reveals that God, as the ever-abundant source of all things, is also their fulfillment. Jesus "baptizes us in the Spirit from the fullness of his own Spirit-led life as the faithful Son of the Father." Just so, Macchia argues, we understand kenosis, or self-emptying, not as the elimination of God, but as the gracious realization of God in creation and creation in God. "This divine self-emptying in Christ imparts to us the flourishing of life in the Spirit, the love of the Father in the image of the faithful Son. This divine self-giving frees us to be ourselves as we were created to be and shows us the wisdom by which that life is to be attained and lived."[42] That is, Pentecost frees us to live as Christ in the power of the Spirit, not in the sense that we merely imitate him, but in the sense that he lives our lives with us and we live his life with him. This is what Paul meant when he said, "I have been crucified with Christ; and it is no longer I who live, but it is Christ who lives in me. And the life I now live in the flesh I live by faith in the Son of God, who loved me and gave himself for me" (Gal 2:19–20 NRSV).

Conclusion

I have asked if a noncompetitive Spirit-Christology is possible, in particular for Wesleyans and Wesleyan Pentecostals. And I have said that it *is* possible. But in conclusion it is worth considering what difference it makes.

---

40 Bulgakov, *The Comforter*, 265.

41 Bulgakov, 250.

42 Frank Macchia, *Jesus the Spirit Baptizer: Christology in the Light of Pentecost* (Grand Rapids: Eerdmans, 2018), 105.

What are its defining features? How is it Wesleyan? How is it Pentecostal?

First, Christ's kenosis is not the "scaling down" of his divinity in order to make his humanity viable. Instead, his humanity is viable precisely because it is fully open to his fulfilling divinity. Christ's humanity is held in full communion with the Father by the Spirit. In the Incarnation, the divine neither recedes nor dominates and the human is neither diminished nor overwhelmed. Christ is fully human because he is fully divine.

Second, because this full and fulfilling communion is true of Christ, we realize it must also be true of God's relation to creation as a whole. That is, God is not the one above the many but the all in all. And that means creatures do not have to be less than themselves in order for God to be God any more than God has to be less than himself in order for creation to be creation. It is exactly the other way around, in fact. Happily, creation is itself just because God is God, the infinite generosity at the beginning, middle, and end of all things.

Third, Jesus is not to be regarded as the model of the Spirit-filled life but as the indwelling source of that life, more intimate with us than we are with ourselves. Jesus is not merely an exhibit of a type but is in and of himself the archetypal reality of life in the Spirit, and as we are in him and he is in us, that reality cannot not come alive in our lives. Therefore, we do not so much seek to do what he did as to let what he is doing happen in us. This is fully in keeping with the centrality of Jesus in traditional Pentecostal theology.

Fourth, given that the fullness of God is in Christ and the fullness of Christ is in us, life is lived always in the unchanging nearness of God. This remains true even though the divine presence is not always experienced as consoling or empowering—some experience nothing at all. But it is essential that we affirm God's constant presence and deny that he is sometimes near, sometimes far from us.

Finally, insofar as the above is true, salvation must take shape over time just by God sharing all of himself with us and we, in turn, sharing all of ourselves with him and one another. Salvation is communion. This is the heart of Wesleyan spirituality, and it requires us to believe that such communion, such interrelatedness, is possible. And I am convinced that a non-competitive, non-dualistic Spirit-Christology shows best how this is true.

11

Methodist Christology After Barth

John L. Drury

Methodist Christology after Barth is an impossible possibility. That is the overarching thesis of this essay. But first, in good Methodist fashion, a word of testimony.

The research for this essay began in the realm of the possible. When the editors of this volume asked me a while ago to write a constructive essay on Methodist Christology after Barth, I explored all sorts of interesting convergences between Barth's Christology and the sorts of Christology operative in the Methodist movement. It was informative, but boring. The boredom ceased only when it dawned on me that I was avoiding the deeper problem: that Barth's way of doing Christology thoroughly undercuts the Wesleyan way.[1] So a much more polemical essay emerged than was originally planned. Yet—thanks be to God—the impossibility of Methodist Christology after Barth is not the final word. Possibility remains—yet, in good dialectical fashion, only by passing through the impossibility. The possibility is only serious if we take seriously the impossibility. To do Methodist Christology after Barth, we must first hear the "Halt!" that Barth's Christology cries out in the wilderness. Hence the governing contention of this essay: Methodist Christology after Barth is an impossible possibility.

The argument for this contention is developed over nine theses. These theses can be grouped into three sets of three. The first three theses concern Methodist Christology in general. The next three explore what it means

---

1 For a whole host of reasons, I use the terms "Methodist" and "Wesleyan" interchangeably throughout this essay.

in general to do Christology "after Barth." And the last three bring these two perspectives into direct dialogue.

Methodist Christology

What is Methodist Christology? The very existence of this volume implies a need for clarification. But the clarification must begin with the noun itself. What do we mean by *Christology*?

The scope of Christology is ambiguous. When we say "Christology," what do we mean? Perhaps more than any other theological locus, Christology suffers from boundary confusion.[2] This need not be a problem, provided we specify our use in each case. Let's begin by identifying three senses of the term. The term Christology can be taken in its wide, its narrow, and its medial senses. We'll take our time with this, because each comes crucially into play in our argument.

The widest sense of Christology is simply Christ-talk. In its most diffuse sense, Christology names whatever persons say about Christ. Any and all talk of Christ is Christological discourse in this loose, wide sense. In this sense, Christology pops up all over a dogmatic system and, moreover, well beyond a dogmatic system. Christology is happening when people sing a song to Jesus, preach a sermon about Jesus, when they converse with Jesus in prayer. All of this is Christology in its wide sense.[3]

But there's also a narrow sense of Christology. Christology in its narrow

---

2 Aside from the word "theology" itself, perhaps its only competitor would be *eschatology*.

3 Note well that this is not an exclusively "theological" or even "Christian" sense of the term *Christology*. In fact, Christology in its wide sense includes Jewish discourse about the Messiah, Islamic doctrines about Jesus, and views of Jesus found in other religions as well as "secular" phenomenology of Jesus and Jesus-traditions. Concerning the problems and prospects of the latter in systematic theology, the works of Ernst Troeltsch remain a watershed worthy of our wrestling. Cf. the essays translated in Ernst Troeltsch, *Religion in History*, ed. James Luther Adams and Walter F. Bense (Minneapolis: Fortress Press, 2007) and in *Writings on Theology and Religion*, ed. Robert Morgan and Michael Pye (Louisville: Westminster/John Knox Press, 1990); and the book-length treatment of Sarah Coakley, *Christ Without Absolutes: A Study of the Christology of Ernst Troeltsch* (Oxford: Clarendon Press, 2003). As we shall see in thesis 3 below, critical appropriation of these methods may prove fruitful for the future development of Methodist Christology. And insofar as Troeltsch stands as the great alternative to Karl Barth in the history of modern theology, this footnote is no mere aside.

sense articulates the ontological constitution of Jesus. Who is Jesus? Or, more to the point: *What* is Jesus? What sort of *being* is Jesus? Christology in its narrowest sense thus engages in a kind of ontological reflection. Professional theologians often refer to this narrow sense as Christology proper. To contemporary ears, the term "proper" may imply an unintended value judgment. So, I've adopted the term "narrow."[4] But Christology in its narrow sense is quite straightforwardly the dogmatic chapter on Christ's person and natures. In classical dogmatics, this locus is then differentiated from the work of Christ. Now, as we shall see, Barth dialectically deflated the person/work distinction. So, for now, we are merely making a phenomenological point: that when theologians say "Christology," they may be using it in this narrow sense.

But there is a third sense of the term *Christology*, which will be indispensable for our argument. This third sense is roughly midway between the wide and narrow senses. Hence the name "medial." Christology in the medial sense corresponds to the whole second article of the creed. It is not as wide as just any and all talk of Christ. But it is also not as narrow as ontological reflection about Christ in abstraction from its wider context. Christology in the medial sense is inclusive of the whole Christ in his being and acting, and thus both his person and his work in their unity and totality. Depending on the theologian, Christology in this sense can even include ecclesiology—reflection on the body of Christ—and eschatology—reflection on the coming of Christ. And this medial sense is crucial for the task at hand because, as already noted, Barth dialectically deflated the person/work distinction, so much so that myopic attention to his Christology in the narrow sense will conceal more than it will reveal. Furthermore, as we shall see soon enough, Methodism makes its mark on Christology primarily in its medial sense.

Thesis 1: Methodism has no distinctive Christology.

Methodists do not have a distinctive Christology. And this applies to every sense of the term *Christology*: wide, narrow, and medial. In any of these

---

4 This may also imply a value judgment, but said judgment is (not un-)intended.

senses, Methodist Christology cannot be definitively distinguished from every other Christian Christology. Whether we regard this as a strength or a weakness of the Methodist tradition, it is a fact with which we must contend.

This is true for Christology in its wide sense. There are not any discernible statements about Jesus that set Methodism apart from every other Christian tradition. Methodist Christ-talk is wonderfully eclectic, and one can find all sorts of borrowings from a wide range of Christian traditions. Now, Methodism does have some distinctive ways of speaking. There is a whole range of lingo by which one can sniff out a Methodist. But these are mostly statements about the Christian life, not Christological statements even in the wide sense of the term.

This is also true for Christology in its narrow sense. Formally speaking, Methodist Christology for the most part inherited the classical tradition—and perhaps intentionally so. The Wesleys and their first companions received and handed on a Christological heritage mediated by way of Western developments in and through the Anglican tradition broadly conceived.[5] Periodic deviation from this tradition is the exception that proves the rule.[6] A review of the Articles of Religion in various pan-Methodist churches bear this out.[7] Furthermore, Methodist dogmatics have not developed a distinctively Methodist approach to the post-Reformation interpretive debates. There is no distinctively Wesleyan third option beyond the Lutheran and Reformed Christological positions. Rather, you'll see Methodist dogmaticians taking one side or the other.[8] So the phrase "Methodist Christology"

---

5   Although his sources and methods predate the more recent critical turn in Wesley Studies, Deschner's work still succeeds in corroborating that Wesley, broadly speaking, inherits a classical Christological tradition. See John Deschner, *Wesley's Christology: An Interpretation* (Dallas: Southern Methodist University Press, 1960; repr. Grand Rapids: Francis Asbury Press, 1988).

6   For example, Adam Clarke's idiosyncratic Christology did not become formally or materially normative ecclesially or academically.

7   For example: The Wesleyan Church, Articles of Religion, Article 3; United Methodist Church, Articles of Religion, Article II; Church of the Nazarene, Articles of Faith, Article II.

8   To take three examples, Pope, Miley, and Wiley discussed these options and locate themselves within the debate, but do not assert a *distinctively* Wesleyan option. See William Burt Pope, *A Compendium of Christian Theology*, vol. 2 (London: Beveridge, 1877), 106–39; John Miley,

is non-informative, at least in the sense of a distinctive Christology. Wesleyans are broadly Nicene and Chalcedonian, just like every other orthodox Christian.

Now, this fact can play out in widely divergent directions. Some Wesleyan theologians take our nondistinctive Christology in the narrow sense as an invitation to retrieval. This line of thinking goes something like this: We have inherited this tradition, we haven't paid a lot of attention to it, but ought to now. So, let us return to the sources of classical Christology in order to exposit our shared orthodox heritage.

Other Wesleyan theologians take our nondistinctive Christology as an invitation to revision. This line of thinking goes something like this: We have inherited this tradition, we haven't paid a lot of attention to it, and therefore we needn't regard ourselves as locked into it. So, let us roll up our sleeves and develop a new Christology, perhaps one that takes its cue from more distinctively Methodist doctrines and concepts.

At least on the surface, both of these can pitch themselves as Methodist, because if Methodism doesn't have a distinctive Christology in the narrow sense, a certain latitude seems to be implied. What neither can do is pitch their approach as the distinctive Methodist approach to Christology. Now, I have my own leanings, but those needn't distract us now. And more to the point, Barth was dialectically sympathetic to both of these directions. But to that we will return later. For now, suffice it to say that the Wesleyan tradition does not have a distinctive Christology in the narrow sense of the term.

But what about Christology in the medial sense? Surely Methodism has something distinctive to say here! Alas, not even here. For what characterizes Methodist Christology in the medial sense is not strictly speaking distinctive. But it is determinately characteristic—which brings us to our next thesis.

Systematic Theology, 2 vols. (New York: Hunt & Eaton; Cincinnati: Cranston & Stowe, 1892, 1894), pt. 4, esp. chaps. 3 and 5; H. Orton Wiley, *Christian Theology*, vol. 2 (Kansas City: Beacon Hill Press, 2013), chaps. 20–22.

Thesis 2: Methodism does have a characteristic Christology in the medial sense of the term: its thoroughgoing commitment to unlimited atonement.

If we take Christology in its medial sense, then we quickly discover a characteristic feature of Methodist Christology. Methodists are thoroughly committed to the doctrine of unlimited atonement. Christ died for all. Whatever their differences on other matters, Wesleyan theologians almost without exception proclaim that Christ died for all. Each and every human being is without exception the actual object of Christ's atoning death. There is considerable diversity in how the mechanics of atonement are conceived. But there is unity—nay, uniformity—on the matter of the scope of atonement. Atonement is for all. On this matter, Methodists speak with one voice.[9]

Here we can see the benefit of differentiating between three senses of Christology. As we saw, Methodist Christology in the narrow sense is derivative. But Methodist Christology in the medial sense is assertive. Whereas with regard to the ontology of the Savior's person, Methodists for the most part simply hand on what has been received; with regard to the scope of the Savior's work, Methodists consistently and vociferously defend the doctrine that Christ died for all without exception.[10]

Now, this does not mean that the doctrine of unlimited atonement is a distinctive Methodist doctrine. Methodists may very well be distinctively emphatic in our articulation of said doctrine. But Methodists are certainly not the only tradition committed to the claim that Christ died for all. So, unlike some of the finer points in the doctrine of sanctification, the doctrine of unlimited atonement is not one of our *distinctive* doctrines. Rather, it is a *characteristic*

---

9   Alas, proving a negative is difficult; but in all my years of study I have not found a single theologian in the Wesleyan tradition who does not emphatically affirm the doctrine of unlimited atonement. The evidence is so overwhelming that any contrary cases would amount to exceptions that prove the rule.

10 Again, it is worth noting that one might call into question a strict person/work distinction in Christology. But it is a useful heuristic at least when discerning that which constitutes a characteristically Methodist Christology. It may turn out that a thoroughgoing commitment to unlimited atonement invites particular developments concerning the being of the atoner. But no such developments currently characterize Methodist Christology. As we shall see, much of my own interest in Barth lies precisely along these lines.

doctrine of Methodism.[11] Methodist Christology can and should be rightly characterized by a thoroughgoing commitment to unlimited atonement.

A brief excursus on prevenient grace serves to corroborate this point. Wesleyans talk a lot about prevenient grace. We appeal to it often to solve theological puzzles.[12] One such puzzle is the eternal destiny of deceased infants. Now, it seems to me that we are right to appeal to prevenient grace in such a case. However, the appeal presupposes a commitment to unlimited atonement. For the Methodist view is certainly not that human beings as such are born good and/or that the divine being is in the abstract obliged to save each and every human. Rather, the doctrine of prevenient grace asserts that the atoning blood of Christ is efficaciously applied to those without sufficient light, including a deceased infant without the mediation of cognitive faith.[13] So the classically Wesleyan doctrine of prevenient grace is decisively not a matter of dealing with cases where the atonement doesn't apply, but rather articulating the variegated manner in which the atonement does apply to each and every case. So even the doctrine of prevenient grace, so beloved of Methodists, is bound up with and even rests upon the doctrine of unlimited atonement.

So, although there is no distinctive Methodist Christology, it does have at least one characteristic feature: a thoroughgoing commitment to unlimited atonement. But beyond this particular feature, Methodist Christology also has a more general orientation that must be articulated.

---

11 I learned this distinction between distinctive and characteristic doctrines from years of delightful dialogue with Jason Vickers. It comes to expression in print via his essay entitled "American Methodism: A Theological Tradition," in Jason E. Vickers, ed., *The Cambridge Companion to American Methodism* (Cambridge University Press, 2013), 9–43.

12 We even occasionally mistake it for a distinctive doctrine. But just like unlimited atonement, prevenient grace is not a distinctive Methodist doctrine. In fact, prevenient grace may be even more widely held, since the prevenience of grace is taught by the selfsame Reformed theologians who assert the doctrine of limited atonement. Perhaps it is distinctive of Wesleyans to appeal ad nauseum to the doctrine of prevenient grace. But that very appeal is a function of responding to Calvinist polemics. The appeal only works if prevenient grace is a shared doctrine, which it is.

13 The connection between prevenient grace and Christ's atoning work appears throughout Wesley's work but can be seen especially clearly in his discussion of sin improperly so-called in chapter 6 of his "Plain Account of Christian Perfection" in *Doctrinal and Controversial Treatises II*, ed. Paul Wesley Chilcote and Kenneth J. Collins, vol. 13 of *The Works of John Wesley* (Nashville: Abingdon Press, 2012). Here and elsewhere Wesley was abundantly clear that even sin improperly so-called is still in need of the atoning blood of Christ.

Thesis 3: The spirit of Methodist Christology consists in its orientation toward transformative praxis.

Up to this point in our analysis, we have attended to Methodist Christology according to the letter. And rightly so, for there is no shame in performing the hermeneutical task of dogmatics, which may and must attend to the letter of church teaching. But precisely as with a hermeneutical task, we must attend not only to the letter but also to the spirit. What is the *Spirit* of Methodist Christology? What does Methodist Christology not only say but *do*? What is its *power*? What is at its *heart*?

Again, we are not searching for a distinctive—something that would set apart Methodist Christology from every other Christology.[14] But we are also not looking for a particular doctrinal assertion, such as the doctrine of unlimited atonement. Rather, we are asking after the spirit of Methodist Christ-talk. The spirit of Methodist Christology consists in its orientation toward transformative praxis.

Besides its distinctive and characteristic doctrines, Wesleyan theology is marked by a consistent pattern of explicitly linking Christian doctrine to the transformation of actual Christians. In keeping with its revivalist roots, there is a recurring expectation among Methodists from the Wesleys through to today that Christian doctrine ought to itself be a means of grace for its recipients. For Methodists, dogmatics is always catechetical. Not only that, but Christian doctrines ought to be exposited and even evaluated in terms of their practical significance in the transformation of people. In fact, this Wesleyan spirit in large measure accounts for the fact that the most distinctive Wesleyan doctrines concern those matters that bear directly on transformative praxis: regeneration and sanctification. But this spirit impacts all Methodist theologizing. Even at its most technical and abstract, Wesleyan theology consistently explicates Christian doctrine in relation to transformative praxis. And this applies no less in Christology.

What makes a Christology Methodist is above all its orientation toward transformative praxis. A Christology that corresponds to the letter of

---

14   In fact, when it comes to its practical orientation, Methodism may simply be a species of Pietism.

Methodist doctrine but fails to make at least some connection to the lived reality of human beings encountering the living Christ has contravened the spirit of Methodist Christology. Such a connection can play out in various ways: perhaps by elevating the life and teaching of Jesus as constitutive elements within Christology; perhaps by speculating on the embodiment of the image of God in Jesus; perhaps by tracing the sacramental relation between Christ as head and the church as his body. Amid wide variation in expositional strategy, the orientation toward transformative praxis is the beating heart of Methodist Christology.

Herein lies a great temptation. Sin is crouching at the door. For a case could be made that ignoring Christology altogether is the natural consequence of this practical orientation. As those who care first and foremost about the formation of individuals, why distract ourselves with medieval metaphysics of the mediator? Why not simply take the contemporary experience of Jesus as the jumping-off point to talk about ourselves? Now, I believe this to be an utterly unconvincing argument. But it is a very Methodist argument to make. There's something true to the spirit of Methodism to raise the objection. The objection can and should be answered. But it can and should be answered precisely in a manner consistent with the spirit of Methodism. The short version goes something like this: It is integral and indispensable to the transformation of humans that said humans grow in the knowledge of the divine-human person who transforms us. We needn't expand the argument, for it suffices to say that the case can be made. But we must acknowledge that it is near and dear to the heart of Methodist Christology to be oriented above all to transformative praxis. Our deepest aversion is to a doctrine that is dead. Only a living doctrine will do.[15] We demand a Christology that lives and enlivens! In other words, Methodist Christology is fundamentally a revivalist Christology.

---

15 John Wesley himself pressed this point very far in his late sermon, "On Living Without God," found in *Sermons IV: 115–151*, ed. Albert C. Outler, vol. 4 of *The Works of John Wesley* (Nashville: Abingdon Press, 1987). I am very thankful to Patrick Eby for pointing this out to me.

Christology After Barth

Having articulated one partner in the dialogue, it is high time to articulate the second. What does it mean to do Christology after Barth? We begin again with some terminological clarification. To do x "after" y is prima facie ambiguous. To do x "after" y can be taken in three senses: subsequent to y, consequent upon y, and transcendent beyond y. So, formally speaking, to do Christology after Barth in the *subsequent* sense is to simply be doing Christology in his historical wake: more or less impacted by Barth, more or less aware of him, and more or less responding to him. However, to do Christology after Barth in the *consequent* sense is to do Christology with the express intention of following his lead: taking seriously Barth's objections to one's own way of doing Christology, incorporating insights from his theology in general and/or his Christology in particular, and perhaps even taking on board his orienting concern(s). Finally, to do Christology after Barth in the *transcendent* sense is to develop a Christology that moves not only through but beyond Barth: connecting yet correcting him, embracing yet expanding him, respecting yet revising him. In each of these senses one may be rightly described as doing Christology "after Barth." Equipped with this formal distinction, let's now explore what it means materially to do Christology after Barth.

Thesis 4: To do Christology after Barth, one must attend to the apocalyptic character of Christology.

Our Christology is after Barth first and foremost because we cannot responsibly ignore the apocalyptic character of Christology. This applies to any of the three senses of "after" outlined in thesis 3. Even those most remotely related to Barth's theology cannot avoid the fundamental revolution in Christology that took place a century ago in which Barth played a/ the crucial role. Whatever we say about Christ today, we must pay attention to the apocalyptic character of Christ's life and teaching and its implications for our own lives and teachings.

Note well: I do not refer here merely to the apocalyptic character of Barth's Christology, but primarily to the apocalyptic character of Christology as such. Barth did not invent apocalyptic Christology. Rather, apocalyptic Christology invented Barth. And apocalyptic Christology in turn was not invented but discovered. At the turn of the twentieth century, Weiss, Wrede, and Schweitzer articulated the "thoroughgoing eschatology" of Jesus's own teaching and expectation. Jesus lived and taught in view of a coming apocalypse and interpreted his own existence in these terms. Now, for these men and their generation, this spelled the end of Jesus's theological significance. Christian theology in its classically liberal mode simply could not abide, let alone be built upon, a Jewish apocalyptic prophet. Although attempts at mediation continued for a few decades, they were conceptually doomed, for an apocalyptic Jesus is no friend to bourgeois family values. But whatever hopes remained were dashed by the event of the Great War, which exposed the rot at the heart of colonialist Christendom.

Enter Karl Barth. The epochal significance of Barth and his erstwhile companions lies precisely in their embrace of an apocalyptic Christology. Instead of trying to build a positive theology on the historical Jesus, they let him apocalyptically shatter their entire theological edifice. If Schweitzer et al. uncovered the apocalyptic character of Jesus's own Christology, it was Barth et al. who rendered the apocalyptic attitude normative for Christian theology. For Barth, the apocalypse that is Jesus Christ just is the engine that both crucifies and resurrects our God-talk. This is the heart of the breakthrough that comes to literary expression in his Romans commentary.[16]

What does this look like in detail? To use one of Barth's favorite images, theology is always trying to paint a bird in flight.[17] There is a cer-

---

16 For example, the justly famous tangent/circle passage in Karl Barth, *The Epistle to the Romans*, trans. Edwyn C. Hoskyns (London: Oxford University Press, 1933), 30: "The Resurrection is the revelation: the disclosing of Jesus as the Christ, the appearing of God, the apprehending of God in Jesus. . . . In the Resurrection the new world of the Holy Spirit touches the old world of the flesh, but touches it as a tangent touches a circle, that is, without touching it. . . . The Resurrection is therefore an occurrence in history. . . . But inasmuch as the occurrence was conditioned by the Resurrection . . . the Resurrection is not an event in history at all." See also Barth, 202–7.

17 Barth famously deployed this image in his crucial 1919 Tambach Lecture entitled "The Christian's Place in Society," the best translation of which can be found in Karl Barth, *The Word of God and Theology*, trans. and ed. Amy Marga (London: T&T Clark, 2011). For the image, see pages 42 and 43. It appears again at the end of his career in Karl Barth, *Evangelical Theology: An Introduction*, trans. Grover Foley (New York: Holt, Rinehart, and Winston, 1964), 9.

tain fixity necessary for theological statements—fixity of reference, fixity of sense, fixity of entailment. But the very subject matter of theology utterly disrupts this fixity. The disruption can be (misleadingly) narrated from God's side or from ours. From God's side, the total alterity of God vis-à-vis creation renders all our creaturely God-talk inherently instable. From our side, the total depravity of the human renders all our God-talk self-serving and so suspect. Again, these are familiar but misleading narrations. These two statements are true, but in themselves one-sided.[18] Yet they cannot be synthesized into a proper whole by us without denying their truth—for even these two statements are subject to the disruption they attempt to narrate. How can we bring to speech the very disruption of our speech?

Here we can see why Christology occupies the center of Barth's theology. For it is in Jesus Christ that the very apocalypse of God takes place. In the crucified and risen Jesus, the disruption of all our God-talk is enacted. And in the selfsame crucified and risen Jesus, the disruption of all our God-talk is overcome. It is precisely in the apocalyptic event of Jesus that theology is punishingly pressed up against its limit, and thereby powerfully pressed into the service of witness. This is what Barth called the *Realdialektik* of Revelation. God's unveiling of Godself occurs precisely in and through the veiling of Godself in the crucified flesh of Jesus. The site in which God is definitively encountered is the very site in which God is the most opposed, unavailable, hidden to us. The revelation of God's being for us occurs in the mode of Godforsaken godlessness. And the unveiling of this veiling in the risen flesh of Jesus does not remove the creaturely veil. Even in the resurrection Christ remains human, and

---

18 Among the many reasons why these two narrations mislead is that neither is remotely original to Barth. The epistemic problematic generated by the infinite distinction between creator and creature was well known to the ancients and developed with systematic precision by the medievals. And the epistemic problematic generated by the total depravity of fallen humanity was discerned by every Augustinian theologian worthy of the name and vigorously deployed by Reformation theology. As we shall see, Barth's epochal significance lies not merely in the emphatic recovery of these old insights but primarily in their radically apocalyptic Christological concentration.

so even in the resurrection God's being-revealed occurs by way of a being-concealed.[19]

Christology in its properly apocalyptic key lives and moves and has its being within this inescapable *Realdialektik*. And I say that not merely as a piece of Barth interpretation. I have sketched this insight in the idiom of Barth's (in)famous doctrine of revelation. We are not obliged to endorse his idiosyncratic epistemology of theology to take heed of the exegetical insight at its heart. For Barth has in fact stumbled onto a crucial insight. This dialectic of revelation is operative on nearly every page of scripture, but especially in New Testament Christological discourse. To take just one example, consider the number of resurrection appearance narratives in which Christ's own do not recognize him until they do, at which point he immediately sends them away and/or removes himself. Once you see it, you can't unsee it. So even if one rejects many of Barth's moves (as I do), one cannot ignore the apocalyptic character of New Testament Christology. On this matter, a century of historical research into early Christianity has not repudiated but rather reinforced this basic insight. And on this matter, I count myself an unrepentant Barthian.

To do Christology after Barth in any sense of the term means taking responsibility for the fact that all our God-talk, with all our Christ-talk at its center, stands under this apocalyptic sword of Damocles. "As ministers we ought to speak of God. We are human, however, and so cannot speak of God. We ought therefore to recognize both our obligation and our inability and by that very recognition give God the glory."[20] Even the slightest awareness of the New Testament means that the conceptual containment that constitutes Christology is called into question. Christ reveals himself.

---

19 The central insight is operative throughout Barth's career, and can be easily traced from the *Romans Commentary* throughout his *Church Dogmatics*, 4 vols. in 13 parts (Edinburgh: T&T Clark, 1956–69, 1975); hereafter cited as *CD*, from its beginning (e.g., *CD* §14) to its ending (e.g., *CD* §69). Despite what the textbooks say, Barth never ceased to be a dialectical theologian even as he developed a more dogmatic approach. On this matter, the definitive study remains Bruce L. McCormack, *Karl Barth's Critically Realistic Dialectical Theology: Its Genesis and Development 1909–1936* (Oxford: Oxford University Press, 2004).

20 Barth, *The Word of God and Theology*, 195.

And so, our concepts are answerable to him. This does not mean that we do not do the conceptual work of Christology. But all such work is destabilized by the livingness of God in Jesus Christ. As Barth soon discovered, doing dogmatics under this sign is a nearly impossible task. But only those who labor under this sign are liberated to do responsible dogmatics.[21] For the very possibility of doing Christology lies precisely in the place where it is rendered impossible.

Thesis 5: To do Christology after Barth in the consequent sense, one must embrace his Christocentric doctrine of election.

Although Barth's doctrine of revelation is the key to his whole theological development, his revised doctrine of election is the key to his mature theology. Sometime in the late 1930s, Barth had another breakthrough. This was decidedly not a break away from his previous apocalyptic insight; rather, it was a breakthrough within his ongoing development of that insight. Barth did not cease to be a dialectical theologian when he became a dogmatic theologian. In fact, even during the 1920s he was experimenting with ways of doing dogmatics within a dialectical frame. Soon after his apocalyptic break with liberalism, Barth was turning his attention to Christology and Pneumatology as the key to doing dialectical dogmatics. But it was his revised doctrine of election that truly centered his theology. From then on, Barth became a properly Christocentric theologian.[22]

How so? According to Barth's revised doctrine of election, Jesus Christ not only reveals God's eternal will to be with us but also is God's eternal will to be with us. And this is because Jesus Christ, truly God and truly

---

21 At the end of the above-cited essay, Barth confessed that perhaps theology could only ever be prolegomena, which in turn would be centered on Christology (198). Although he soon found a way past this counsel of despair, he never ceased to identify Jesus Christ as the condition for the possibility of doing theology.

22 The plot of this story told here exposes a great irony of recent academic theology. Barth's Christocentrism is constantly criticized in favor of a more balanced Word-and-Spirit approach, as if such an option didn't occur to him and as if such an option didn't in fact structure nearly two decades of his theological development. Barth tried this approach and then deliberatively chose to abandon it. Perhaps he was mistaken, but he had his reasons. Have we seriously attended to those reasons? If not, then we must ask ourselves whether this line of revision is merely a regression to an earlier Barthian position, rather than a genuine advance beyond it.

human, is both the subject and the object of election. First and foremost, God is the one who from and to all eternity elects himself to be God with us in Jesus Christ. And simultaneously God elects us to be with him in Jesus Christ. Jesus Christ is both the electing God—the God who chooses himself to be with us and chooses us to be with him—and the elected human—the human being whom God chooses and who in response chooses God—in one person. This multilayered but singular act is an act of divine self-determination. God eternally determines himself to be the God he is in Jesus Christ. Thus, both the deity and humanity of Jesus are constitutive of his identity as the second person of the Trinity from and to all eternity. Jesus is the "Lamb slain from [before] the foundation of the world" (Rev. 13:8 KJV). Jesus is the beloved one in whom we were chosen (see Eph. 1:4–6). Jesus is the Word that was with God and was God in the beginning, who in time became flesh and dwelled among us; and we have beheld his glory, glory as of an only son, full of grace and truth (see John 1:14). This glory, this revelation, this making-known of the eternal God is an utterly new apocalyptic event. And yet it is an event that makes manifest the eternal truth and grace of God.[23]

Here we can see that the epistemological revolution of Barth's apocalyptic doctrine of revelation finds its ontological basis in Barth's Christocentric doctrine of election. We can trust the revelation of God in Jesus Christ because the eternal will of God just is Jesus Christ. The correspondence between God in himself and God for us is no blind faith or vain hope, but rather the very story and substance of the gospel itself. Without ceasing to be utterly dialectical, the apocalypse of God does not leave us suspended in midair but directs our attention to the history of the covenant fulfilled in Jesus the Messiah. The election of Jesus, the election of the community, and the election of individuals—this unfolding of election in time is the very revelation of God's eternal act of self-determination in Jesus Christ. So, we can say with humble boldness that God is from and to all eternity a human God. Now, this does not mean that the Incarnation didn't take place at a

---

23 In this paragraph as well as in the next, I am attempting to summarize the whole of *CD* §§32–35.

particular place and time in our human history. But it does mean that that particular event is the very enactment of the singular event of God's choosing himself for us and us for himself in his Son Jesus Christ.[24]

Now, it should be clear at this point that Barth's revised doctrine of election has massive material implications for the development of an entire dogmatic system. According to this doctrine of election, no theological statement stands outside the impact of Christology. All God-talk is determined by Christ-talk, because God has determined himself in Christ. On this account, it is irresponsible (both epistemically and ontologically) to speak of God in abstraction from Christ. Even the doctrine of creation must come under Christological control. And that is precisely what we see in the immediately subsequent volume of the *Church Dogmatics* (III/1–4). Therefore, to do any theological work after Barth in the consequent sense requires that one embrace Barth's revised doctrine of election.

This applies above all to Christology. One cannot do Christology consequent to Barth without embracing his doctrine of election. Barth spent the last decade of his professoriate developing a robustly Christocentric Christology.[25] Now, the phrase "Christocentric Christology" may seem redundant. But, alas, so little Christology takes its bearings from the apocalypse of God in Jesus Christ. Rather, so much Christology (in the narrow sense of the term) brings in from elsewhere a conception of deity and a conception of humanity and then asks how these two can both be predicated of Jesus Christ. Barth invites us to turn that procedure on its head: to define true deity and true humanity on the basis of the story of Jesus. Because, according to his revised doctrine of election, Jesus Christ doesn't just *have* true deity and true humanity, but in fact *is* the truth of deity and the truth of humanity.

The same goes for Christology in the medial sense of the term. Barth tried his best to ensure that our conceptions of Christ's work are filled out

---

24 Barth here borrows the *logos incarnandus* concept from the Protestant Scholastics: the eternal Son is not always already a creature, but he is always already the one who was going to become a creature.

25 *CD* IV/1–4.

in terms of the actual life history of Jesus Christ. And this means that Christ's temptations, teachings, miracles, and missionary existence are constitutive of Christology, rather than mere appendages to the atonement.[26] It also means that the nature and scope of Christ's atoning work cannot be restricted by the syllogistic entailments of divine sovereignty and/or human responsibility considered in abstraction from Christ as the one true living God and the one true living human.[27] Finally, it means that even the transition from Christ's own life history to our own is enacted by Christ himself in his risen life.[28] At each and every point, Barth attempted to think through the problems of Christology in terms of the revolutionary insight articulated in his Christocentric doctrine of election. If one wishes to do Christology after Barth in the consequent sense, one must embrace this very insight.

Thesis 6: To do Christology that transcends Barth, one must become more thoroughly ecumenical.

But what about those of us who wish to learn from Barth but then move beyond him? Are we simply compelled to repeat his own Christology? Is the fourth volume of the *Church Dogmatics* the only way to do Christology after Barth? The launching pad for transcending Barth may be found in the ecumenical intention of his mature Christology. In *Church Dogmatics* IV, Barth deployed a tripartite structure with the express intention of staging a critical dynamic synthesis of the Christian traditions known to him. To do Christology after Barth in the transcendent sense of the term requires one to become far more receptive to a wider range of sources and styles both past and present. And this would almost certainly require a revision in the basic structure of Christology. In what follows, I will first survey this structure before identifying its blind spots.

Barth's mature Christology unfolds according to a three-part structure (see figure 1). Each part is designed to incorporate the themes of different

---

26 Cf. esp. *CD* §64.3 and §69.3.

27 Cf. esp. *CD* §59.2 and §71.2.

28 This is the basic structure of the argument of the "transitional sub-sections" of *CD* 4: §59.3, §64.4, and §69.4.

voices in Christian scripture and tradition in correlation with the various aspects within Christology. The first part develops the Pauline theme of the *descent* of Christ—the downward movement of God to the human (chapter 14). The second part develops the Lukan theme of the *ascent* of Christ—the upward movement of the human to God (chapter 15). And the third part develops the Johannine theme of the *glory* of Christ—the forward movement of the God-human (chapter 16). Barth correlates these three parts with the three basal elements of Christology in the narrow sense: true deity, true humanity, one person. Barth further correlates these three parts with the threefold office of Christ: priestly, royal, and prophetic. And this entire development is explicitly designed to give voice to three clusters of Christian tradition: the magisterial Protestant emphasis on justification by faith; the monastic, Anabaptist, Pietist, and Methodist emphasis on sanctification through love; and the modern missiological emphasis on vocation in hope.

What should immediately strike the reader is the beautiful breadth of Barth's vision. He neither ignored nor conflated these three sets of voices, but rather leveraged his dialectical imagination toward a critical dynamic synthesis of these three streams of Christian thinking and living. And he did so at a structural level, so that the ecumenical engagement is not mere window dressing but built into the very architecture of his Christology. Those of us who wish to do Christology after Barth in the sense of moving with and beyond him would be wise to adopt such a substantive structural strategy for listening to the voices of others.

What also immediately strikes the reader is the disappointing dearth of marginalized voices. Barth has gathered the usual suspects: the Reformers, the Romans, and the Revisionists. What is utterly necessary in our time is a radical expansion of sources, streams, and styles of theology. Barth has for the most part ignored the Eastern Churches in this schema. And the voices of the Global South were only beginning to be heard in Barth's time, but we in our time are without excuse. To do Christology after Barth in the sense of transcending him requires that we engage in a far more radical ecumenism than he ever dreamed of.

But how? How might we develop a critical dynamic synthesis of global Christology? Precisely by adopting Barth's structural strategy yet by adapting to a more rigorously global ecumenism. Now, I am far from ready to propose a fully developed alternative structure. But I can suggest one experimental possibility. It would be inspired by the original threefold movement of Christianity into Africa, Asia, and Europe. A triad could be developed within each, forming an ennead. The first triad could draw on different themes from both ancient and modern African Christianity. The second triad could do the same from both ancient and modern Asian Christianity. And the third triad could be a version of Barth's own triadic Christology, reshaped in light of the themes of Latin American Christianity. Again, this is just an experiment, intended to demonstrate the possibility of a global Christology after Barth. My primary hope under this thesis is that catching the breadth of Barth's Christological vision will inspire us to broaden our horizons far beyond his limitations.

Figure 1. The Architectonic of Barth's Doctrine of Reconciliation (CD IV).[29]

	Chapter 14 (IV/1)	Chapter 15 (IV/2)	Chapter 16 (IV/3)
Chapter Title	"Jesus Christ, the Lord as Servant"	"Jesus Christ, the Servant as Lord"	"Jesus Christ, the True Witness"
Idiom (Dialogue Partner)	Pauline (Magisterial Protestant)	Synoptic (Monastic/ Methodist)	Johannine (Modern/ Missiological)
Perspective	⇩ God Humbled	Man Exalted ⇧	➡ God-Man Revealed ➡

---

29 Originating from E. Jüngel, *Karl Barth, a Theological Legacy*, trans. G. E. Paul (Philadelphia: Westminster, 1986), 48–49, revised in light of Daniel Migliore's unpublished handout, and further revised by me in accordance with my dissertation research published in John Drury, *The Resurrected God: Karl Barth's Trinitarian Theology of Christ's Resurrection* (Philadelphia: Fortress, 2014).

	Chapter 14 (IV/1)	Chapter 15 (IV/2)	Chapter 16 (IV/3)
Christology	"The Obedience of the Son of God" (§59)	"The Exaltation of the Son of Man" (§64)	"The Glory of the Mediator" (§69)
Subject Incarnate Person of Christ	*Deity*: "The Way of the Son of God into the Far Country" (§59.1)	*Humanity*: "The Homecoming of the Son of Man" (§64.2)	*Unity*: "The Light of Life" (§69.2)
Act Reconciling Work of Christ	*Priest*: "The Judge Judged in Our Place" (§59.2)	*King*: "The Royal Human" (§64.3)	*Prophet*: "Jesus Is Victor" (§69.3)
Goal Christ's Resurrection as Transition	*Raising*: "The Verdict of the Father" (§59.3)	*Arising*: "The Direction of the Son" (§64.4)	*Parousia*: "The Promise of the Spirit" (§69.4)
Sin	Pride & Fall (§60)	Sloth & Misery (§65)	Falsehood & Condemnation (§70)
Soteriology	Justification (§61)	Sanctification (§66)	Vocation (§71)
Pneumatology: Community: Individual:	Awakening Gathering (§62) Faith (§63)	Quickening Up-Building (§67) Love (§68)	Enlightening Sending (§72) Hope (§73)
Chapter 17 (IV/4): Ethics	Foundation: Baptism (§75)	Fulfillment: Lord's Prayer (§76–8)	Renewal: Lord's Supper

Methodist Christology After Barth

It is high time for us to place Methodist Christology and Barth in direct dialogue. Of course, we've already done much of the work implicitly above by simply placing the two next to each other. The dissonances and resonances, the problems and prospects, the hopes and fears—these are all bubbling just beneath the surface. But now they must burst forth. And so, let us bring this conversation to a close with three final theses, which together substantiate the main thesis of this essay: that Methodist Christology after Barth is an impossible possibility.

Thesis 7: The apocalyptic character of Christology disrupts Methodist Christology in both its retrievalist and its revisionist modes.

To do Methodist Christology after Barth, we must wrestle with our classical Christological inheritance. We cannot simply take for granted an orthodox Christology, as if such matters can be assumed without further articulation. Too much has happened in our own Methodist history, let alone the wider history of the church, to assume all is well here and move on. We must engage with this heritage directly.

Furthermore, we must engage the Christological heritage not only directly but also dialectically. We cannot simply repeat old Christological formulae, just asserting that it has always been there. The apocalypse of God in the story of Jesus places a question mark around any such easy orthodoxy, for knowledge of God dispossesses us of our confidence in any "always been there." To know God in Christ is to know God not as a mere given but as a giving. And so even the best of Methodist retrievalism must begin again and again at the beginning with the living God known in the face of the living Jesus Christ, crucified and risen.

However, the dialectic cuts both directions. We must wrestle with our classical Christological inheritance with the hopeful expectation that it will prevail over us! The apocalyptic character of Christology, at least as discerned and developed by Barth, does not permit an unbridled revisionism any more than an untroubled retrievalism. For the severe limitations of human knowledge of God apply first and foremost to us! And so, we have no reason to expect that our ingenuity in divine things is any better than our forebears. In fact, we have reason to expect ours to be worse. And so, the dogmatic tradition is always the basis of theological reflection, including especially Christological reflection.

This is one of the many reasons why we should continue to dialogue with Barth. For Barth's critical stance toward the classical Christological heritage cannot be dismissed as revisionist liberalism. His respect for and embrace of Christian tradition is far too deep. Rather, Barth stands as a sign of the living self-development of the Christian tradition. Barth's revisions are always placed in the hermeneutical and even homiletical context of saying the old in a new way. In this we would be wise to heed his example, even if we do not embrace his every proposed revision.[30]

Thus, we can see the first layer of the impossible possibility of doing Methodist Christology after Barth. It is impossible for Methodist theologians to continue to take for granted the classic Christological dogma as a given. Yet it is also impossible for Methodist theologians to discard that very given in favor of our own idiosyncratic innovations. It is precisely in the face of this impossibility that we encounter the possibility of Christology, which rests not in us but in God alone, who has made himself known in the dying and rising of Jesus, who calls us to him and sends us out to speak responsibly of him in the church to the world. When we do Christology, we may and must do it under the weight of this responsibility. But we really may and must do it!

Thesis 8: Methodist Christology's characteristic commitment to unlimited atonement is radically affirmed by Barth yet grounded in such a totally other doctrine of election so as to be unrecognizably Methodist.

In doing Christology after Barth, Methodists find a powerful ally on at least one front. Barth is one of the few theologians who can compete with Wesleyans in terms of a thoroughgoing commitment to unlimited atonement. This makes him especially unique among his fellow Reformed theologians.

---

30 A classic example of this sort of respectful revision of classical conceptualities can be found in *CD* IV/2, §64.2. See especially the meta-commentary on page 106.

And so, unlike the previous thesis, we begin here with possibility. It seems quite possible that a Methodist Christology could draw from otherwise foreign Barthian wells in the development of a rigorous articulation of this beautiful doctrine. We might even find fresh ways of reading scriptural texts, appropriating ancient traditions, and constructing rational arguments in support of this doctrine.

However, the possibilities here run up against a troubling impossibility, for his doctrine of unlimited atonement is embedded within his doctrine of election. Although his doctrine of election is a sharp break within his Calvinist and Reformed tradition, it is nevertheless a break *within* that tradition. Barth remains a supralapsarian in Christology, such that the whole history of God with us occurs within the one eternal covenant fulfilled in the dying and rising of Jesus. This remains a discourse foreign to Wesleyan ways of thinking.[31] Of course, we do have a doctrine of election; but the concept of foreknown faith plays such a crucial part that embracing Barth's doctrine of election would require a total overhaul. Divine foreknowledge notwithstanding, Methodist Christology is overall structured to take the created image of God as our starting point, such that Jesus is the restoration of an original design that enables the fulfillment of an original intention. For Barth, even creation is an event ordered by the covenant.[32] The precedence of creation is only chronological according to Barth. So, despite our deep concurrence on the unlimited scope of the atonement, a genuine rapprochement between Methodist Christology and Barth seems next to impossible. The only live options seem to be the lopping off of Barth's arguments from their larger systematic context or locating Methodist doctrine within a form of thought so foreign that it ceases to be Methodist.

This is the second layer of the impossible possibility of Methodist

---

31 Wesley and the early Methodists did make use of "covenantal" themes and practices; but that is a far cry from the ontological priority of the covenant within Barth's theology. There is an essay by my wife's husband that speaks more to this issue, entitled "Promise and Command: Wesley and Barth on Matthew 5:48," in W. Travis McMaken and David Congdon, eds., *Karl Barth in Conversation* (Eugene, OR: Cascade Press, 2014).

32 Cf. esp. *CD* III/1, §41.3.

Christology after Barth. On the one hand, he is a great non-Wesleyan ally for our ongoing development of the great Wesleyan doctrine of unlimited atonement. On the other hand, his version of this doctrine is so deeply rooted in his doctrine of election that we may cease to be Methodist if we take it on board. And so here we are faced with a choice: either converse with Barth as an ally, knowing full well the temptation of his thoughtform to wreak havoc on ours; or set Barth aside, knowing that doing so means abandoning one of the greatest defenders of unlimited atonement in the entire Christian tradition. Neither option seems wise, hence the impossibility. The only possibility that remains is to labor under the hope that the choice is not in fact as stark as it seems.

Thesis 9: The Methodist orientation toward transformative praxis can find an unlikely ally in Barth.

As argued above, the spirit of Methodist Christology consists in its orientation toward transformative praxis. Contrary to much received wisdom, Barth was not absolutely opposed to such an orientation. All of Barth's thought flowed from and to praxis. He was deeply critical of a static objectivism in theology, whether in classical scholastic or in modern liberal form. The subject matter of theology is always the living God encountering living humans. And the space of theology is always the living church bearing witness in a living world. In this highly specified sense, Barth was an existential theologian. He was not merely cataloguing doctrines and unfolding syllogisms, but rather *practicing* missionary faithfulness under the aspect of critically reflective speech.[33] Thus Barth is an ally to Methodism in its fight against dead dogma and in its fight for a praxis-embedded dogmatic enterprise.[34]

---

33 This commitment is expressed in the opening *Leitsatz* of the *CD*: "As a theological discipline dogmatics is the scientific self-examination of the Christian Church with respect to the content of its distinctive talk about God" (§1 [*CD* I/1, 3]). A particularly striking development of this is Barth's decision to locate theology as the sixth of twelve practices of the Christian community's service in *CD* §72.4 (IV/3.2, 879–82).

34 Barth famously united dogmatics and ethics in his *CD*. In this paragraph I am attempting to sketch a picture of Barth between two opposing interpretations of this unity: one that claims that if we just get our dogmatics right, the ethics will naturally follow, and another that claims that ethics are necessary to get our dogmatics right. Barth believed neither of these things,

However, for all his existentiality, Barth remained doggedly determined against any theology based on experience. For the praxis at the center of Barth's thought is divine praxis—or, more precisely, the divine-human praxis enacted in Jesus Christ. According to Barth, we may and must again and again take our bearings from this singular event. This Christo-centric actualism critically distances itself from not only static objectivism but also experiential subjectivism. And so, Barth's entire project cuts against the Wesleyan orientation toward praxis, at least as it is usually conceived.

But could the Wesleyan orientation toward transformative praxis be conceived otherwise? Could it be that at its best Methodist theology draws from human experience precisely because of its orientation toward the divine praxis of the Holy Spirit? Could it be that Barth's late-career olive branch to Schleiermacher could be offered as well to the Wesleyan tradition?[35] And could this not in turn be fruitful for Methodist Christology after Barth, in which we take seriously that the work of the Holy Spirit in our lives today just is the living encounter with the risen Jesus Christ, who is our justification and sanctification? Perhaps precisely on this question of the relation between theology and practice we will discover the most mutually fruitful encounter between Barthian and Wesleyan habits of thought. For in the end, we share a childlike wonder at the amazing love of God in Christ, and wish our theological explorations to be in service of that wonder, rather than the other way around. And so, despite genuine impossibilities on this and many other fronts, Methodist Christology after Barth is a possibility worthy of ongoing exploration.[36]

---

because he conceived of dogmatics as itself an ecclesial practice that is before but never independent of ethics.

35 During retirement Barth commented that Schleiermacher's *Glaubenslehre* could be charitably read as a theology of the third article, rather than reducing it to a phenomenology of human religious experience. Karl Barth, "Concluding Unscientific Postscript on Schleiermacher," trans. George Hunsinger, *Studies in Religion* 7, no. 2 (1978): 117–35.

36 I am exceedingly grateful to editors of this volume for their initial input into this essay and to Bud Bence, Keith Drury, and Patrick Eby for their feedback on an earlier form of this essay; alas, any remaining errors of style, of fact, or of judgment are all mine.

12

Methodist Christology After Oden

Justus H. Hunter

I n a programmatic essay on canonical theism, William Abraham gives a litany of theologians "hard at work refurbishing and replenishing the intellectual treasures of the church."[1] But only one is a Methodist: Thomas C.
Oden. Indeed, no scholar of the last Methodist generation pursued theological retrieval more aggressively, and more successfully, than he. Today's
retrieval projects in Methodist theology are fortunate to set out *after* Oden.

Thomas C. Oden was born in Altus, Oklahoma, on October 21, 1931,
to a pious Methodist family, his father a lawyer and his mother a music
teacher. After graduate degrees at Perkins School of Theology at Southern Methodist University in Dallas, Texas, and Yale Divinity School, Oden
taught, briefly at Perkins, then for a decade at Phillips Graduate Seminary
in Enid, Oklahoma, before joining the faculty of Drew University in Madi-
son, New Jersey, from 1970 to 2003. Over the course of his career, he published more than fifty books. Most significantly, he served as the general
editor for the thirty-volume Ancient Christian Commentary on Scripture.

Beginning early in his appointment to Drew, Oden's theology was a theology of retrieval. But what sort of retrieval? He repeatedly asserted that
he sought to teach nothing new. His memoir hinges on a transition, provoked by a dream: "In the season of Epiphany 1971 I had a curious dream
in which I was in the New Haven cemetery and accidentally stumbled upon

---

1 William J. Abraham, "The Emergence of Canonical Theism," in *Canonical Theism: A Proposal
for Theology and the Church*, ed. William J. Abraham, Jason E. Vickers, and Natalie B. Van Kirk
(Grand Rapids: Eerdmans, 2008), 154. Since Oden, Abraham's canonical theism has emerged as
an alternate, though closely related, project in retrieving the Christian tradition for the present.

my own tombstone with this puzzling epitaph: 'He made no new contribution to theology.' I woke up refreshed and relieved."[2] As he put it elsewhere, "Since 1979 I have earnestly pledged to my readers that I intend to propose nothing original as if it might be some improvement on apostolic teaching and its early exegesis."[3] At first glance, then, Oden's retrieval is simply repetitive. This produces problems for those of us who come after. Is theological retrieval simply repetition? As much is suggested by Kenneth Collins, who offers common criticism to both Tom Oden and William Abraham's projects:

> A number of similarities yet emerge when the works of Oden and Abraham are compared. Both, for example, are backward looking in that they privilege a golden age (the first millennium) in which the messiness of doctrinal disputes has all been settled such that the task of contemporary theologians is greatly simplified and reduced. And both maintain, in one form or another, all that is left for contemporary theologians to do is to bring forward the finished theological products of the dead to new social locations.[4]

But is it the case that carrying forward the legacy of Tom Oden, in theology in general or Christology in particular, is simply to repeat the "finished theological products of the dead?"

I think not. In the essay that follows, I will advance two claims.[5] First, "going on" after Oden cannot be simply repetitive. A closer look at what Oden was actually doing bears this out. Second, Oden's work was primarily preparatory. Those of us who would pursue Methodist theological retrieval

---

2   Thomas C. Oden, *A Change of Heart: A Personal and Theological Memoir* (Downers Grove, IL: InterVarsity, 2014), 143.

3   Thomas C. Oden, *John Wesley's Teachings*, vol. 2, *Christ and Salvation* (Grand Rapids: Zondervan, 2012), 29.

4   Kenneth J. Collins, "Review of *Canonical Theism: A Proposal for Theology and the Church*," *Asbury Journal* 63, no. 2 (2008): 105.

5   I am grateful to the participants of the Wesleyan Studies Summer Seminar, Asbury Theological Seminary, and Drs. Kenneth Collins and Russell Richey for the time and support to pursue the research that underlay this essay.

must go on after Oden. We must go on, continuing in a direction prepared and suggested by Oden himself.

Toward these ends, the argument that follows will, first, survey Oden's Christological writings. Second, I will briefly characterize Oden's approach to Christology. Third, I will probe more deeply into Oden's concept of "consensus" before turning to his utilization of this concept in his Christology. Finally, I will argue that, while his project is not simply repetitive, it does present perplexities for those of us who work after Oden. Somewhat surprisingly, I will briefly suggest that a guide for moving past these perplexities can be found in the work of the late-nineteenth-century Methodist theologian William Burt Pope, whom Oden dubbed "the most brilliant of Methodist theologians."[6]

Oden's Christological Writings

Oden did not devote significant attention to Christology before his aforementioned dream in 1971. Afterward, he only gave sustained treatment to Christological topics on four occasions. He devoted an entire volume of his magisterial three-volume *Systematic Theology* to Christology.[7] That volume was later edited into the shorter *Classic Christianity.*[8] He also gives an extended excursus on John Wesley's Christology in *John Wesley's Scriptural Christianity.*[9] That volume was later expanded into the four-volume *John Wesley's Teachings*, the second volume devoted to Christology and soteriology.[10] And, it is worth mentioning, though he only penned a four-page introduction, he also edited the Christological writings of Albert Outler, his "first and best theological teacher."[11]

---

6   Thomas C. Oden, *Classic Christianity: A Systematic Theology* (New York: HarperOne, 2009), xxviii.

7   Thomas C. Oden, *Systematic Theology*, 3 vols. (San Francisco: Harper & Row, 1987–1992).

8   See n. 6 above.

9   Thomas C. Oden, *John Wesley's Scriptural Christianity: A Plain Exposition of His Teaching on Christian Doctrine* (Grand Rapids: Zondervan, 1994).

10   Thomas C. Oden, *John Wesley's Teachings*, 4 vols. (Grand Rapids: Zondervan, 2012–2014).

11   Albert Cook Outler, *Christology*, ed. Thomas C. Oden, The Albert Outler Library, vol. 4 (Anderson, IN: Bristol Books, 1996), 18.

On each occasion, Oden's Christology was deliberately derivative. His method was, on the face of it, the re-presentation of the thought of those who went before. In the case of *Systematic Theology* and *Classic Christianity*, he sought to represent the position of what he called the "classical consensus." In *John Wesley's Scriptural Christianity* and *John Wesley's Teachings*, it was the teaching of John Wesley.

The heart of Oden's work was his conception of the "classical consensus." When Oden turned to the subject of Christology in *John Wesley's Teachings*, he immediately adverted to the classical Christian tradition:

> Wesley prayed that the people in his connection of spiritual formation might be saved from supposed "improvements" on the apostolic testimony or presumed christological innovations. Wesley at no point hinted that there is a needed purification, progression, or remodeling of ancient ecumenical christological definitions. There is very little of that in magisterial Protestantism. The Reformers gladly accepted ancient ecumenical definitions of the apostolic church, and Wesley followed in their steps.[12]

Unsurprisingly, Oden's subsequent treatment of Wesley's Christology is largely derived from what Oden would come to call the "classical consensus." It is, therefore, the three-volume *Systematic Theology*, later edited and published as *Classic Christianity*, that sets out Oden's Christology, a Christology shared by John Wesley himself.

In the twenty-year period between *Systematic Theology* and *Classic Christianity*, Oden wrote extensively on the decline of mainline Protestantism, theology after modernity, early African Christianity, and the renewal of Christian orthodoxy.[13] He also worked tirelessly, beginning in 1988, to conceive, organize, and edit the Ancient Christian Commentary on Scripture. Thus, when it came time to revise and republish *Systematic Theology*, a text still in demand twenty years after its publication,

---

12 Oden, *John Wesley's Teachings*: *Christ and Salvation*, 2:39.

13 A bibliography of Oden's major publications can be found in Oden, *A Change of Heart*, 337–40.

Oden drew upon his substantive textual study, his ability to write for pop-ular audiences, and a sharper grasp of his most fundamental theological commitments. As he put it, *Classic Christianity* "deepened the patristic roots, tightened the systematic structure and reached out for general lay leaders."[14]

Classic Christianity is marked by its expanded interest in early Chris-tian thought and a sharper, more integrated focus. On the latter, Oden refined many of his earlier intuitions into a central concept he called "clas-sic consensual ecumenical teaching," the first line of his text.[15] His orien-tation was not to the peculiar teachings and practices of, for instance, United Methodism, but to the "deeper consensus that has been gratefully celebrated as received teaching by believers of vastly different cultural settings, whether African or Asian, Eastern or Western, sixth or sixteenth century."[16] Though his motives were no doubt shaped by his Methodism, his constructive pursuits drew primarily from the broader Christian tradi-tion. At least, such was his claim. We will see later that the claim requires careful scrutiny.

A few points should be made regarding Oden's concept of the "clas-sical consensus." By this phrase he was not thinking primarily of the doc-trinal deliverances of the early Christian ecumenical councils. His primary interest was the founts of theological insight that produced those conciliar doctrines. In fact, Oden was more likely to recite early Christian commen-tary on scripture than rehearse the creeds and canons of early councils. In speaking about the creedal deliverances, he was not afraid to name them as foundational to his project. But he also clarified the manner in which they function: "(This effort) proposes to follow that ancient ecumenical consen-sus of Christian teaching of God as seen in earliest creedal summaries. . . . These confessions still embrace and empower not only centrist Protestants and traditional Roman Catholics and Orthodox but also great numbers of

---

14 Oden, *A Change of Heart*, 300.

15 Oden, *Classic Christianity*, xiii.

16 Oden, xiii.

evangelicals, liberals, and charismatics."[17] That is, while Oden was thoroughly committed to these creeds as deliverances of particular doctrines—no doubt true—he was more fundamentally interested in that which is seen through them: the consensus. It is this consensus that served his aims of continued theological and spiritual nourishment for the church today.

This subtle distinction is crucial, though often overlooked, when considering the aims, structures, and contents of Oden's Christology. It is also crucial for discerning what it would mean to go on after or beyond Oden.

Oden's Approach to Christology

Christology is the central topic of *Classic Christianity*. Book 1 treats "the Living God," covering the divine essence, existence, persons, and creative work of God. Book 3 treats "Life in the Spirit," covering the person of the Spirit, the way of salvation, ecclesiology, and eschatology. In between these two books falls *The Word of Life*, Oden's exposition of Christology according to the classical ecumenical consensus.[18]

The Christology is creedal in structure, with an important caveat. While several chapters move through the standard order of topics—person, incarnation, life, death, resurrection, ascension, and session—his first chapter reflects at length on the question, "Why Christ?"[19] A look at this section reveals several distinctives of Oden's Christology.

One of the most notable, and striking, transitions between the earlier *Systematic Theology* and later *Classic Christianity* is Oden's decreasing emphasis on polemical engagement with twentieth-century liberal Protestantism. Those engagements are present, but they are more subdued, more generalized, more marked by the wisdom of lessons learned and battles

---

17 Oden, *Classic Christianity*, xiii.

18 Those familiar with classic texts in theology will not be surprised by this order, as it follows the structure of the Apostles and Nicene Creeds, and is evident in such classical expositions as Thomas Aquinas's *Summa Theologiae*, as well as many others. Among Methodist theologians, Oden's structure is highly imitative of William Burt Pope's three-volume *Compendium of Christian Theology*.

19 Oden, 213–30.

exhausted. A typical example can be seen in his discussion of the distinction between the person and work of Christ. Consider these paragraphs from the earlier *Systematic Theology*:

> Classic exegetes characteristically began their reflection with a discussion of the distinctive *identity* of Christ, or the *person* of Christ as truly human and truly God—who he is (Augustine, *Trin.* IV, *FC* 45, 129–179; cf. Novatian, Hilary, and Gregory Nazianzen on second [*sic*] article of the Trinity). If this cannot be systematically established, it is doubtful that there is any viable alternative way to speak of divine-human mediation or of the mediator's activity. This sequence runs counter to the prevailing modern procedure insisted upon by Harnack, Bultmann, Bousset, Tillich, Pannenberg, Marxsen, and many others, which is characterized by the notion that it is necessary to speak first of the historical activity of Jesus before speaking of his being recollected as the Christ.[20]

We can see several key features of Oden's project here. First, Oden's Christology is profoundly conscious of, and explicit about, its reliance upon the thought of the past. In *Classic Christianity*, he began referring to this theology as a "compendium."[21] Repeatedly he deflected attention away from his explanations, and toward the body of literature and conviction they sought to explain. Second, while his project prioritized the past, it did not do so without a particular justification. He was explicit about his privileging the sources of the past over the present, and the older over the newer. The rule applies all the way down, with the greatest deference paid to scripture and early Christian exegesis of the same scripture. "The most authoritative affirmations of classic Christian doctrine hinge on the best and most widely received scripture interpretations of the classic exegetes."[22] But why privilege the past? Here, like Vincent of Lérins, he appealed to the studied judgment of the church over time under the guidance of the Holy

---

20 Oden, *Systematic Theology*, vol. 2, *The Word of Life*, 17.

21 Oden, *Classic Christianity*, xx.

22 Oden, xxiv.

Spirit.[23] Those same authoritative affirmations of classic Christian doctrine "are the views that have been happily received by the *consensus fidelium*."[24]

When Oden revised the aforementioned passage for *Classic Christianity*, he dropped the paragraph on the countertendencies of modern Christology. While the former explication (including the citation of Augustine, Hilary and Gregory Nazianzen) remains, Oden made no mention of modern Protestant obligation to speak first of the historical Jesus before dealing with his recollection as Christ.[25]

Oden's "Consensus"

By the time Oden was editing *Classic Christianity*, the theological trajectory of liberal Protestantism was in shambles. This was due, not only to the criticisms arising from contextual theologies, but also due to the widespread interest in theological retrieval among the evangelical, Roman Catholic, and Orthodox scholars with whom Oden spent decades collaborating. A few years before publication of *Classic Christianity*, Oden published *One Faith: The Evangelical Consensus* with J. I. Packer.[26] Around the same time he completed his general editorship of the Ancient Christian Commentary on Scripture. His audience had moved from mainline Protestantism, where declamations were necessary, to an emerging orthodox ecumenical community.

Understandably, then, Oden's interest was shifting toward the constructive project of articulating a "classical consensus." The orthodox ecumenical community emerging after the decline of the mainline required an articulate defense of the labor for retrieval now necessary in light of a century-long disintegration of the classical Christian heritage. He spent the 1990s publishing *After Modernity . . . What? Agenda for Theology* (1990), *Two*

---

23 Thomas Guarino has published a helpful study of Vincent's views in *Vincent of Lérins and the Development of Christian Doctrine* (Grand Rapids: Baker, 2013).

24 Oden, *Classic Christianity*, xxiv.

25 Oden, 224.

26 Thomas C. Oden and J. I. Packer, *One Faith: The Evangelical Consensus* (Downers Grove, IL: InterVarsity, 2004).

Worlds: Notes on the Death of Modernity in America and Russia (1992), and *Requiem: A Lament in Three Movements* (1995). In the 2000s, he moved on to *The Rebirth of Orthodoxy: Signs of New Life in Christianity* (2003), *Turning Around the Mainline: How Renewal Movements Are Changing the Church* (2006), and *How Africa Shaped the Christian Mind: The African Seedbed of Western Christianity* (2007). That is, he moved from critical to constructive projects, and *Classic Christianity* morphed with him.

The concept of "consensus" and its emerging significance in Oden's thought over several decades is essential for understanding his constructive work, and therefore the Christology of *Classic Christianity*. In his memoir, Oden credits his introduction to the historic Christian faith to his Drew colleague Will Herberg, a conservative Russian Jewish theologian. Like Oden, Herberg had spent his early years interested in radical politics but grew skeptical of modern trends in politics and education. It was Herberg who challenged Oden: "You will remain theologically uneducated until you study carefully Athanasius, Augustine and Aquinas."[27] Before this, Oden admitted, "I had never crawled through patristic texts with a listening heart. I had never truly inhabited that timeless, sacred world."[28]

Herberg's encouragement led Oden to reexamine the Christian tradition. And that reexamination reversed the course of his work. "The classic texts reshaped my mind."[29] His study of these classic texts produced confidence in their power. "I came by grace to grasp the distinctive way of consensual reasoning that had ripened within classic Christianity. I became fascinated with the social dynamics of orthodoxy, the process of transmitting apostolic tradition and coming to trust the reasoning of classic consensual teaching."[30] For Oden, his interest in consensual reasoning was always wedded to a rejection of mainline academic trends from the outset. "Those who absolutely adored absolute toleration began to notice

---

27 Oden, *A Change of Heart*, 136.

28 Oden, 137.

29 Oden, 139.

30 Oden, 139.

I was suffering fools a little less gladly."[31] These wedded commitments remained integral throughout his life. However, they were not always emphasized evenly. Over time, his confidence grew in the simple power of the classic texts. "Since meeting and dwelling with the Christian exegetes through their writings in their own words, I came to trust the very orthodoxy that I had dismissed."[32]

The 1970s and '80s were a period of Oden's growing confidence in the classical consensus. *Systematic Theology* marks a watershed in both his study and articulation of that consensus. His confidence grew over the 1990s and 2000s, as did his grasp of (1) what that consensus consisted in and (2) what marked it as distinctive from what was on offer by other trends in academic theology.

On the former, Oden came to conceive of the consensus as a gift inspired and preserved by the Spirit, clarified by the church's broad spatial and temporal acceptance, and evident across myriad artifacts produced and preserved by Christians. Though modern theology had grown uninterested in exhibiting such a consensus, it was, according to Oden, "the task of the science of theological reasoning as viewed classically" to show the unity of classic Christian teaching. Moreover, the classic texts themselves often sought to show this unity by demonstrating "textual interconnections," the primary objective of *Classic Christianity*. These textual interconnections, for Oden, were the methodological pathway for demonstrating both the unity and power of classic Christianity, the same unity and power that had reshaped his mind. By demonstrating the consensus via textual interconnections, Oden argued, he was following the example of classic Christian theologians themselves:

> (Classic theologians) all showed these textual interconnections. They focused on delivering accurately the authoritative texts in a plausible, thoughtful arrangement and in an uncomplicated, readable style in

---

31 Oden, *A Change of Heart*, 139.

32 Oden, 140.

order to show forth their cohesiveness as a demonstration of the work of the Spirit. There was no accent on the individual virtuosity of individual thinkers or on those who were putting the pattern together. The pattern arose out of a worshiping community. The important thing was not the brilliance of any individual's arguments but the shared pattern formed by the conflation of texts themselves, radiating the power of the Spirit.[33]

While his conception of the consensus grew, and his method for demonstrating it refined, his interest in the consensus as an alternative to trends in academic theology remained. And there remained Oden's enduring concern to distance his thought from liberal Protestantism.

Oden's Consensual Christology

We see this twofold emphasis in the Christology of *Classic Christianity*. Oden went to some length to show how and why he structured it according to the Nicene Creed.[34] Nevertheless, when he turned to his first topic—the deity of Christ—Oden focused on rebutting modern skepticism. He first recounted biblical questions: "Who is this who forgives sins? Who is this I hear such things about? Who do you say that I am?"[35] Then he turned to "the question today" and lingered.[36]

Oden supplied warrant for his extended investigation. "Is it possible to set forth credible evidence that Jesus is the one he is attested to be? . . . If this proves right, then all else follows; if this proves wrong, then nothing else could possibly avail to make Christianity worth pursuing."[37] But what sort of investigation was this? Oden spent the remainder of the chapter giving warrant for the classic Christian claim that Jesus is, in fact, "the One

---

33 Oden, *Classic Christianity*, xix.

34 Oden, 228–30.

35 Oden, 233–34.

36 Oden, 234–35.

37 Oden, 234.

and Only God become fully human, a historical individual personally uniting two distinct natures, human and divine."[38]

He enfolded both historic and modern objections. He briefly recited, first, Arian, Ebionite, and biblical objections. Then he pivoted to Ritschl's liberal culture-Protestantism, in which Jesus merely shared an ethical purpose with God. The treatment of the question that ensued layered classical texts in response to a host of modern and classic objections to Christ's divinity. Against Ritschl he cited Augustine and Chrysostom alongside Joachim Jeremias and Ferdinand Hahn.[39] Later, against the *Religionsgeschichtliche Schule* he cited Isaac of Nineveh and Ambrose alongside Karl Barth.[40] Thus he addressed the conflict between liberal Protestant theology and the classical consensus.

Similar emphases are evident in Oden's discussion of the Incarnation. He opened with an argument that "both genders were honored equally in the incarnation."[41] He called on the Cappadocians, Augustine, Theodoret, Leo, and Julian of Norwich in support.[42] Oden was on solid ground here. The tradition has long seen fit to argue that Jesus's maleness does not prevent salvation from extending to all. And Oden chose his sources well. But we also see his underlying concerns about modernist objections. Once again he treated the modern anxiety by appeal to classical texts first, only then turning to a straightforward description of the doctrine under consideration. Only once he had handled the worry about gender did he turn to biblical and doctrinal explication of the Incarnation itself, and the historic speculations over its reasons and necessity.[43]

Of course, modern objections are just objections, and a contemporary Christology is right to take them up. Moreover, it is in the tangles with

---

38 Oden, *Classic Christianity*, 234.

39 Oden, 237.

40 Oden, 244–45.

41 Oden, 265.

42 Oden, 265–67.

43 Oden, 268–74.

modern sensibilities that Oden's concept of "consensus" is often most rewarding. Consensus on questions like the divinity of Christ or the extent of salvation possible for a male savior are rather easy to establish in classic texts when viewed in relation to modern rejections of these teachings. At these moments Oden's method of demonstrating textual interconnections by layering classic texts is most potent. And this is Oden's definitive contribution to Methodist Christology. He returned us to the great classical tradition. He returned us to uncompromising confidence in the hypostatic union, to Christ's divinity, to utter confidence in the realities opened up by the particular revelation of God in Jesus Christ.

But Oden's consensual Christology has other perplexities. These are particularly evident when, modern objections overcome, he moved to the explication of the doctrines he had by now warranted. He sometimes articulated arguments and positions that the classic texts leave open to speculation as if they were constitutive of a binding consensus.

Consider Oden's treatment of the question, "Was the incarnation necessary?" Oden first argued for an essential connection between sin and incarnation, citing a litany of early Christian sources. When he moved into the modern period, he recited Calvin's infralapsarian assertion in the *Institutes*—the Incarnation would not have been if there had been no fall.[44] But he overlooked the well-documented equivocation in Calvin often cited by Reformed supralapsarians.[45] Moreover, his early and medieval references are standard infralapsarian fare—Augustine, Rupert of Deutz, Hugh of St. Victor.[46] But he made no mention of classic supralapsarians like Augustine (in other texts), Robert Grosseteste, or Duns Scotus.[47]

It is simply implausible to take such a contested position as part of the

---

44 Oden, *Classic Christianity*, 272–73.

45 See, for instance, Oliver Crisp's treatment of Calvin's apparent equivocation in his essay "John Calvin (1509–1564) on the Motivation for the Incarnation," in Crisp, *Revisioning Christology: Theology in the Reformed Tradition* (Burlington, VT: Ashgate, 2011), 23–42.

46 Oden, 273.

47 For more on the history of the motive for the Incarnation, see Justus H. Hunter, *If Adam Had Not Sinned: The Motive for the Incarnation from Anselm to Scotus* (Washington, DC: Catholic University of America Press, 2020).

"consensus." The classic texts are equivocal on such questions. Augustine is regularly cited as warrant for both positions.[48] So it is perplexing to see one particular speculative position elevated as if it were constitutive of "consensus."

This raises a second issue with Oden's concept of consensus. He asked, "Does God (become incarnate) often?"[49] It is the sort of question one expects in a scholastic treatment of incarnation. Once the possibility of the de facto incarnation has been defined and defended, questions regarding particular features of the Incarnation, and a range of other possibilities, are considered.[50] Oden noted that Augustine gave an argument in defense of the fittingness of the time of the Incarnation "after man sinned, and not in the beginning."[51] In keeping with the classical Christian consensus, Oden held that the incarnation, in all its particularities, was suitably, fittingly done. Oddly, though, when Oden then turned to this issue of the possibility of multiple incarnations, he did not follow the concerns of the scholastic thinkers who clarified arguments about the Incarnation's fittingness and suitability. Those scholastics would turn to the possibility of multiple incarnations to refine their understanding of possibility, necessity, and fittingness in relation to divine operations *ad extra*. Scholastic theologians like Thomas Aquinas would turn such questions over on the basis of the internal logic of Christian theology. Instead, Oden returned to his worries about the *Religionsgeschichtliche Schule*:

> Was the incarnation unique—once for all times? If so, why did God become human only once? [*sic*] Or can we expect repeated incarnations?

---

48 For a clear demonstration of disagreements in the early Christian literature, see the entry "Incarnation" by A. Michel in *Dictionnaire de Théologie Catholique* 17 (1923), 1445–1539, especially the treatment of the *possibilité, convenance, et nécessité de l'incarnation* on pp. 1462–82.

49 Oden, *Classic Christianity*, 274–78.

50 See, for instance, the structure of Anselm of Canterbury's *Cur Deus Homo?* in *Anselm of Canterbury: The Major Works*, ed. Brian Davies and G. R. Evans (Oxford: Oxford University Press, 1998), esp. II, 8–9.

51 Oden, *Classic Christianity*, 275. See a similar question in Thomas Aquinas, *Summa Theologiae* III, q. 1, aa. 5–6. Thomas cited the exact same text, Augustine's *in libro octogintatrium quaest.* 44, as that cited by Oden, in a. 6, *ad* 1.

Nothing is more characteristic in the history of religions than the thought of the union of God and humanity. . . . These views differ markedly from the incarnation, which speaks of the one true God who becomes flesh and suffers and dies in history without ceasing to be God. . . . The once-for all condescension of the one and only Son to assume human nature was understood to be a [*sic*] unique, singular, and not needing to be duplicated since the sacrifice once made does not need to be reoffered redundantly (Heb. 9:25-28; Chrysostom, *Hom. On Hebr.* 17.4-6). He is the only Mediator, not one among many (Tho. Aq., *ST* 3 Q26; Calvin, *Inst.* 3.20.19).[52]

His final citation of Thomas Aquinas is most strange, insofar as Thomas was quite explicit that more than one incarnation was possible. For Thomas, not only is the incarnation of other triune persons possible; so are multiple incarnations of the Son himself: "Whatever the Father is able to do, the Son is able to do. But after the Incarnation the Father of the Son is able to assume another human nature distinct from that which the Son assumed; for in no way is the power of the Father or the Son diminished by the Incarnation of the Son. Therefore it seems that the Son, after the Incarnation, is able to assume another human nature than the one He had assumed."[53] Here we detect fundamentally different orientations in Oden's project and a project like Thomas's. And this orientation is not reducible to a disagreement about the "consensus" on matters like the Incarnation. After all, Oden's substantive positions are entirely commensurate with Thomas's when it comes to fundamental matters of Christology. Oden cited Thomas no fewer than sixty times in the Christological chapters of *Classic Christianity*. However, where Thomas was ordered to speculation on the holy teaching (*sacra doctrina*) given in Scripture, Oden's aims were to set the classical Christian tradition over against the academic judgments of liberal Protestantism. And in this difference lies a path for going on after Oden.

---

52 Oden, *Classic Christianity*, 275.

53 Thomas Aquinas, *Summa Theologiae* III, q. 3, a. 7, *sed contra*. Translation my own.

After Oden

Oden's reading in classic Christianity extended primarily to early Christian texts. One encounters Anselm of Canterbury or Thomas Aquinas, but nowhere near so frequently as Augustine of Hippo or the Cappadocians. Magisterial Reformers like Luther, Calvin, and Ursinus are cited here and there. But there is rarely mention of the scholastic traditions, Lutheran or Reformed, that followed in their wake.

In sum, Oden's chief objects for retrieval were early Christian texts, texts he had neglected in his early theological work. His theology was oriented around the diverse, sometimes conflicting positions in early Christian texts.

Of course, Christians have long recognized there are diverse, sometimes conflicting positions in early Christian texts. The medievals worked these into grand syntheses. Early scholastic texts of the Latin Middle Ages, such as Abelard's *Sic et Non* or Peter Lombard's *The Sentences*, reckoned seriously with the diversity of opinion in early Christian sources. And scholastics such as Peter Lombard sought out a unified speculative vision underlying this diversity of positions. That diversity in early Christianity provoked the practice of gathering "sentences," authoritative snippets of text that expressed with particular clarity the theological positions of luminous early Christian thinkers. Some of those sentences demanded fundamental assent. But some of them produced puzzles. Peter Lombard, in *The Sentences*, sought to consider systematically the unity of this diverse body of doctrines. He organized all of theology into fundamental divisions, turning over key sentences in each area, sometimes clarifying, sometimes speculating, and sometimes leaving behind puzzles for others to continue pondering. In this way the sentences were layered and drawn together, thereby showing fundamental areas of consensus, while leaving other points open to further development.

If the *Sentences* merely served to lay out that which was consensual, it is unlikely that it would have become the standard text for training theologians at Paris and at Oxford in the thirteenth century. Lombard also sought to develop speculative resolutions to some of the dilemmas in the classic texts themselves. When Augustine apparently gave three possible ways for understanding the metaphysics of the hypostatic union, Lombard took a closer look at the historic teaching of the conciliar tradition to sort out which position we ought to pursue.[54] His three opinions proved irresistible for the speculations of subsequent scholastic theologians.[55]

When he encountered puzzles in the classic texts, Lombard read carefully and thought deeply and creatively with the classic Christian tradition. He speculated. He sought to understand that which he received. This was the same point of departure for the great schoolmen of the middle ages. Like Anselm of Canterbury's, theirs was a "faith seeking understanding."[56] The best scholastic receptions of classic texts, with all their diversity and complications, have been marked by a freedom to speculate within the world of thought opened up by the consensus of early Christian teaching. And in this way, I submit, those of us interested in retrieving the historic Christian teaching about Christ to which Thomas C. Oden returned us ought to go on. We ought to accept his conclusions: the classic texts and their consensus are true. And we ought to go on to develop a Methodist Christology with the same spirit of speculative energy that early Christians left to their great medieval and modern followers.

Ironically, going along this path after Oden might require going behind him. Methodists are not without theological exemplars who share Oden's confidence in a consensus yet move on into the domain of the speculative exploration of the word opened up by that consensus. The very theologian Oden dubbed "the most brilliant of Methodist theologians," William Burt Pope, pursued such a project in his three-volume *A Compendium of*

---

54 Peter Lombard, *The Sentences*, bk. 3, *On the Incarnation of the Word*, trans. Giulio Silano (Toronto: Pontifical Institute of Mediaeval Studies, 2008), dist. 6.

55 Walter Principe's studies of the theology of the hypostatic union lays out much of the early developments of the three opinions. Walter Principe, *The Theology of the Hypostatic Union in the Early Thirteenth Century*, 4 vols. (Toronto: Pontifical Institute of Mediaeval Studies, 1963–1975). More recently, Richard Cross has given a rigorous analysis of the positions developed later in the thirteenth century in *The Metaphysics of the Incarnation: Thomas Aquinas to Duns Scotus* (Oxford: Oxford University Press, 2008).

56 Anselm of Canterbury, *"Proslogion,"* in *The Major Works*, 82–83.

Christian Theology.[57] And, I submit, it is to such a position that Methodist Christology should return: confident in the received tradition, clarifying that consensus which the Spirit gives and preserves, and speculating within it in line with the peculiar doctrines of our heritage.[58] In this way we can continue along the path Oden was preparing for us.

---

57 William Burt Pope, *A Compendium of Christian Theology*, 3 vols. (London: Wesleyan-Methodist Book-Room, 1880).

58 On Methodism's peculiar doctrines, and Pope's theological analysis and justification of them, see his essay "Methodist Doctrine" in *The Wesley Memorial Volume*, ed. J. O. A. Clark (New York: Phillips & Hunt, 1880). See also Justus Hunter, "A Defense of William Burt Pope's Confessional Methodist Theology," *Wesleyan Theological Journal* (2019): 7–17.

13

William Burt Pope and the Future of Wesleyan Theology: The Work of Christ in Dogmatic Perspective

Jason E. Vickers

He is himself before all things, and in him all things hold together.
—**Colossians 1:17** (NRSV)

And here lies the unutterable preciousness of the Triune Essence. . . . The glory of the future cross already shines upon the chaos of moral disorder."
—**William Burt Pope,** *A Compendium of Christian Theology*

f Wesleyans want to do serious work in Christology, then we are going to need to take a theological sabbatical from John Wesley. I am well aware of how bizarre this will sound in some ears. We have invested enormous amounts of time and energy over the last century retrieving and promoting Wesley's theology.[1] This was a right and good thing to do. For that matter, it is still a right and good thing to do. Taking a sabbatical doesn't mean abandoning one's regular work forever. Wesley is to Wesleyan theology what teaching classes is to the professorial life; reading Wesley is and should be a routine feature of our work. But just as we take an occasional break from

---

1 I myself have participated in this important enterprise. See Jason E. Vickers, *Wesley: A Guide for the Perplexed* (London: T&T Clark, 2009); Randy L. Maddox and Jason E. Vickers, eds., *The Cambridge Companion to John Wesley* (New York: Cambridge University Press, 2009); and Kenneth J. Collins and Jason E. Vickers, eds., *The Sermons of John Wesley: A Collection for the Christian Journey* (Nashville: Abingdon Press, 2013). I also teach a required master's level course on John Wesley's theology at least once per year at Asbury Theological Seminary.

teaching classes in order to get other work done, we need to take a break from Wesley in order to undertake serious theological reflection on the person and work of Christ. Why?

Wesleyan Theology and the Culture of Anxious Narcissism

There are two major reasons why Wesleyan theologians need to look elsewhere for help in Christology. First, John Wesley was not a systematic theologian. He was an occasional and practical theologian chiefly concerned with equipping and enabling the church for preaching, evangelism, missions, discipleship, and the like. Accordingly, his main interests were soteriological, not Christological. This doesn't mean that Wesley didn't think about the person and work of Christ. It simply means that he did not develop a well-organized, thorough, and carefully nuanced Christology. Even if we comb through all of his works, accumulating the most minor Christological scraps as we go, we would be hard-pressed to produce such a work. For instance, we would have very little material from which to construct an account of the unity of Christ's person and the distinction of his two natures (notoriously, Wesley's account of Christ's human nature is woefully underdeveloped).[2] Equally problematic is the fact that Wesley has comparatively little to say about Christ's resurrection. Put simply, there are significant gaps here. Acknowledging this in no way diminishes Wesley's importance. Rather, it honors him by not asking him to do something that he did not set out to do.

The second reason that Wesleyans who want to do serious work in Christology need to look to someone other than Wesley for help is intimately related to the first. As already noted, Wesley was primarily interested in soteriology, which is to say, in the doctrines of justification, regeneration, sanctification, and Christian perfection. These are his long suits as a theologian. Wesley was concerned with the *subjective appropriation* of the work of Christ and the work of the Holy Spirit. This is perfectly understandable when we recall that, from his perspective, the chief problem the church

---

2 For more on this, see Jerome Van Kuiken, "Deschner's Wesley and the Monophysite Meme," *Wesleyan Theological Journal* 54, no. 2 (Fall 2019): 37–55.

faced was nominal Christianity, not heterodox belief. Thus, he stressed that true or *real* Christianity involved more than mere assent to the Thirty-Nine Articles of the Church of England and the creeds of the early church. What really mattered was whether or not one had come to know Jesus in a way that was truly life changing. Put simply, Wesley was a Pietist and a revivalist.

Why is this a problem for Wesleyan Christology today? In one sense, it isn't. Indeed, we need to be careful not to lose touch with the Pietistic and revivalistic aspects of our tradition. Woe be unto us if we trade our warmed hearts for dead orthodoxy! At the same time, there is no reason to set these things at odds with one another. We need clear heads and holy hearts! Unfortunately, Wesley's emphasis on the subjective appropriation of the faith has led, albeit unintentionally, to what Phillip Cary has aptly named a culture of "anxious narcissism."[3] When asked the question, "What is your faith about?" we Wesleyans, like our Protestant counterparts in the Reformed and Lutheran traditions, respond by making it fundamentally about ourselves. This is true of both the evangelical and liberal-progressive wings of Wesleyanism.

For evangelical Wesleyans, the Christian faith is primarily about repenting of sin and accepting Jesus as one's personal Lord and Savior. To be sure, these actions—repentance and profession of faith—presuppose prior actions on God's part. Yet, the focus in evangelical circles is clearly on what people must do to be saved rather than on what God in Christ has done once and for all for us and for our salvation. Anxious narcissism occurs because, unlike God's decisive and irreversible action in Jesus Christ, human repentance and profession of faith are subject to scrutiny, self-doubt, wavering, backsliding, and the like. Evangelical Wesleyans are plagued by the following questions: Were we sincere enough in our repentance? Were our motives pure? Do we really trust Jesus? Have we really given God our whole hearts, or are we holding back a part of ourselves? Is our faith strong enough? Can we lose our salvation? Is faith enough, or are works necessary? In the worst

---

3 Phillip Cary, *The Meaning of Protestant Theology: Luther, Augustine, and the Gospel That Gives Us CHRIST* (Grand Rapids: Baker Academic, 2019), 2.

cases, a preoccupation with such questions can be spiritually disabling. Our narcissism and anxiety undermine our confidence and trust in the Lord.

Liberal-progressive Wesleyans do not fare better. Like their evangelical counterparts, liberal and progressive Wesleyans frequently make the faith fundamentally about themselves. Instead of repentance and personal faith, the focus now is on social justice or social reform. Anxious narcissism occurs because we are given to scrutinizing and doubting our own efforts to combat the many forms of social injustice in the world. Social evils like racism and sexism, we are told, inhere in societal structures and are virtually impossible to eradicate. We can never repent enough or do enough to bring about real and permanent change. Here, too, questions abound: Have we sufficiently condemned racism, sexism, and other social injustice? Have we sufficiently confronted social injustice in our workplaces? In our churches? In our homes? In what ways do we ourselves remain complicit in social injustice? In the worst cases, a preoccupation with these questions can be spiritually disabling. Our narcissism and anxiety prevent us from seeing who we truly are in Christ.

At this stage, someone is likely to object that we Wesleyans believe that salvation is a matter of divine-human cooperation. We are synergists! In theory, this should make us immune from anxious narcissism. We know that we cannot save ourselves. We know that the gospel declares that "while we still were sinners Christ died for us" (Rom. 5:8 NRSV). We simply believe that God's grace requires our response. At our best, we even know that our response, including our most basic profession of faith in Jesus Christ, is God-enabled. We know that "no one can say 'Jesus is Lord' except by the Holy Spirit" (1 Cor. 12:3). Yet, the problem remains. We are given to anxious narcissism because we lack order and discipline in our theology.

Like Wesley, Wesleyans today tend to be in a rush to move past what God has done for us in Christ to questions pertaining to how we should respond to God's saving actions. Our motives for doing so are no doubt pure, but that doesn't mean that we don't create problems along the way. The best place to see this is the doctrine of the atonement. Rightly understood, the atoning work of Christ on the cross should be a bulwark against anxious narcissism. Unfortunately, that is not the case. In a particularly damning assessment, George Lindbeck observes that both evangelical and liberal forms of synergism shift the focus of the doctrine of the atonement away from the objective work of Christ on the cross and toward our subjective appropriation of it. He writes:

> Those who continued to use the *sola fide* language assumed that they agreed with the reformers no matter how much, under the influence of conversionist pietism and revivalism, they turned the faith that saves into a meritorious good work of the free will, a voluntaristic decision to believe that Christ bore the punishment of sins on the cross *pro me*, for each person individually. Improbable as it might seem given the metaphor (and the Johannine passage from which it comes), everyone is thus capable of being "born again" if only he or she tries hard enough. Thus with the loss of the Reformation understanding of the faith that justifies as itself God's gift, Anselmic atonement theory became culturally associated with a self-righteousness that was both moral and religious and therefore rather nastier, its critics thought, than the primarily moral self-righteousness of the liberal Abelardians. In time, to move on in our story, the liberals increasingly ceased to be even Abelardian.[4]

At the risk of oversimplification, much contemporary theological reflection on the atonement shifts the emphasis away from the question, "What has Jesus done?" to the question, "What would Jesus do?" The objective work of Christ on the cross recedes into the background to the point that it is barely perceptible.[5] As Colin Gunton observed, "In place of an act of God" centered in the "historic life and death" of Jesus "towards the otherwise helpless," the emphasis is now on "those who by appropriate action [can] help themselves."[6]

---

4 George Lindbeck, "The Theology of Justification in Dogmatic Context," in Mark A. Husbands and Daniel J. Trier, eds., *Justification: What's at Stake in the Current Debates* (Downers Grove, IL: InterVarsity, 2004), 207.

5 The best place to see this is in the increasingly widespread aversion among Protestant theologians to classical models of the atonement in favor of so-called nonviolent views.

6 Colin Gunton, "The Sacrifice and the Sacrifices: From Metaphor to Transcendental?" in Cornelius Plantinga and Ronald J. Feenstra, eds., *Trinity, Incarnation and Atonement: Philosophical and Theological Essays* (Notre Dame, IN: University of Notre Dame Press, 1989), 211.

Synergism is neither inherently anxious nor narcissistic. It leads to anxious narcissism when we fail to develop and articulate a robust account of God's eternal nature, purposes, and saving actions in Jesus Christ because we are in such a rush to discuss the role that is ours to play, whether in personal salvation or social ethics. More broadly, synergism becomes a problem when we lack dogmatic discipline. Without dogmatic discipline and order, we end up talking primarily about ourselves.

The good news is that, within the Wesleyan theological tradition, there are ample resources to help us combat and eventually overcome the culture of anxious narcissism. In the remainder of this essay, I want to retrieve and explore one such resource, namely, the work of the nineteenth-century British Methodist dogmatic theologian William Burt Pope. My goal in doing so is not to advocate for the creation of a new sub-discipline within Wesleyan theology, that is, Pope studies. Rather, it is simply to provide an example of how dogmatic discipline can prevent synergistic understandings of salvation from a seemingly inescapable drift into anxious narcissism by anchoring them in a bracing account of God's eternal nature, purposes, and saving actions in Christ. Given his obscure status in our tradition, it may help to say a few words about Pope's dogmatic approach to theology. I will then examine Pope's account of the work of Christ, highlighting the ways it both requires and inspires humble gratitude (rather than anxious narcissism). I will conclude by offering some reflections on the importance of dogmatic discipline for the future of Wesleyan theology.

The Rise and Fall of Methodist Dogmatic Theology: William Burt Pope (1822–1903)

Until recently, William Burt Pope has been a forgotten figure in the history of Methodist theology.[7] In the mid- to late nineteenth century, Pope

---

7   In the last few years, there's been a resurgence of interest in Pope's theology. For example, see John L. Drury, "Scholastic Eschatology in the Wesleyan Tradition: The Case of William Burt Pope," *Wesleyan Theological Journal* 54, no. 2 (Fall 2019): 18–25; David N. Field, "Prevenient Grace and Universal Atonement in the Theology of William Burt Pope," *Aldersgate Papers* 11 (June 1015): 33–52; and Justus Hunter, "A Defense of William Burt Pope's Confessional Methodist

was easily the most gifted and important theologian in British Methodism. He taught for decades at Didsbury Methodist College in Manchester, and his three-volume *Compendium of Christian Theology* (1875–1876; revised 1877–1879) was a major theological text in Wesleyan/Methodist educational institutions in America until the early decades of the twentieth century, when his influence declined rather dramatically. What happened? Why are so few Wesleyans familiar with Pope today?

In an essay on Pope's Christological eschatology, John Drury observed that Pope's approach to theology had "deep roots in the protestant scholastic era." Pope himself was working two centuries after Protestant scholasticism's peak, but the scholastic approach "fit the needs of his time." Drury continued, "In the mid-nineteenth century, British Methodism was coming of age as a distinct confessional community, not unlike the Lutherans and Reformed in the seventeenth century. Pope drew on their methods as he sought to clarify, consolidate and defend Methodist theological identity. In many ways, Pope was to Wesley what Gerhard was to Luther and what Turretin was to Calvin."[8]

The strengths of Pope's scholastic approach to theology were its dogmatic discipline and conceptual clarity and consistency. With respect to dogmatic discipline, the doctrine of the Trinity orders and governs Pope's *Compendium* from start to finish. For example, as we will see below, the account of God's eternal triune nature orders and governs Pope's understanding of the doctrine of the atonement. The same can be said for virtually every doctrine in the system. And it is precisely this discipline that leads to moments of extraordinary clarity and insight on a wide range of topics ranging from providence and prevenient grace to eschatology and Christianity's relationship with other world religions. For instance, with respect to other religions, D. N. Field wrote, "Remarkably, his theology of religions,

---

Theology," *Wesleyan Theological Journal* 54, no. 2 (Fall 2019): 7–17. In addition to these publications, a new dogmatics working group affiliated with the Wesleyan Theological Society has recently completed the second year of a four-year annual seminar focused on Pope. Plans are underway to publish the proceedings of this seminar when it is completed.

8   Drury, "Scholastic Eschatology," 19–20.

which in some ways reflects his colonial context and in other ways transcends it, anticipates developments that have emerged in the twentieth century, often related to the proposals of Vatican II."[9]

Despite these strengths, Pope's classical dogmatic approach was "far too passé for the emerging academic liberalism of mainstream Methodism."[10] As Justus Hunter has recently shown, early twentieth-century Methodist theologians like Alfred Knudson dismissed Pope's theology as a "form of authoritarian rationalism" that failed "to integrate faith and religious experience." With respect to Pope, this criticism is unfounded. Hunter continues, "Pope's theology places heavy emphasis upon the Spirit's gift of faith and tends to describe its scientific character in terms of its consistency and coherence with its foundations."[11] Pope himself put it this way: "In theology, which seeks in all truth its relation to God and eternity, there is the guarantee of a special guidance of the Holy Spirit of God. His witness is not given only to the personal acceptance of the believer; it is a testimony to *the doctrine on which his experience rests*."[12]

Whereas Pope's account of the work of the Spirit clearly stipulates that experience rests upon doctrine, the criticism and rejection of Pope's theology (and of dogmatic approaches to theology generally) paved the way for appeals to "unthematic, or pre-linguistic experience, intended to carve out space for the religious in the wake of Kant's critical philosophy." To be sure, the turn to experience as foundational for theology can be viewed as an apologetics for the Christian faith at a time when appeals to divine revelation were increasingly being met with indifference, skepticism, and even mockery. But it was also inherently narcissistic, making knowledge of God primarily a matter of reflection upon our own experience. When the concept of experience proved "incapable of discriminating between beliefs,

---

9 Field, "Prevenient Grace," 34.

10 Drury, "Scholastic Eschatology," 19.

11 Hunter, "Defense," 14.

12 William Burt Pope, *A Compendium of Christian Theology: Being Analytical Outlines of a Course of Theological Study, Biblical, Dogmatic, Historical* (New York: Hunt & Eaton, 1889) 1:31, italics mine.

and therefore of determining for or against any particular belief," it was only a matter of time before anxiety set in.[13] At best, reflection upon pre-linguistic and unthematized religious experience leads to affirmations of the existence of a generic and nameless deity, a far cry from the triune God of the Christian faith.

The Work of Christ in Dogmatic Perspective: Pope's *Compendium*

By contrast with approaches to theology that begin with unthematized religious experience *and* culminate in anxious narcissism, Pope's approach to theology begins with God and both requires and culminates in humble gratitude. He writes, "God is the source and the subject and the end of theology." Theology is "from God in its origin, concerning God in its substance," and "leads to God in all its issues."[14]

Pope's insistence that God is "the source" of theology and that theology is "from God in its origin" provides a firm check against anxious narcissism at the outset of theological reflection. No longer the source of theology, the theologian finds herself in a position of humility and trust where knowledge of God is concerned. If she is to know anything whatsoever about God, she can only receive such knowledge *from God*. This is even true (for Pope) of so-called natural revelation. She is dependent upon God's self-disclosure from the word go. The reason for her dependency is plain to see. God is "incomprehensible and unsearchable." Even when God draws near to us in the person of Christ, he does so "dwelling in the light which no man can approach to search." Pope continues, "In the profoundest sense He is ever THE UNKNOWN GOD. It is His glory that He must conceal Himself."[15] In a particularly beautiful image, Pope went on to compare theology to a "temple which is filled with the presence of God." Theology

---

13 Hunter, "Defense," 15.

14 Pope, *Compendium*, 1:3–4.

15 Pope, 1:4.

is a "hidden sanctuary, into which no high priest taken from among men can enter," but *from which* "issues a light which leaves no part dark save where it is dark with excess of glory." In other words, the knowledge of God is not something that we can secure for ourselves. Rather, we can only wait upon it and receive it *from God*. Consequently, said Pope, "all fit students" of theology "are worshippers as well as students."[16] Theology both requires and culminates in humble gratitude.

As for the knowledge that shines forth from the sanctuary, Pope warned against the presumption of comprehensiveness or mastery. The knowledge we receive is "sufficient" insofar as "nothing that it concerns us to know has been or will be hidden from us." But because what concerns us has to do with such God's "surpassing majesty," we must strive to maintain a proper balance between confidence in that which we have received and the "deepest humility."[17] We must always remind one another that "mystery is everywhere in this knowledge: its simplest elements are things unsearchable by the faculties of man."[18]

So where does this shining forth take place? Pope is clear: "Jesus Christ is Himself in Person and in Word the revelation of God."[19] So Christology isn't just central to Pope's theology; it is its controlling norm. Both in his person and in the scriptures (which are "under the control and supervision of the Holy Spirit"), Jesus Christ simply is God's self-revelation to humanity. As such, the first question that theology must answer is not a question about our response to the coming of God in Jesus Christ. Rather, it is a question about what the revelation of God in Christ tells us about God's eternal nature and purposes.

When Pope wrote that Jesus Christ is the revelation of God, he did so with the suffering and death of Christ specifically in mind. In other words, Pope didn't begin with a conception of deity in the abstract, which is to

---

16 Pope, *Compendium*, 1:5.

17 Pope, 1:9.

18 Pope, 1:29.

19 Pope, 1:10.

say, deity conceived apart from God's concrete actions in Christ. Rather, Christ's incarnation and especially his work on the cross stands at the center of Pope's Christology, governing all that comes before and after. Put simply, the cross is the key for understanding God's eternal nature and purposes. Thus, Pope said, "Before the world existed, Christ was ordained to take human nature in order to its renewal."[20] He continued, "Redemption is in the New Testament declared to have been a purpose of God in or from eternity. This design, having reference solely to the Saviour's work, and *apart from its application by the Spirit*, is regarded in Scripture as an absolute decree of man's salvation virtually accomplished from the beginning: a mystery reserved for gradual revelation, but a reality underlying all human history."[21]

Next, Pope explained that, as an eternal decree, the motive for the incarnation, suffering, and death of Christ is a love that is both spontaneous and absolute. It neither takes counsel from nor gives an account to anyone "outside of Himself." Rather the "counsel of His own will is simply the decree of His supreme volition. . . . It represents our redemption as the primitive norm or rule according to which God *worketh all things*," not a scheme or expedient "evolved in the Divine mind." What is subject to change or evolution in the divine mind are "the conditions on which personal salvation is suspended, and the methods of the Spirit's administration." In other words, there is a "plan of salvation" but not, strictly speaking, a "plan of Redemption." The latter, said Pope, "is as simply a fiat of will as creation."[22]

This is truly a remarkable passage. Pope went out of his way to bracket any discussion of our response to God's work ("apart from its application by the Spirit"). To be sure, he would take up our appropriation of the Savior's work in due course. Yet, one gets the sense that Pope was well aware that Methodists tend to be in a hurry to move past what God has decreed in Christ from all eternity in order to talk about our role in the economy of

---

20 Pope, *Compendium*, 2:90.

21 Pope, 2:91 (italics mine).

22 Pope, 2:91.

salvation. A model of dogmatic order and discipline, Pope named and re-sisted this temptation, insisting that we linger here, contemplating Christ's work on the cross as a matter of eternal decree that, as such, is not contin-gent upon our response to it. In fact, there's a real sense in which we have no say in the matter. As a matter of eternal decree Christ's work on the cross is the condition under which "the whole world has lived and moved and had its being. . . . [It is] the testimony in time of an eternal act in the Divine counsel."[23] Strictly speaking, it is not subject to change. God has never been or intended to be anyone other than who God is on the cross. The economic Trinity really is the immanent Trinity.

The decretive will of God to redeem human beings is therefore not something that God arrives at gradually, say, through negotiation or af-ter a season of anger for which God needs to apologize. God decrees and acts in accordance with God's nature and not due to our suasion. We can-not persuade God to redeem us because God has elected to redeem us from eternity. Nor is our redemption an emergency measure to salvage an unanticipated fall. "The redemption of mankind," said Pope, springs from "the eternal purpose of God the Triune: *Let Us Redeem Man!* was silently one with *Let Us make man!*"[24]

When Pope turned to the doctrine of the atonement proper, he con-sidered it under three aspects: (1) the results of Christ's work as to God; (2) the results as to God and man; and (3) the results as to man. With respect to God, the work of Christ is "the supreme manifestation of the glory and consistency of the Divine attributes." In a truly beautiful passage, Pope said, "But, in the mystery of the Atonement, the provision of eternal mercy, as it were, anticipates the transgression, and love in every representation of it has the pre-eminence. The passion is the exhibition rather than the cause of the Divine love to man."[25] He then added, "But it is the glory and unity of

---

23 Pope, *Compendium*, 2:92.

24 Pope, 2:101 (italics original).

25 Pope, 2:263–64. Pope offered a beautiful extended reflection here on the unity of divine love and holiness made manifest in the cross of Christ.

all the attributes that the work of Christ exhibits in their perfection. There is nothing that belongs to our conception of the Divine nature which is not manifested in His Son . . . and we must receive Him as He is made known to us through the mystery of the Atoning Mediation of His Son. His Name is proclaimed only in the Cross."[26]

The second aspect of the atonement, which is to say, as it relates to God and man, Pope termed "reconciliation." The closely related third aspect is called "redemption." Pope explored the objective and subjective dimensions of each of these two aspects. With respect to reconciliation, Pope stressed the overcoming of the enmity that exists between God and man. In the cross of Christ, God objectively reconciled "the entire world of mankind" to himself, including all those who lived before Christ, as well as all those who live after. The cross "belongs to all the world. Its two arms stretch backward and forward, to the beginning and to the end of time."[27] As for our subjective appropriation of God's reconciling work in Christ, Pope declared that it is "no other than the personal assumption of the benefit of general reconciliation."[28]

With respect to redemption, Pope stressed the deliverance of the whole human race from the bondage of sin, which is conceptually different from the overcoming of enmity (reconciliation). Here, Pope explored the ransom theory of the atonement at length, stressing that humankind is ransomed primarily from sin, "subordinately and indirectly, from captivity to Satan and to death the penalty of sin."[29] Ultimately, however, the emphasis falls on redemption as a divine transaction and not on our subjective appropriation of it. When reconciliation and redemption are received in penitent faith, they become the life of righteousness, the discussion of which Pope promised to take up in a future section of his dogmatics. In the meantime, the discussion of redemption focuses on the fact that it is

---

26 Pope, *Compendium*, 2:279.

27 Pope, 2:285.

28 Pope, 2:287.

29 Pope, 2:289.

"altogether a divine transaction." Concerning the *origin* of redemption, Pope declared that "the love of the Triune God is its source, the justice of the Triune God [its] necessity, and the wisdom of the Triune God its law." Concerning the *method* of redemption, he observed that it is accomplished "in the mediatorial revelation of the Trinity," which is to say, the Father who sends His Son, the Son who "takes our nature that in it He may redeem us," and the Holy Spirit who "orders the process of our salvation." Finally, concerning the *results* of redemption, Pope exclaimed, "The acceptance of the ransom-price of mankind is the accomplishment of a Divine purpose, which needed nothing out of God for its attainment, and by nothing out of God could be frustrated."[30]

To summarize, Pope treated the work of Christ on the cross under three aspects: (1) God; (2) God and man; and (3) man. The order is instructive. The doctrine of the atonement is first and foremost a word about God. More specifically, it is about the glory of God and the unity of the divine attributes made manifest in the cross of Christ. Even when the doctrine of the atonement speaks to man, it does so in terms of what Christ has done to reconcile and redeem human beings through his atoning sacrifice on the cross. Exploration of the subjective appropriation of Christ's work, which is to say, the work of the Spirit, is purposefully delayed. This is a matter of dogmatic discipline and order, but the effect of that order on the theologian is monumental. By fixing our gaze upon the cross, Pope facilitates a surrendering of all anxiety and narcissism and the adoption of a posture that balances proper confidence with humble gratitude. The true student of theology is also a worshipper.

The Future of Wesleyan Theology: Proper Confidence and Humble Gratitude

When it comes to Protestant theology, we Wesleyans like to think that we are exceptional. We believe that our approach to and emphasis upon the

---

30 Pope, *Compendium*, 2:293.

doctrines of unlimited atonement, regeneration, assurance, and entire sanctification is unique. And perhaps it is. But our commitment to synergism makes us just as susceptible to anxious narcissism as our Protestant neighbors in the Lutheran and Reformed traditions.

As mentioned above, synergism is *not* inherently narcissistic. Rather, anxious narcissism happens when we fail to cultivate and maintain a robust vision of God's eternal triune life and purposes and then to carefully and consistently think about salvation from the standpoint of that vision. I believe this is precisely what has happened to us in the Wesleyan theological tradition. Across space and time, we have become more adept at talking about ourselves than talking about God. Why is this?

We Wesleyans are prone to making the faith fundamentally about ourselves because we have abandoned serious work in dogmatic theology.[31] If Wesleyan theology is to be truly *theological*, then we are going to have to undertake the slow and difficult work of dogmatic theology.[32] We can learn a great deal about how to do this work by reading someone like William Burt Pope. The goal in doing so is not to make Pope himself or some other theologian an object of study. Rather, it is to allow him to model for us the ways in which order, discipline, and consistency bring clarity to theological reflection. Ultimately, we must learn to do this work anew and afresh for ourselves. We must learn what it means once again to attend to the grammar of the Christian faith in an orderly manner.

If order and discipline bring consistency and clarity to theology, then they also affect the posture of any would-be student of theology. The brief sampling of Pope's reflections on the work of Christ provided above illustrates this. On the one hand, the cross of Christ stands at the center of Pope's theology, exercising control over all that comes before and after it.

---

31 A telling indicator of how long we have forsaken the work of dogmatic theology is the sheer number of Wesleyan theologians today who, when hearing the phrase *Wesleyan dogmatic theology*, will insist that no such thing exists. Dogmatic theology, they will insist, is native to the Reformed tradition, not the Wesleyan.

32 See the symposium "What Makes Wesleyan Theology *Theological*?" in *Wesleyan Theological Journal* 52, no. 2 (Fall 2017): 7–46.

On the other hand, the prior doctrines of the divine nature and election entail that Christ's atoning sacrifice on the cross is unconditional in every sense of the word. It is freely decreed by God from all eternity. All of human history takes place within the horizon of the cross. Contemplation of these mysteries leads simultaneously to proper confidence and humble gratitude. As a result, dogmatic theology can be seen as an antidote to the anxiety and narcissism that plague Western culture at large, as well as our beloved Wesleyan tradition.

Finally, as we have seen, dogmatic theology culminates in worship. Rightly undertaken, it fixes our gaze on the glory and beauty of God made manifest in the cross of Christ. Here, divine love and holiness along with all of the other divine attributes are in perfect harmony. Here, God's eternal nature and purposes are on display for the world to see. Here, God reconciles and redeems lost humanity. Here, God's steadfast love is made known once and for all. And we can surely trust it!

Contributors

Reginald Broadnax is Chair of the Department of Religious Studies, Clinton College (Rock Hill, SC), and author of *The Category of Freedom in the Thought of Charles Hartshorne: A Neoclassical Metaphysics* (2009).

Paul W. Chilcote is retired professor of historical theology and Wesleyan studies at Asbury Theological Seminary. He has authored and edited numerous books on the Wesleys, Wesleyan spirituality, women's studies, and evangelism, including the award-winning *A Faith That Sings: Biblical Themes in the Lyrical Theology of Charles Wesley* (2016), *Singing the Faith: Soundings of Lyrical Theology in the Methodist Tradition* (2020), and volume 13 of *The Works of John Wesley* (2013), coedited with Ken Collins.

Edgardo Colón-Emeric is Irene and William McCutchen Associate Professor of Reconciliation and Theology at Duke Divinity School. He is the author of *Óscar Romero's Theological Vision: Liberation and the Transfiguration of the Poor* (2018) and *Wesley, Aquinas, and Christian Perfection: An Ecumenical Dialogue* (2009).

John L. Drury is associate professor of theology and Christian ministry at Wesley Seminary of Indiana Wesleyan University. He is the coeditor of *Karl Barth and the Future of Evangelical Theology* (2018) and the author of *The Resurrected God: Karl Barth's Trinitarian Theology of Easter* (2014), winner of the Wesleyan Theological Society's Smith-Wynkoop Award.

Chris E. W. Green is professor of public theology at Southeastern University (Lakeland, Florida) and author of *The End Is Music: A Companion to Robert W. Jenson's Theology* (2018), *Pentecostal Ecclesiology: A Reader* (2016), and *Foretasting the Kingdom: Toward a Pentecostal Theology of the Lord's Supper* (2012).

Justus H. Hunter is assistant professor of church history at United Theological Seminary (Dayton, Ohio). He is the book review editor for the *Wesleyan Theological Journal* and has published articles and book reviews in a variety of professional journals.

Michael Lodahl is professor of theology and world religions at Point Loma Nazarene University. His books include *Shekhinah/Spirit: Divine Presence in Jewish and Christian Traditions* (1992; 2012) and *Relational Holiness: Responding to the Call of Love* (2005), coauthored with Thomas Jay Oord.

Thomas H. McCall is professor of theology and scholar-in-residence at Asbury University. His books include *Jacob Arminius: Theologian of Grace* (2012), coauthored with Keith Stanglin, and *Which Trinity? Whose Monotheism? Philosophical and Systematic Theologians on the Metaphysics of Trinitarian Theology* (2010).

Mark K. Olson is an instructor at Nazarene Bible College. His books include *Wesley and Aldersgate: Interpreting Conversion Narratives* (2018) and *John Wesley's Theology of Christian Perfection: Developments in Doctrine and Theological System* (2007).

Thomas Jay Oord directs doctoral students at Northwind Theological Seminary and the Center for Open and Relational Theology, and he is the author or editor of numerous books, including *The Uncontrolling Love of God: An Open and Relational Account of Providence* (2015) and *Thy Nature and Thy Name Is Love: Wesleyan and Process Theologies in Dialogue* (2001), coedited with Bryan Stone.

Christina M. Smerick is professor of philosophy and religion at Northwest Nazarene University. She is the author of *Jean-Luc Nancy and Christian Thought: Deconstructions of the Bodies of Christ* (2017) and the coeditor of *This Is My Body: Philosophical Reflections on Embodiment in a Wesleyan Spirit* (2016).

Jerome Van Kuiken is dean of the School of Ministry and Christian Thought, Oklahoma Wesleyan University, and an adjunct professor at Wesley Biblical Seminary. He is the author of *Christ's Humanity in Current and Ancient Controversy: Fallen or Not?* (2017).

Jason E. Vickers is professor of theology, Asbury Theological Seminary, Wilmore, Kentucky. He is the author of *Minding the Good Ground: A Theology for Church Renewal* (2011) and coeditor (with Randy Maddox) of the award-winning *Cambridge Companion to John Wesley* (2009).

CPSIA information can be obtained
at www.ICGtesting.com
Printed in the USA
LVHW051639060222
710367LV00014B/1280